Criminal Identities and
Consumer Culture

Criminal Identities and Consumer Culture

Crime, exclusion and the new culture of narcissism

Steve Hall, Simon Winlow and Craig Ancrum

Routledge
Taylor & Francis Group

LONDON AND NEW YORK

First published by Willan Publishing 2008
This edition published by Routledge 2012
2 Park Square, Milton Park, Abingdon, Oxon OX14 4RN
711 Third Avenue, New York, NY 10017

Routledge is an imprint of the Taylor & Francis Group, an informa business

ISBN 978-1-84392-255-1 paperback
      978-1-84392-256-8 hardback

British Library Cataloguing-in-Publication Data

A catalogue record for this book is available from the British Library

Project managed by Deer Park Productions, Tavistock, Devon
Typeset by TW Typesetting, Plymouth, Devon

The best lack all conviction, while the worst
Are full of passionate intensity

W.B. Yeats

Contents

Preface

As we were writing the final few pages, the British media reported the latest estimates supplied by the British Crime Survey. Crime, we are told, is going down. However, all criminologists know that the 'the crime figures' are not accurate representations of reality but dependent on incidents reported to and recorded by the police, or on samples of victims selected and interviewed by researchers. Lying in the background of these discussions is the tacit assumption that current policies on policing, criminal justice and punishment, supplemented by advances in the security industry, are actually bearing fruit; the forces of law and order, we might think, are winning 'the war on crime'. However, illegal activity is locally differentiated, and crude national or regional statistics tell us very little about what actually goes on in the nooks and crannies of everyday life. In some of Britain's economically marginalised locales numerous activities that, should they be reported, would appear in the statistics as 'crimes' persist relentlessly as an undercurrent; unrecorded, unpublicised and seamlessly woven into the fabric of everyday economic life. Although it is not the focus of this book, the same could be said of the arteries of global trade, the corridors of bureaucratic power or the boardrooms and offices of big business. The current sociological trend indicates that elusive illegal economic activities, which continue largely under the radar of government bureaucracies and statisticians, are merging with the everyday flows and eddies of what is rapidly becoming a globally networked market-driven way of life. These activities are more widespread and intense in regions and locales whose socio-cultural fabrics have been disrupted by neo-liberal economic policies. The aim of this book is to explore in depth and detail 'criminal life' in a few of these nooks and crannies, and to allow what we find there to enlighten us about the general ethico-cultural direction in which

Britain is heading, and indeed where it might have been heading for some time.

We have also been told that the crime problem is essentially a social construct, as many liberal criminologists have maintained for decades, and thus the real task for the 'critical criminologist' is to investigate why 'the crime problem' is constructed in the way that it is, and how these constructions are presented to the public by an illiberal, irresponsible and sensationalist mass-media to fuel anxiety, justify authoritarian governance and reproduce the dastardly 'culture of control'. Is it not really the case, however, that things are more complicated and criminology is trapped in an ideological stand-off? One can only marvel at the crudity of the long-running liberal–conservative slugging match that structures both popular and academic discourses. The liberal-left's dated yet still iconic notion of the 'moral panic' is in essence nothing more than a simplistic conspiracy theory given a sophisticated appearance by decades of devoted intellectual cake-decorating. We should swiftly add the caveat, however, that this pales into insignificance when compared to the right's lurid counter-claim that for decades the liberal-left have been, in the name of irresponsible social engineering, conspiring in a treasonously subversive manner to destroy personal responsibility along with the nation's traditional and precious organic culture, creating 'feral youth' on the way. Supporting one side or the other is the easy way for academics and journalists to toe their respective lines, guarantee publication and forge safe and easy careers, especially now that academia is rapidly becoming another intrusively over-managed commercial industry just like the mass media have been throughout their collective history. As conservative declinists stage an outlandishly theatrical fiend-fest hoping to get the thumbs-up for yet another crackdown that will prove ineffective in the long term, worried liberals jump up and down in front of reality like goalkeepers facing penalty kicks, waving their arms and shouting 'look away, there's nothing to see here' lest someone might score a goal by actually understanding what's going on and what needs to be done about it. In this book we will make every effort to transcend this impasse and, in the true traditions of ethnography and critical theory, to aid a resurgent crop of criminological ethnographers and theorists in their efforts to reopen the investigation of what is actually happening out there and why.

Readers of this book will quickly learn that despite diminishing crime statistics in Britain, in many economically marginalised locales everyday harms and illegalities continue, incidents of serious and fatal violence simmer away, young lives drift perilously close to nihilism, and anxiety pervades the populations. In these places crime and violence are largely unrecorded yet fundamental constituents of everyday life, and if we are to address this reality and its underlying motivations we must also address directly the brutal yet symbolically creative essence of the culture that accompanies liberal-capitalism and the post-political neo-liberal state. If we can guarantee one thing, it is that whatever snapshot 'figures' the crime statistics suggest, and whatever meanings and practices our research and that of other criminological ethnographers throws up, things won't stay the same. History did not end, as much as neo-liberals wanted it to in the 1990s after the collapse of the Soviet Union. It goes on, and the impending energy crisis, the downturn in the global economy, the credit crunch and the big scare-word 'recession' – or, even worse, 'depression' – currently on the lips of economists augur a very different future, which might well be upon us before we know it. Recession means reduced opportunities in the legal sphere. How those individuals whose expectations have been elevated in a culture that glorifies the well-taken economic opportunity as a right, a good, a status-symbol and an ego-boosting individual achievement will react can only be estimated with the aid of an honest account of how some individuals are reacting *now* in the localised previews to the impending main event. All of this and, as we shall see, a good deal more besides leaves our discipline lagging behind and once again failing to take the lead in explaining the big issues of our time. However, if one peruses some of the excellent new thinking coming on line, which we discuss throughout this book, and some of the more penetrative essays in collections such as Sumner's *The Blackwell Companion to Criminology*, which are now filtering through into the new textbooks, there are signs that the worm is turning and the discipline is waking up. The heartfelt beliefs that the sacred human subject can never be truly dominated by ideology, cultural hegemony and economic compulsion, that despite its environment 'social agency' is always an indelible and dynamic feature of everyday life in late modernity, and that the exercise of power automatically produces resistance without real politics and the mature mind rescued from narcissism and inspired by the spirit and language of radical subjectivity, have all had their day. We need to explore new intellectual paths and begin the process of rehabilitating criminology if it is to have any hope of ensuring its relevance in what look like rather turbulent times ahead. Our aim here is to make a small contribution to that rehabilitation.

Acknowledgements

Firstly, as the main theorist on the job here I would like to thank co-authors Simon Winlow and Craig Ancrum, two of the best criminological ethnographers in the business, for allowing me to work alongside them. Without data that represent faithfully the ongoing reality of life in advanced capitalism even the best theoretical explanations can over time stagnate and degenerate into inter-textual abstractions. The immense hard work and ethnographic expertise provided by Simon and Craig save us from that fate. Also, I would like to thank a number of fellow academics, who, despite the edicts of those who would restrict our thoughts to empiricist particularism, encouraged me to develop and persevere with my ideas, especially Colin Sumner, who supported my early publishing career, and also Robert Reiner, Nigel South, Kevin Stenson, Betsy Stanko, the late Ian Taylor, Tim Newburn, Tony Jefferson, Mark Little, Peter Francis, Mike Randall, Steve Taylor, Rob Horne, Graeme Kirkpatrick, Ronnie Lippens, Keith Hayward, Stephen Tomsen, Katherine Watson and Chris Greer. Special thanks to Jeff Ferrell, Mike Presdee and Wayne Morrison for supporting the publication of some of our research team's central themes despite, we suspect, disagreeing with most of what we say. Very special thanks to all my M.A. and PhD students for so many stimulating conversations, especially Mark Horsley, and Anna Millington for the great help she gave our researchers, and to the staff in the Division of Sociology and Criminology at Northumbria University, especially John Stirling for support through a difficult time, and all the criminologists for taking the weight during my sabbatical: Peter Francis, Pam Davies, Sarah Soppitt, Louise Ridley, Jamie Harding, Rob Hornsby, Wendy Dyer and Faye Dolman. Most of all, thanks to my family, Chrissie, Chris and Alex, for tolerating my grumpiness and the irritating tap-tapping on my keyboard until the early hours.

Steve Hall

My colleagues and I must offer our sincere gratitude to those who facilitated the fieldwork. Becoming older and increasingly middle class has distanced me from many of the people quoted in these pages, and much of the fieldwork would have been impossible without the help of a number of key gatekeepers whose continued involvement in the North East's criminal markets enabled the ethnographic process to begin. I'd like to thank Steve Hall for his continued support and friendship, and Craig Ancrum for sharing the research burden and making those journeys through the Tyne Tunnel to provide me with the details of recent changes in the north east's drug markets. I'd also like to reiterate Steve's thanks to the cultural criminology contingent, especially Keith and Jeff, and thank Colin Webster for looking through the first draft of this book and offering his encouragement. But, most of all, my thanks go to Sara for putting up with me.

Simon Winlow

I would like to thank Steve Hall and Simon Winlow for seeing enough in me to give me a chance, for pulling me into the academic world, and for always being willing to advise and support, I owe you both a whole load of pints. Thanks to all my colleagues at Teesside and especially John Harrison, Mark Simpson and Mark Cowling. Massive thanks to those who can't be named, this is your book. May you do what you do for as long as you can. Thanks to Dawn and Callum who make it all worth it. Thanks to my mam who didn't get the chance to see where I ended up, I owe you and dad everything.

Craig Ancrum

Chapter I

Introduction: the return to motivation

There is little doubt that crime is now a central issue of our times. From the gang cultures and outbursts of interpersonal violence that pervade some economically run-down locales (Dorling 2004) to the systematic gangsterisation of the global economy (Woodiwiss 2005), crime occupies a prominent place in public discourse. Criminology's more critical attempts to identify and explain the social and politico-economic roots of the crime problem have been rich and varied, although perhaps not quite so successful as they once promised to be. If for the moment we avoid launching ourselves hastily into the extremities of the postmodernist denial of truth and knowledge, we might suspect the principal reason for this disappointment is that in the post-war era critical criminology largely avoided talking too much about crime and its harmful effects, preferring instead to focus on the contested political language of crime and the 'conservative' establishment's unjust practices of criminalisation and labelling. However, since the mid 1980s a growing current within critical criminology, beginning with the left realist and feminist breaks with left idealism, has shown increasing awareness that the discipline has since the late 1960s relied too heavily on useful but limited concepts such as 'moral panic' (Cohen 2002) and 'authoritarian populism' (Hall 1980, 1985). This focus displaced the exploration of the motivations behind the harmful acts that constitute criminality itself with relentless critiques of the practices of punitive reaction and the language/imagery with which the hegemonic apparatus of politics, law and mass media constructed public perceptions of crime. Although we certainly must not lose sight of the important issues of social inequality, unequal power to define and the political function of the 'politics of fear' in the legitimisation of the sort of authoritarian governance that can directly threaten civil liberties, this core liberal-left argument, on its own, has only limited explanatory power. Pleasingly, however, critical criminology is now getting into its stride down an alternative path, along which it can draw more attention to the crime explosion that characterised Britain and the USA from the late 1960s to the late 1990s as a reality inextricably linked to the increasing dominance of neo-liberal political economy.

The evidenced argument that increased equality across the economic, political and cultural dimensions of the social universe can indeed reduce crime, punitiveness and general incivility is still powerful and persuasive (Reiner 2007). However, just as the liberal-modernist hope that increased opportunities for prosperity and freedom would reduce crime floundered as rates rose in Britain and the USA in the 1960s and 1970s, the sharp rise of intra-class crime and violence among a depoliticised working class and the continuation of fraud and corruption among the wealthy business/political class in the 1980s and 1990s cast doubt on the efficacy of the whole project of social equality in the context of our current core values, begging the very basic question, 'Equal rights to what?' Just as global warming and other ecological problems cast doubt on the industrial-capitalist route to prosperity and happiness, the crime explosion cast doubt on all variations of the modernist politico-cultural route to solidarity. Today's world, as Alain Badiou (2007) remarked, seems to be all about the language of formal liberty and equality in the absence of real fraternity, or solidarity, to use the gender-neutral term. As we write, news reports of white-collar fraudsters popping out of the woodwork and the deaths of young people at the hands of others wielding firearms and knives dominate the media in Britain, even in the 'quality' liberal press. Three young men are beginning lengthy sentences for kicking to death a father who remonstrated with them after they had committed an act of petty vandalism, while another three are receiving the same punishment for beating to death a young man with learning difficulties to 'see who could knock him out first'. The general sentiment that something somewhere is going badly wrong can no longer be passed off as the mere product of a conspiratorial attempt to generate fear among the population with the aim of legitimising current modes of authoritarian control. The explosion in genuinely harmful forms of crime and violence in Britain has been undeniably real:

> It seems that the broad pattern of change over the last half century is clear. The overwhelming, most dramatic change is the huge increase in recorded crime. Probably a significant (but ultimately unascertainable) proportion of this was due to reporting and police recording changes up to about 1980, so the statistics exaggerate the

increase in crime. After 1981, with the advent of the BCS, it is possible to be more certain, especially about the 1980s when the two statistical series went in the same direction. Although a small fraction (about a fifth) of the recorded doubling of crime was attributable to more reporting by victims, *there can be no doubt about the crime explosion that took place.* (Reiner 2007: 75, our italics)

Despite ostensible decreases from the late 1990s, which correlate with large rises in the prison population and the intensification of surveil-lance, risk management and correctional practices, the situation still remains problematic. Reiner (*ibid.*), in an expertly assembled digest of criminological work done so far on the relationship between crime and political economy, reminds us of the important details that lie under-neath the general statistics; although the crime rate in England and Wales diminished after 1992, violence diminished only a little, while some forms of serious violence, such as robbery, continued to rise. Dorling's (2004) detailed demographic work highlights the fact that in many troubled locales blighted by permanent recession, unemployment and burgeoning criminal markets the murder rate is six times the national average. However, simply blaming unemployment is no longer adequate; some forms of property crime actually tend to decrease in economic recessions because more people remain at home to bolster informal methods of control (Box 1987), and of course for a long time during the industrial-capitalist era unemployment, economic instability and social inequality were the spurs to working-class political solidarity and action rather than ethico-social implosion.

That said, what we saw in the 1980s was not merely another structural adjustment of the economy and the labour market leading to another standard recession. Rather, it was a radical shift in political economy and culture, a move to the unprecedented domination of life by the market, which created a large number of locales of permanent recession across Britain and the USA. As we shall see, the criminal markets developing in these areas now tend to operate in the relative absence of the traditional normative insulation that thinkers such as Polanyi (2002) and Galbraith (1991, 1999) – drawing upon the initial warnings of Adam Smith in his *Theory of the Moral Sentiments* – regarded as essential to the restraint of the inherently amoral and socially disruptive logic that lies at the heart of the liberal-capitalist market economy. Contrary to the prognostications of some (see Friedman 2000; Murray 1988, 1997), the 1980s was not a time of vigorous and inherently progressive cultural change. Although we do acknowledge – and we will get this in early for the sake of some of our less thoughtful and attentive critics who seem unable to deal with paradox (see for instance O'Brien 2007) – that there has been some progress in some dimensions, especially race/ethnic and gender relations and tolerance of different forms of sexuality, *at the same time as this progress* the Anglo-American world has also experienced the restoration of purified classical liberal-capitalism as we entered a period of intensified ideological control (Harvey 2007; Badiou 2002). We were told in a way that grabbed the imagination of a politically significant majority of the population that the unhindered market would work its magic and deliver us from the evils of economic stagnation and lack of opportunities for personal prosperity. In our para-political liberal-democratic system, increasingly atomised, nihilistic and cynical electorates needed to be persuaded either not to vote, or to vote for parties and politicians whose interests were in direct opposition to the mutual interests of the vast majority. The personal interests of competing individuals took centre stage as Anglo-American culture became dominated by ubiquitous and powerful ideological messages that stressed self-interest, acquisition and social competition.

In this period deep political regulation – of both the economy and the important institutions of cultural reproduction that characterised the post-war social democratic era – was rapidly replaced by deregulation on behalf of the needs of business. Acquisitive individualism was systematically embedded as a psychocultural driver in a global monet-arist economic project that was more concerned with finance capital than productive capital (see Schumpeter 1994; Harvey 2007). To cut a long story short, the upshot is that investment in traditional industry declined, resulting in the loss of huge sectors of the North American and British industrial heartlands and the emergence of a large, insecure service sector of casual, low-paid workers and a so-called 'underclass' of long-term unemployed struggling for significance and prosperity in a fragmented social system characterised by deepening and widening inequality. This, passed off by neo-liberal ideologues as an act of 'creative destruction' promising better things to come, occurred alongside the continuing expansion of consumption and consumer credit, the increasing reliance on a buoyant housing market to guarantee personal loan repayments, and the flooding of the high streets with a vast array of cheap goods manufactured in low-wage economies abroad. The socially deleterious effects of this change were insulated only by a rationalised welfare system in combination with newly developed strategies of risk-management (see Hughes 1998; Beck 1992; Giddens 1998, 2007).

It was on this radically altered terrain in the 1980s that the most resounding phase of the 'crime explosion' took place, and it presents new challenges for criminological theory. Reiner (2007) outlines five necessary conditions for crime: labelling, motivation, means, opportunity and the absence of ethical and situational controls. Perhaps the least understood and most neglected is motivation, which tends to be approached at the individual psychological level. While psychologistic explanations can often bear fruit in the investigation of less common and more serious crimes, the psychosocial and cultural explanations that we need to explain the explosion in common forms of crime, whose perpetrators do not usually suffer from clinically diagnosable psychological or psychiatric problems, have been limited. Anomie, labelling, relative deprivation, sub-cultural differentiation, discursive subjectivity and their various derivatives have all had their moments, but have never offered really satisfactory explanations, even when attempts were made to integrate them. Even the more sophisticated new psychosocial studies now coming on line to construct integrated theories (see for instance Gadd and Jefferson 2007), while extremely useful for examining relational dynamics across various social and cultural axes and throwing light on specific case studies, are perhaps supplementary to the deeper exploration of what should be regarded as direct yet complex relationships between our core values and practices, our current conditions of existence and the individual's motivation to commit crime.

In a tradition that stretched from Bonger (1916) to Ehrlich (1973), early criminological work correlating crime rates with poverty, inequality and unemployment was largely ignored and dismissed as 'reductionist' by both the Left and the Right, of course for entirely different reasons. The Left were keen to downplay working-class deviancy and focus on the crimes of the powerful, and the Right were keen to ignore consumerist values, political economy and the social conditions of existence in order to press their traditional case for personal responsibility and the rebuilding of traditional moral discipline along with its essential transmission mechanisms, such as the Arnoldian canon of high culture, the family, the church and the juridical disciplinary state. Most feminist and pro-feminist criminologists have been keen to shift the focus to male privilege and competitive, acquisitive masculine culture, despite the fact that most males commit no crime and female competitiveness and acquisitiveness are hardly invisible or controversial aspects of contemporary life. Neither side of the political divide appeared especially keen to develop more sophisticated analyses that addressed political economy and its underlying values, or to draw upon classic social and critical theories, which from the 1980s onwards were often dismissed as obsolete. Most work tended to focus on subjectivity, gender, language, discourse, bio-power, conflicting sociocultural relations, imbalances of politico-discursive power and the roles of policing, punishment and rehabilitative techniques; all fascinating and important topics, but topics that nevertheless failed to confront squarely the core problematic. The powerful, generative politico-economic, cultural and psychosocial currents that were gathering strength underneath what now seem like relatively petty conflicts over industrial capitalism's booty were largely ignored, possibly because in the midst of our post-war complacency and optimism we imagined these currents to be either under control or reduced to mere residues by the progressive forces of liberal democracy. 'Capitalism has its nasty side, but don't worry, we "smart liberals" are on top of it'; perhaps we should imagine that ubiquitous little lullaby spoken by the voice of an airline pilot addressing the passengers before entering a zone of turbulence. However, now that real rises in violent crime and renewed fears about social disorder, geopolitical conflict, cultural disharmony and economic instability have cast doubt upon the inevitability of that progress, we must move back to a more critical mode of analysis and explore with renewed vigour – and perhaps with a little more respect for classical discourses and a little less for some of the more novel post-war thinking that has let us down quite badly – the deep generative relationships that exist between political economy, culture, psychology and harmful crime. These factors intersect and converge in consumer culture, as Reiner explains:

> The emergence of a globalized neoliberal political economy since the 1970s has been associated with social and cultural changes that were likely to aggravate crime, and to displace all frameworks for crime control policy apart from 'law and order'. The spread of consumerist culture, especially when coupled with increasing social inequality and exclusion, involved a heightening of Mertonian 'anomie'. At the same time the egoistic culture of a 'market society', its zero-sum, 'winner-loser', survival of the fittest ethos, eroded conceptions of ethical means of success being preferable, or of concerns for others limiting ruthlessness, and ushered in a new barbarism. (Reiner 2007: 109)

This was accompanied, he goes on to argue, by the reversal of the 'solidarity project' and a common sense of citizenship; a reversal that occurred, we will emphasise again, *despite* progress in some quarters, which seems to suggest that progressive liberalism might have been compromised in an important way as it capitulated to competitive individualism. As Rose (1996) claimed, the post-1980s era has seen the 'death of the social' and the fracture of relations of mutual reciprocity that have always existed in one form or another across our diverse anthropological histories. These important social goods have now been replaced by what is quite possibly the most complete and pervasive form of atomised competitive individualism yet seen in British culture. As we have argued at length elsewhere (see Winlow and Hall 2006; Hall and Winlow 2007), we regard as extremely naive the notion that, in the midst of this atomisation and actuarial control, traditional communities are being replaced by new do-it-yourself symbolic communities that can revive relations of morality, respect and obligation and foster effective political opposition via myriad cultural micro-transgressions. The system cannot suffer 'death by a thousand cuts' because, as we shall see later, in the Lacanian sense these 'cuts' are exactly what it needs to breathe and reproduce itself. However, what we shall argue in this book is that in a very different way the social *has* been maintained; the corollary of the advanced capitalist economy is the colonisation of the former life-world by consumerism's symbolic system, which seems to be constituted by images of a simulated social life and all the paradoxical struggles for both distinction and community that a real traditional social life entailed. Maybe the social is not as dead as Rose thought, and the *truly* atomised life exists only in specific dimensions of reality; perhaps the social lives on in a collectively imagined, mass-mediated form as a site for symbolic and para-political struggles that can be harnessed to the economy. Perhaps it is not simply the lack of a real social life but the emergence of an imaginary social world to replace it and organise atomised individuals into a frenetic competition that is the most criminogenic aspect of life in advanced modernity: this is the principal theme we want to explore throughout the book.

If we put political economy aside for a brief moment, in the post-war era there seems to have been a notably strong link between rising crime and consumerism. Earlier but less abrupt rises in the crime rate also correlated with the early twentieth-century phase of consumerist development in the 1920s, where the acquisition and display of wealth, performative ability and social distinction – in the form famously named by Thorstein Veblen (1994) as 'conspicuous consumption' – began to diffuse further outwards in the social body than it had done after the bourgeois revolutions in the eighteenth century. The practice of acquiring primarily for the purpose of display began to break down the traditional restraining cultures of asceticism and collectivism, disrupting the fragile project of political solidarity, undermining the vital functional, status-enhancing and identity-providing role of production in the realm of material reality and becoming the most common measure of value (Hall 2000). In what follows we will argue in more detail that when the formative pressure generated by this homogenising quasi-cultural method of measuring value combines with the social divisions, impoverished culture and competitive narcissistic individualism that characterise societies based on classical liberalism's purified form of market capitalism, the result is, inevitably, criminogenic at the main points of disruption and opportunity. The main generator and conduit of this pressure is the consumer culture that throughout the twentieth century has become increasingly important to the expansionary logic of our post-needs capitalist economy. The evidence we present throughout the book suggests that this metaculture has clearly assimilated young people involved in crime. As each generation passes, living in this culture is increasing the number of individuals who lack the political and symbolic resources necessary to resist its compulsions and myths, and who therefore readily subscribe to its more deleterious tendencies. For instance, the 'live now – pay later' norm encourages the short-cut mentality and ratchets up consumer debt as well as cultivating egoism and an irresponsible, instrumental attitude towards others. Vital aspects of traditional working-class cultures that are now being systematically jettisoned by consumerism once constituted an anti-utilitarian buffer against the forces of augmented egoism, narcissism and competitive individualism, forces that are active in the legitimisation and normalisation of criminogenic practices in everyday economic and cultural interaction (see Barber 2007; Bakan 2005). It might be worth stating here, again for the benefit of some of the less thoughtful critics of this position (see, for example, O'Brien 2007), that we do not see the culture of the British post-war working class as an alternative candidate for Fukuyama's (1993) 'end of history', and nor do we see it as a flawless model of human existence, better in every way than today's cultures, to be deified, returned to in a romantic homecoming and exported across the known world. Nor do we deny that some aspects of today's culture are indeed better. Caricatures such as this one are predicated on a poor understanding of history and culture; a more useful conception of historical change would lie somewhere between Braudel and Foucault, a mixture of continuities and discontinuities. What we claim is that the cultural ethos of anti-utilitarian solidarity that was recognised and cultivated by the socialist and social democratic political projects, and which had a fragile existence in some working-class cultures, was a vital quality that should have been a principal continuity, but it was placed under systematic attack by the forces of neo-liberal ideology in the 1980s, and significantly eroded in the socio-economic reality these forces brought upon us.

The dominant discourses of liberal-left labelling theory and conservative or neo-classical control theories colluded in the marginalisation of concentrated criminological explorations of motivations and 'root causes'. The aetiological explanations of social democratic criminologists were denounced by both parties in what amounted to a quintessential 'straw man' argument, accusing them of pathologising individuals, culture and society and making crude and unsatisfactory mechanistic links between poverty, egoism and crime. In fact, as Reiner (2007: 9) argues, most of these criminologists 'always stressed the importance of culture and morality in shaping how economic circumstances were experienced and interpreted, and thus in mediating any link with crime'. However, the liberal symbolic interactionist perspective, wherein meaning and morality are socially constructed in negotiations between groups that have different degrees of definitional power, unwisely assumed that these interpretations are relatively 'free'. The conservative position, wherein they are constructed in the eternal Manichean battle between good and evil (with humans, of course, inclining towards the evil), unwisely assumed fixed tendencies, which required constant discipline by an elite class. In comparison to these positions, we will argue, what we might call the 'radical social democratic' school's attempt to account for all variables from political economy to culture, psychology, social relations and statecraft was from its very beginnings (see Bonger 1916; Merton 1938) always far more comprehensive, rounded and sophisticated.

Reiner (2007: 24) argues further that in a materialistic culture there is no end to the generation of aspirations, and consequently no end to their pursuit. While we fully agree with this basic assertion, the term 'materialistic', we suggest, is problematic. It is not the material aspect of consumer goods that provokes desire and ambition but the social symbolism they carry, and so in a very important way the problem is the opposite: cultural life in the consumer era has become *far less materialistic* and *far more symbolic* than it should be, a move mirrored in the macro-economic shift of emphasis from the reality-bound realm of productive capital to the fictitious realm of finance capital that we mentioned earlier. As the French philosopher Alain Badiou (2002, 2007) warns, for the sake of embracing a corrosive form of social symbolism that serves the interests of advanced capitalism and its plutocratic elite, we have entered a stage in our historical trajectory where we are devaluing all aspects of nature's material world and the human labour performed in it; an attitude we will unavoidably come to regret. A greater appreciation of the material elements of our life-world might considerably improve contemporary social life, and it's our contention that many of us are drowning in a sea of economically energising but socially dysfunctional symbols while a small minority float comfortably on its surface. Reiner's (2007: 15) point that a culture obsessed with material goals can offer no compensation for those who fail to achieve them because there are no alternative values of comparable stature is a very good one; if we add to this the sociological fact that in a post-needs, desire-driven economy these 'material' goals are first and foremost symbolic goals, we see immediately that the first move in any strategy to reduce criminogenic consumer pressure would be to change our interpretations of, and attenuate our emotional attachments to, the symbolism that now orders our relationship to material goods. As we shall see later, the principal problem is not how we might become 'less materialistic' but how we might reconstruct what Jacques Lacan (2006, see pp. 125–49) might have called a Symbolic Law that can prohibit pathogenic desires and attach meaning to and encourage emotional bonding with alternative sources of value; an order of signs and values in which the individual is able to enter into a more reflexive and rational relationship with consumer products and the symbolism they inevitably carry.

In this important aetiological dimension of criminology the most powerful and enduring explanatory concept to date has been Robert Merton's (1938) version of the Durkheimian concept of *anomie*, a condition of discontent and social disorder that results from society's failure to reconstruct and maintain a set of norms to regulate the 'malady of infinite aspirations' that has been released from its formerly rigid regulatory framework in the transition from mechanical to organic societies. The basic condition is one of 'normlessness', which, when partial, disorders society, but if it ever became total it would render society and its individual members uncontrollably psychopathic (Horne and Hall 1995). We do not want to get involved in a lengthy discussion of Merton's work in this book except to reiterate his basic point that the American Dream of a classless system of opportunities for personal prosperity and status belies the institutionalised structural reality of unequal opportunities in which the majority exist, consequently rendering the majority unable to achieve this prosperity and status. However, this is a departure from Durkheim, who argued that the psychological root of anomie is the 'malady of infinite aspirations', and the social stimulus that invokes and manifests this malady is the *lack* of consensus on fundamental goals and values, which results in an ineffectual normative framework that fails to regulate human desire and the social interactions between individuals. Here we find the beginnings of a conceptual separation of values and norms, if we define 'values' as a set of underlying moral principles and 'norms' as the everyday rules that guide the expression and practice of values. In Merton's version the conception of the social organisation of values is different and, by extension, so is the relationship between values and norms; fundamental values remain consensual and the lack of consensus is to be found in the mixture of socially approved and disapproved normative means of remaining true to values and achieving the goals they encourage. Thus for Merton it is the differentiation of the normative means of achieving goals that gives society its 'pluralistic' appearance and causes problems. Liberal-pluralists, on the other hand, in a discourse that became dominant in the 1960s and displaced strain theory, naturalised and celebrated what Durkheim saw as problematic and argued that societies are culturally plural down to their boots, and that a monolithic set of values and goals has never really existed. This was taken to a position of extreme constructivism and relativism by postmodernists. However, we will argue that in criminology these positions miss the point; because values and norms have been confused and conflated, often talked about so vaguely that they seem interchangeable, the functional dynamic tension that has been cultivated in the relationship between tacit value consensus and explicit normative differences has been missed.

The data we present in the coming chapters essentially suggests that although there is little contestation of core values in the narcissistic world of consumerism, it is nevertheless anything but 'normless'. In fact it demands a remarkable depth, complexity and diversity of normative strategies that arise in various social positions and geographical locales, accompanying and guiding biographical paths. An entirely normless society, driven exclusively by the brutal underlying logic of capitalism along with the raw psychological motivations and cultural values of utilitarianism, would be a psychopathic dystopia, beyond even the fevered imaginations of the scriptwriters who dream up the storylines for post-apocalyptic B-movies, and as such it would destroy itself virtually overnight. In the criminal worlds we explored there was actually a surfeit of meanings and norms that operated around a tight constriction of active values and practices; neither freely negotiated alternative goals and values, as the sub-culturalists and liberal-pluralists argue, nor practical adaptive means, as Merton argued, but normative strategies that flirt precariously with both normlessness and unrefined conformity, attempting to both cope with and fuel underlying impera- tives by structuring and ordering simulated worlds in which narcissistic fantasies and struggles for social distinction are played out using the symbolism of consumer goods. Thus, for us, as we explain in more detail later, consumer culture's norms are neither absent nor adaptive and plural; for the very reasons that they can be proliferated and can appear *in the imagination* to be seductively plural, adaptive or even absent, they are an integral and functional part of advanced capitalism's economic dynamism.

Norms, as we shall see, have become rules created in fantasies rather than traditional symbolic practices, and these fantasies can be crimi- nogenic in that they are now the primary site in which the identification process takes place, and as such they are detaching some young people from the 'real world' of social relations, symbolic prohibitions, con- science and physical reality. In this process there has been no 'de- subordination' of working-class youth; that claim is a pernicious myth, and what we have seen is a shift in the relation of subordination, from that which once confronted traditional authorities with malice aforethought to that which accepts marginalised assimilation and con- fronts the new authority by indulging in its fantasies, which are populated by the images of the conspicuously wealthy winners in a system of ruthless interpersonal competition. We would also suggest that internalised morality and controls have not necessarily been 'weakened' as such; rather, as Žižek (2002, 2007) has argued, we have witnessed a crucial historical shift in the constitution of the super-ego. Internal motivations and controls have been significantly reoriented, and the fundamental force of the super-ego – guilt – now has less energy to carry out its traditional duty of bearing down upon the failure of the individual to be civilised and sociable. A new concern now demands its attention: the failure to enjoy. It seems that today we are more likely to experience guilt as a result of our failure to experience all the indulgent pleasures laid out for our delectation by the culture industries than we are as a result of trampling over the interests of others in our relentless struggle to acquire and display. As a direct consequence of this shift, the super-ego now partners the essential instrumentalism of the ego in driving home the core ethics of contemporary capitalism. Reiner (2007), following Bonger, Tawney and many others, is unerringly correct in his claim that egoism now dominates advanced capitalist culture. However, as we shall see, we cannot talk about the culture of egoism without making the Rousseauian distinction between the healthy egoism of *amour-de-soi*, which can engender respect for others, and the pathogenic egoism of *amour-propre*, which sees the success of the self in the relative downfall of others, and also including a critical assessment of its new dancing partner the *reoriented super-ego*, which together constitute a further step in the development of what Lasch (1991) called the 'culture of narcissism'.

The book is organised in the following way. In Chapter 2 we focus on 'the great change' from traditional forms of capital, community and politics to an increasingly competitive global economy, supported by highly unstable labour markets and administered by a new para-political system grounded in neo-liberalism and increasingly beholden to the interests of the market. The emergence of insecure and hyper-competitive labour markets has widened social divisions, marginalising a rump of the old traditional working classes to a position of near total social and economic insignificance. The encouragement of competitive individualism, consumer desire and instrumental egoism has badly corroded old systems of reciprocal individualism and mutual obligations, replacing them with the personal project as the cultural norm. Increased geographical and social mobility has emptied many areas of competent politico-cultural leaders, and the remaining husk of the old working class has become something to escape from as an individual, rather than fight for and improve as a collective. Some initial data presented here shows that the emptying of value and meaning from local cultures has contributed to the general climate of escapist dreams and social simulations on which consumerism is founded. The casualties of this epochal shift have fallen into an urban 'underclass', out-competed, left behind by historical currents, social fragmentation and the death of the political, but not essentially different in their basic motivations from those who inhabit the mainstream. In these disastrous locales we have seen the growth of criminal markets, predatory crime, violence and a raft of well-documented social problems. Here we also see a complex hybrid of cultural breaks and continuities across the generations, which have resulted in the end of class-based 'social crime' and a shift to crime as an instrument for achieving fantasised positions of social distinction and 'respect' in consumer culture. The reworking of traditional forms of working-class toughness that were cultivated for functional roles in the past has been useful as a normative strategy for relative success, and this combines with turbulent childhoods, an atomised and instrumentalised sense of relative deprivation, consumer fantasies and a reoriented super-ego to motivate the subject in a struggle for social distinction and the retention of a narcissistic identity in the fantastic realm of money, designer clothes, gadgets, elite shopping experiences and conspicuous consumption.

In Chapter 3 we introduce more data, which shows a growing contempt for the collective and a ubiquitous preference for low-level criminality as the means to gratify hedonistic drives. So many are convinced that by employing these methods they will escape and reach the heights of an imaginary society, and this indicates that the particular cohort of young people we interviewed have entirely bought into the dual ethos of entrepreneurialism and consumption. Many were motivated by the dream of becoming a famous criminal businessman, a star in that particular localised sky, although others were content to 'live the dream' literally, in a passive manner, lazily plodding on in the expectation that a lucky 'big break' will appear one day soon, as if by magic. Wealth and conspicuous consumption were the sole sources of value, and these young people experienced constant discontent, unhappiness and a general 'absence of life' without it. The fear of humiliation was extremely powerful and deeply internalised, functioning as a dynamic force in interpersonal relations. There was also a constant obsessive focus on money, and on freedom as lived by the 'cool' fashionable icons of the media, and this fed into expectations of rewards in work and business that, in their relatively impoverished locales and market sectors, were entirely unrealistic. The relationship between work and reward has been severed, ripped away from reality into a fantasy realm of ludicrously high expectations and pleasures that come complete with numerous short cuts to their achievement and gratification. To these ends, the most common economic activity is drug distribution, and, even in this illegal business, sentiments of luck, fate and providence have returned to displace the planning and control that had characterised business, work and their accompanying ways of life in the industrial era. The moods of our respondents tended to swing between fatalism and optimism, driven constantly by suspicion, hostility and quite notably negative conceptions of the 'other'.

In Chapter 4 we outline two case studies, which reinforce the points made above in more depth and detail and show how tightly connected individuals actually are to fundamental consumerist and neo-liberal values. The evidence suggests that their position is far more complex than 'social exclusion'. The majority do not perceive themselves to be in this position, yet neither do they feel wholly 'included' in either the structural or cultural senses; they seem to perceive themselves as being active in a social struggle, driven not simply by a positive belief in bourgeois values, but by their enrolment in a fantasised simulation of its raw, uninhibited possibilities and excesses practised on their own terms. These two men were not simply subjects of 'hegemony'; their lifestyles have been internalised and naturalised beyond that to a *doxic* condition where they are not the reluctant and politically volatile targets of hegemonic cultural influence but the enthusiastic agents of a fantasised version of it; in this fantasy, despite setback after setback, they are always on the path to a position of social distinction in its elite upper echelons.

In Chapter 5 we introduce the idea of the diffusion of the desire to stand out from the 'herd' as a distinguished individual, and how this has developed into a potent form of assimilation and motivation as it has been harnessed and systematised by consumer culture, a process that has poisoned some sectors of traditional working-class culture and postponed any struggle for social justice that might have once existed within them. Some schools of liberal sociology attempted to recast the diffusion of the decadent and atomising ethos of social distinction as the creative urge to resistance, subversion, transgression and ultimate freedom, and here we stage a critique of this move. Consumerism is now targeting very young children, and it has muscled its way into traditional institutions such as the family, the community and the school to become the primary form of socialisation and the primary source of identity. 'Cool', rugged individualism is the main selling point, the structured value-form reflected in most consumer products, and it is now liberal-capitalism's primary cultural icon. Despite its superficially attractive properties, this form is responsible for the destruction of childhood and the loss of respect for adults and the Symbolic Law, as well as being a motivational source of unforgiving competition and humiliation. All this, as we shall see, points to the poverty of the notion of 'resistance at the point of consumption'. The diffusion of this form has been reinforced since the late 1950s by the hegemonic and eventual *doxic* practice of the 'counterculture', which, as an invention of the marketing industry and the libertarian Right rather than an organic politico-cultural form emerging autonomously from the 'street', has replaced traditional radical collectivism and in so doing temporarily disrupted all effective forms of political and ethical resistance. It cleared the way for a culture driven by hedonism and narcissism, which over the final decades of the twentieth century mutated into an atomised competition in a bogus realm of *aristos*, creating a lack of trust and respect between competing individuals and fomenting anxiety, suspicion and hostility, the basic triggers for both violent criminality and increased punitiveness and surveillance.

In Chapter 6 we continue this critique and turn its gaze on liberal-pluralist criminology, which became influential in the 1960s, overwhelming and displacing integrationist, interventionist and structuralist accounts based on political economy and collectivist politics, thus acting as an unwitting justifier of the market-driven chimera that was the counterculture. Here we trace the roots of this movement in the USA, whose mainstream culture is still tied to libertarian individualism, anarcho-capitalism and an underlying Manichean conception of the state as 'absolute evil' in contradistinction to the entrepreneurial individual as 'absolute good'. In this climate criminological theory itself was assimilated into the primary strategy of valorising the ethos of 'cool individualism', an iconic form required by the marketing industry to increase consumer demand by manipulating the processes of identity construction. In this process of atomisation and manufactured disobedience, cultures external to the consumer market were losing their ability to mediate, reproduce and stamp their authority on meanings and values, and the ongoing stimulation of ambition itself in the context of consumerism was becoming toxic. Here we see a culturo-economic process wherein narcissistic self-assessment in relation to market performance and fantasised positions of distinction is replacing the moral sentiments required to sense narcissism and social injustice as fundamentally wrong. We also extend the critique into liberal-pluralism's unhelpful conflation of norms and values and its accompanying misrecognition of their relationships. Criminological theory right across the political spectrum became bogged down in this misrecognition, along with the Manichean battle between two conceptions of 'absolute evil' and the opposing sources of 'moral panic' that they sustain in public discourse: the pathological state and the pathological individual. These intellectual currents, we argue, dominated political and popular discourse, nourishing the emergence of para-politics and the growing inability to do anything at all about the underlying forces and processes that cause crime.

In Chapter 7 we explore theoretical criminology's technical failure to deal with the functional paradoxes and dynamic tensions that constitute advanced capitalism's system of social positions and relations and energise its consumer culture. In our formulation the categories of 'exclusion' and 'inclusion' work in this constitutive and energising way, and we look at how consumerism transcends yet harnesses as a simulation the real social conflict and the tension once created in the gap between these two positions, merging narcissistic competitiveness with existential rebellion. This process has created a rebellion/conformity hybrid that functions in the normative order as both a secondary mediating and motivational driver and an extremely risky and diaphanous restraining and ordering mechanism. Was there really a post-war cultural revolution, we will ask, and if so what did it create, what did it destroy and what did it bequeath us? For us, it bequeathed to our culture this volatile rebellion/conformity hybrid that has become the principal criminogenic force in specific cultural and material circumstances. To those involved as active subjects in this game, the objective situation of 'exclusion' has a weaker existence as a perceptual category in the minds of most of the excluded, and the canards of inevitable organic resistance, subversion and transgression have left criminological theory unprepared for the assimilative power of consumerism's current sociogenetic and psychogenetic processes; a power that has been seriously underestimated. Enforced optimism has prevented us from seeing the 'structure of unequal opportunities' and the positions of 'exclusion' and 'inclusion' as functional aspects of a dynamic system that lays down the foundations for social hostility and the chaotic processes of identity construction, which have now been so long 'in harness' that they have become normalised and virtually invisible. However, the good sign is that stringent critical analysis is filtering back into criminological theory, and this, we contend, needs to be built upon before criminological theory loses its reputation as the supplier of feasible explanations of the causes of crime and gives way entirely to the liberal critique of criminal justice.

In Chapter 8 we extend our critique of criminological theory and get down to the psychosocial nub of our argument. For us, what we call the 'ghost revolution' against 'totalitarian evil' still pervades liberal criminology, and visions of the pathological state are still used as a buffer to insulate public opinion from the admittedly dangerous and regressive concept of the pathological individual existing on a mass scale. However, despite the good intentions, left-liberalism has helped its right-wing libertarian cousin, operating now in the guise of neo-liberalism, to destroy legitimate collective authority alongside its illegitimate oppressive forms, forcing what's left of institutional governance to become smaller yet more draconian and intrusive in the way that neo-liberals prefer. In the political tumult of the post-war decades the whole traditional symbolic order was torn to shreds, losing its vital prohibitive ability and allowing the proliferation of narcissism, the generative psychological force behind the forces of *thymos* and the malady of infinite aspirations, which were erroneously seen by many on the Right as timeless and naturalistic and others on the Left as 'socially constructed'. In a consumer culture where aesthetic display now overrides character and deeds as a source of value and status, most anterior forms of social identity have been lost, apart, ironically, from the most reactionary, which refused to go with the flow and whose continuing existence further discredits the whole principle of a symbolic order. In the absence of a functioning symbolic order, many young people are now dependent on narcissistic identification, which sustains a terrifying sense of lack and a fetishised desire to identify throughout the life-course with the fantasised social symbolism carried by consumer goods, reviving in simulated form the historical *ideal ego* and *ego ideal* of aristocracy. Consumerism's 'capture' of the subject by the prolongation of the narcissistic identification process and the merging of the imaginary *ideal ego* with the symbolic *ego ideal* has been joined, as we have already seen, by the systematic alteration of the conscience; the super-ego injunction to enjoy. Consumerism now has a firm grasp on both the ego and the super-ego, which operate together as a joint psychodynamic force rather than as oppositional forces in tension. Thus infantile narcissism is now part of our way of life, and the conscience is merged with the aggressive quest for recognition in the social mirror, interfering with the fragile Enlightenment project of autonomous, ethical self-governance. This, we argue, has profound criminological implications.

In Chapter 9 we conclude by demonstrating how the ubiquitous sentiment of 'hatred of losers' is a cultural manifestation of a new historical round in the veneration – by newly atomised individuals who in the objective structural sense are themselves losers – of the new barbarian 'aristocrats' who have risen to prominence in the advanced capitalist marketplace. The current release of narcissism and the struggle for social distinction from modernism's ascetic cage is a product of the diffusion throughout the social body of drunken fantasies and brutal power-plays that were once exclusive to the social struggles that took place with spectacular violence in the domain of the elite. Now that rebellion and disobedience are hopelessly confused in popular culture, as are exclusion and inclusion, it becomes apparent that the harder our young criminals are marginalised, the more they imagine themselves to be conforming to the mainstream culture of social distinction via the display of 'cool' individualism, and, perversely, the more they imagine themselves to be worthy of conformity's instant rewards. This suggests that much of today's criminality is the result of the breakdown of the *pseudo-pacification process* (see Hall 2007). This long-term historical process was based upon the transfer of the entitlements to deploy physical violence from the private and arbitrary realm of the aristocracy to the state, combined with the gradual diffusion of entitlements to symbolic violence – the main instrument in the struggle for social distinction and the sociological counterpart of *amour-propre* – throughout the social body to be harnessed as an energy source for capitalism's economic engines of production and consumption. The process is now

17

breaking down as it overheats in the aftermath of the neo-liberal restoration and consumer culture's further democratisation and intensification of the struggle for social distinction; we now encounter the revival of the cult of barbarism as each and every atomised individual is encouraged to reach the highest pinnacle of society by not really being part of it. Much of the criminality committed by our interviewees was driven by the infantile narcissistic imaginings of those who would be the elite in a simulated aristocracy harnessed to the consumer economy. We offer no detailed solutions, which will be the subject of further work, only the suggestion that consumerism should now take its place as a primary issue in criminological theory, and as a primary political issue for anyone sufficiently brave or foolish to declare an intention to revive serious intervention in economy and culture.

Methodological note

The data contained within these pages is drawn from a broad-ranging and ongoing ethnographic study focused on criminal identities in the north-east of England. We can see little use in endlessly recapitulating for what we assume to be an informed and critical readership the various snakes and ladders of ethnographic method, but we would like to clarify a few points relating to our study before the reader encounters the words of our interviewees in the next three chapters. It is perhaps most important to acknowledge from the outset that some of those we spoke to have a long-standing and ongoing relationship with our researchers. We continue to rely heavily on personal connections and the introductions made by key gatekeepers to develop and expand our research cohort and begin the process of setting up interviews. This is, of course, a haphazard way of doing things, but for us it continues to be the best of a mediocre bunch. We take it upon ourselves to contextualise critically the spoken words of our respondents; we have no interest in simply reproducing our conversations for voyeuristic consumption in empirical sociology's zoo. Our interviewees have things to say and so do we, and if the meaning fits the analysis we carry on. We do not unnecessarily prompt our interviewees or set them up with leading questions, and over the years the remarkable homology between what they say about their worlds and what we are saying about the world in general has reinforced our belief that we're on the right track and are entirely justified in our severe criticism of some of social science's prevailing orthodoxies. We're happy to admit that our previous knowledge of these environments inevitably shaped our expectations of the research itself, but in this particular study our findings prompted forms of analysis that are new to us and have significantly extended our previous attempts at theorising subjectivity under neo-capitalism. As always, we attempt to remain true to our data as it was spoken, report our findings as accurately as possible and deploy the theoretical framework that makes sense to us, because that, after all, is all one can do.

There were one or two moments of discomfort, but for the most part the actual interview process was remarkably straightforward. The research, as it was lived, was often a rather fitting act of personal entrepreneurship as we attempted to make our respondents comfortable with our presence, happy to talk to us and ready to help us with our project. If the interviewee preferred us not to use a recording device, then we quickly put it away and focused on the business of asking the kind of questions likely to produce a meaningful and considered response which may be analysable at some point in the future. Throughout this book the interview data we managed to get on tape is dispersed among data taken from field notes. When we were not permitted to use recording equipment, or on those occasions we chose not to, we attempted to transcribe verbatim accounts of the interviews directly afterwards and consolidated this information with detailed ethnographic accounts of the entire encounter. Still, many of the quotes we offer over the coming pages are taken directly from taped interviews, and those that aren't are very accurate reflections of what interviewees had to say. In many cases, short phrases or accounts of crimes clearly stood out in the minds of our researchers and were easily reproduced, and it is these particular quotes we tend to utilise throughout the book.

We have disguised the identity of all our respondents, and we have also done everything possible to ensure that nothing contained in these pages can come back to haunt them. We do not intend to display these men and women as heroic rebels battling against an oppressive social order or minimise the socially corrosive nature of their crimes, but despite the general critical tone of much of what we have to say, nor do we intend to demonise our respondents or portray them in a wholly negative light. Some of those we spoke to revealed to us their involvement in very serious crimes that severely harmed individual victims, and while we were occasionally ill at ease with the nature of these revelations, we were always mindful of the broader forces that brought these men to this point. Some inspired a deep sense of sympathy, others didn't. Some of the situations we entered into made us feel uncomfortable and more than a little angry, whereas others made us laugh and supplied us with a useful stock of amusing anecdotes and one-liners. Some of our interviewees were always forthcoming and keen to help, others took their time to get to know us before consenting to an interview, and of course many others who we met would have nothing to do with us at all. Some scared us so much that we would not even dare insult their photographs, while others were just everyday young men trying to scramble together a living in some of the most dangerous places in Britain.

In methodological terms, the tediously predictable critical response to our general thesis is that our results are not generalisable: our sample is small and localised, and contains few women and no ethnic minorities, and consequently cannot be taken as an accurate reflection of criminal cultures on a global or even national scale. To us this would be a rather petty cut-and-paste observation made about a book that contains within it more than enough contentious argumentation to provoke far more insightful criticism. Clearly we believe that our results might actually be generalisable; we suspect that the motivations, values, normative strategies and orientations displayed by those we spoke to are similar to those of a broad range of criminals throughout the Western world, particularly in Britain and the USA where neo-liberal capitalism appears to be at its most advanced. Certainly, we build a weighty thesis on a relatively small amount of data, but this is entirely in keeping with the long traditions of ethnography and sociological criminology; a fact that increasingly appears to escape many critics of this kind of social research. If we had the time, energy and funding to broaden our study, we are pretty certain that our central thesis would be proven correct by data gathered by streetwise female researchers or data gleaned from similar locales populated by other ethnic groups.

At this stage in our careers we have only a passing interest in the institutional rules of criminological empiricism, and we are not especially concerned about the restrictive doctrines of contemporary social research. To us what matters is presenting an accurate reflection of the environments, the cultures and the sentiments and expressions of the individuals we researched, and ultimately the conclusions to be drawn from the data we have managed to accumulate. We believe the data we offer in the following pages, when coupled with our previous research in similar environments, entirely justifies some of our bolder claims. We think our times demand serious, penetrative theoretical engagement and necessitate a wilful disregard for the restrictive administrative and conceptual orthodoxies that continue to prevent criminology from advancing from its current position and making real suggestions about what has to be done to reduce crime and improve everyday social life. This is certainly one topic we were unwilling and unable to be dispassionate about, and we hope the reader can see why.

Chapter 2

Life on the precipice: economic change and acute marginalisation

The world changes . . .

While we do not want to take up too much space retelling the story of the epochal shift from industrial to consumer capitalism, it's crucial to make the connection between the wholesale economic change that occurred across the West during the 1980s and the acute marginalisation that followed in its wake. As we have suggested in much greater detail elsewhere (Hall 1997; Winlow 2001; Hall and Winlow 2003; Winlow and Hall 2006), the rapid withdrawal of traditional forms of paid employment profoundly affected the practical life-world, moral codes and the *habitus* of a traditional industrial working class whose temporary and partial stability had provided generations of men and women with a suite of dispositions that enabled them to cope with the practical and cultural pressures they faced. It also furnished the majority with clearly defined and dependable identities, and imbued them with a responsive and highly nuanced feel for the world around them. Despite its many local and regional variations, the basic form of the productivist working-class *habitus* guided the majority of individuals along clearly identifiable and reasonably predictable biographical trajectories, providing them with the wherewithal to construct meaningful and fulfilling lives in the face of their ongoing subjugation to and exploitation by those who owned and controlled the means of production. Some liberal commentators have emphasised the insular, regressive and reactionary tendencies of working-class culture, in which progressive liberal values could often be held back, but there is no denying that until the 1980s many individuals were comfortable living within its parameters, to the extent that they were willing to engage in political struggle to ensure the historical continuation of their way of life. From the mid nineteenth century many modern working-class lives tended to unfold within a communal context of interdependency and mutuality born not only of practical circumstances but also of a tacit recognition of shared prospects and hardships, and this cultural awareness of common interests and common fate was also institutionalised at the political level. In the Heideggerian sense working-class being was 'thrown into the world' as a product of the anarchic dynamism of the developing forces of production, but how individuals eventually came together to make their home in it as moral, social and political beings is yet to be fully understood.

Since the heyday of classical industrial capitalism in the nineteenth century, working-class life has revolved around the certainty of paid employment and a specific mode of exploitation. The basic economic principles of wage-labour are unchanged, but in reality the nature of paid work has changed considerably and not necessarily for the better, which casts a shadow over some liberal commentators' celebration of the opening up of opportunities for individual expression and so-called 'new communities'. Furthermore, it's now clear that pockets of acute marginalisation have developed in locales of permanent recession throughout Britain, creating a distinct section of British society that has little or no formal interaction with the legitimate economy. Those who constitute this social group are not simply a contemporary manifestation of the dispossessed poor of the modern era, and the key issue relating to their place in society is not the continued ability of those with social power to negatively portray and categorise the lower echelons of the 'working class' as pathological, violent and criminal barbarians, as some still argue (see, for example, Bagguley and Mann 1992; Welshman 2006). In a society held in thrall by the spectacle of western culture and intoxicated with the promises of indulgent consumerism that now extend some considerable distance beyond needs (Debord 1984; Žižek 2002; Barber 2007), acute marginality can be understood only by means of a penetrative critique of the deeper culturally constitutive and reproductive forces that underlie our current social and economic order. As we shall see in following chapters, the economic logic underneath the mode of social competition and self-interest, which structures and drives market capitalism and its liberal democratic culturo-political system, has actively sought to create winners and losers, carefully and diligently diffusing throughout the social body a cultural code that justifies and naturalises a narrative of interpersonal struggle, success and failure, and which, with the full force of a recast super-ego, compels the majority to throw themselves into the mêlée. While the market has created more affluence, it has also systematically encouraged most individuals to be discontented and dissatisfied with their lives, thus maintaining the 'dream' and the steady flow of money into consumer markets (see Lane 2001).

Of course, those individuals who 'fail' to engage successfully with the consumer economy are easily dismissed as feckless, uneducated and lazy (Murray 1990, 1994), but this should not draw our attention away from the blunt realities of a global economy that has severely reduced its need for the relatively expensive mass industrial workforces that once were the backbone of the old industrial nations of the West. The labour market in Britain is now 'flexible', open to global competition and highly unstable, constituted by a sizeable low-paid casual service sector containing an increasing proportion of exploited migrants alongside enclaves of occupational specialists. The economy is administered by corporate high-flyers and ruled over by a new breed of globally-oriented business oligarch, many of whom have shown tendencies to corruption (Woodiwiss 2005). The days of organised trade unions bargaining with traditional industries and imposing their collective will upon a social democratic state are at an end. Most consumer items can be made far more cheaply in developing countries, and as a consequence, the forms of production that remain in a country such as Britain tend to be highly specialised or significantly downgraded in terms of status, job security, pay levels and other benefits.

It's worth reminding ourselves that the first two-thirds of the twentieth century saw significant leaps forward in social justice as the working classes were able to organise political representation to intervene on their behalf. Once the horror of war faded, the political consensus in the era of post-war reconstruction encouraged full employment, and a comprehensive welfare system bonded most citizens to mainstream civil society and rapidly expanding forms of public culture (Hobsbawm 1995). This modern social democratic order was founded upon the belief that in order to create the conditions in which freedom could flourish we must first enable those at the bottom to meet their immediate needs, and provide them with the economic opportunities to fashion a reasonable way of life in a regulated market system. However, as we reached the final third of the twentieth century and neo-liberalism's ideological control approached the absolute – expressed for the popular ear by Mrs Thatcher's 'there is no alternative' slogan – 'freedom' would come to mean something very different (Harvey 2007; Murray 1988). From the 1960s onwards, as consumerism became more central to economic growth it also became an increasingly important constituent of the evolving working-class *habitus* as the mass-media's manufactured cultures and technological innovations began to transform identity and citizenship across the West. From the 1980s in particular, economic necessity and rapidly developing cultures of self-interest and narcissism (see Lasch 1991; Hayward and Yar 2006) began to erode the embedded but still rather fragile forms of togetherness that had provided the vital platform on which the working class had been able to organise a meaningful and effective political resistance to the unrelenting edicts of modern capitalism: competition, cost-cutting, efficiency, productivity, growth. A new era of ideological control cultivated intense social competition and instrumentalism at the very heart of British culture as the logic of the market rapidly filtered into the working class's social locations, institutions and cultural traditions, which in its heartlands had built up a resistance to this malign influence and grown the fragile saplings of a genuine 'otherness'. To lubricate this cultural sea change, we were told by the increasingly shrill voices in neo-liberal academia and popular culture alike that enduring bonds would inhibit rather than enrich, that commitment to any collective project would impinge upon 'personal freedoms', and that the virtues of reciprocity and community involvement would give way to the calculated, instrumental and strategic sociocultural engagement of the individual (Bauman 2000, 2006; Beck and Beck-Gernsheim 2001).

The rapid erosion of traditional labour markets further withered modernist community, as 'the family wage' (Fraser 1994; Montanari 2000; see also Shulman 2003) was consigned to history and mobility and flexibility became essential requirements in postmodern labour markets. The 1980s also witnessed the end of the parallel biographies usually associated with working-class life (Winlow and Hall 2006) as workers were ushered into the rapidly expanding service sector and became conversant with its new instrumental ethos and forced 'emotional' commitment to the corporate image (*ibid.*; see also Taylor and Bain 1999). The fact that this new workforce wore ties instead of overalls did not herald a new era of 'civilised labour', or an end to exploitation, or indeed indicate a shift in the balance of power between employers and employees (see Angell 2001; Friedman 2000). The promise that the new economic era would be characterised by bright ideas, brisk innovation and new technologies that would propel the whole society into a new era of freedom and prosperity was, for all but a small number, a sham. After the disappearance of the heavy industry that constituted the practical point of existence for the world's oldest working class (Byrne 1989) and made Britain a global industrial superpower (Hobsbawm 1989), more and more people were drafted into the ranks of a new, downgraded and depoliticised workforce in the service industries. The sexy hi-tech media and information jobs that were believed to typify Britain's new economic dynamism were in reality few and far between (see, for example, Brown and Hesketh 2004). Women did not suddenly storm boardrooms and nor did significant numbers of the ex-working classes find themselves dragged into a slipstream that helped them upwards through the post-16 education system towards a nirvana built upon individual skill and tenacity. Instead, significant numbers of working people were forced to cope with the drudgeries of the rapidly growing McJobs sector: minimum wage, part-time and non-unionised employment often coupled with anti-social work shifts and oppressive management strategies. These new working lives were often devoid of the enduring friendships and forms of mutuality, resistance and humour that once made the industrial workplace bearable. According to Ames (2007), the American 'workplace shooting' phenomenon that began in the 1980s is an indication that, after the Reaganite economic reforms, working lives in many occupations engendered interpersonal disdain and hostility to an extent unprecedented in the history of modern industrial capitalism between individuals of the same or similar rank, individuals who once might have become close workmates. Among the Western European nations, Britain has been the most enthusiastic importer of this intensified work culture.

The defeat of organised labour, abetted by an increasingly sophisti-cated meaning system that stressed instrumental self-interest and pen-etrated into the deepest recesses of culture and psyche, ushered the workforce-citizenry into an advanced phase of the liberal-capitalist project. As the new 24-hour information society (Castells 1997) kicked into gear, the traditional Monday to Friday, nine to five working week became increasingly rare as shift patterns adapted to the rigours of the global consumer/service economy. For many full-time employees work-ing hours increased significantly, and for others insecure part-time labour became unavoidable as employers sought to further cut back on costs with the hope of expanding profit. From this historical juncture, increasing numbers of workers would attempt to construct a viable income by maintaining more than one job (see Toynbee 2003), further eroding modern presumptions about job stability, 'family time', rest, relaxation, and the balance between work and consumption, which were all essential to 'the good life' (see Warburton 2006). In a general atmosphere of increased competition, employers could demand and receive more from their employees without risking the threat of industrial unrest. Within the new consumer-led growth areas of the economy short-term, hourly-paid contracts became standardised, often accompanied by wages that failed to reflect the cost of living (Ehrenreich 2002; Newman 1999). For many, this effectively meant a reversion back to the raw exploitation of early capitalism as workers were once again cast as totally expendable and exploitable units of production without a stable platform of functional value and political solidarity from which they could attempt to change their situation. The wreck of the formerly strong platform that working-class culture and politics certainly once had been – dealt its final blow in the defeat of the striking miners in 1984/85 – became something from which to escape rather than stay and fight for. Rather than petition for change as a collective, the response of most low-grade service workers to personal dissatisfaction appears to have been to move on to pastures new. Many workers who negatively appraise their current employment often seek to remedy the situation by moving on to yet another employer, usually in the same sector, but rarely at increased levels of pay. Our recent research (see Winlow and Hall 2006) has revealed that many young service workers understand this process as essentially progressive, as each employer is cast as a staging post on the onward journey to higher social status, greater freedom and material prosperity, despite rather stark indications that in reality this dream almost never comes true. There is no doubt, however, as the cultural studies theorists have been keen to remind us (see McGuigan 2006), that both the collective loss and the individual frustration are compensated by the availability of a vast array of cheap consumer goods, both physical and virtual, that saturate the high streets, living rooms and TV screens that constitute the everyday vista of late modern life.

The flexibility of these new labour markets and the expanding diversification of lifestyles in popular culture emboldened a broad range of cultural commentators to proclaim that things were getting better and the Western population was scaling new heights of liberation: the whole way of life was becoming more open, more fluid, more dynamic, driven by healthy open competition in a new meritocracy (see Friedman 2000). However, for most of those who were economically active in these developing sectors of the economy a depressing and anxiety-inducing work experience became coupled with the expectation of continual consumption during time spent away from work. Work and commercial-ised leisure became locked together and normalised as life's principal effort/reward dyad, and from the 1980s onwards the majority of workers, who lacked entirely the political power to change any of the main coordinates of their existence (Žižek 2006c), were to be controlled and exploited both at work and in their leisure time more completely than at any other time in Western history. Established forms of cultural identity were rapidly remoulded to fit in with the new disciplines of advanced consumerism, and while some adapted and prospered, a growing number found themselves to be downwardly mobile and freefalling perilously close to a bare minimal functional existence as socio-economic and cultural beings and total irrelevance as active ethico-political beings. More importantly, as we will discuss later, they were being shown a way of dreaming that allowed them to enjoy this existence, which was ushered in by the remarkable recuperation of the artistic 'social critique' that had once been aimed at capitalism itself (Boltanski and Chiapello 2006).

The casualties of 'the great change'

Alongside the elite of mega-winners, technocrats and a proletarianised middle class (Lea 2002), the rapid shift from industrialism to the new consumer/service economy produced many casualties (Agamben 1998; Žižek 2008), but those who concern us here inhabit the moribund cultural sectors of the working class that were unable to adapt to – and which were deliberately discarded by – this new phase in the history of the capitalist project (Hall 1997; Winlow 2001). The inability or reluctance of some to retrain and prepare themselves for the new functional demands of the service sector created pockets of long-term unemployment, often in residential areas that once serviced heavy industry or in low-income estates within or on the outskirts of the larger cities. For Thatcher and the other ideologically driven neo-liberals who followed in her wake with religious zeal (see Gray 2007), a high rate of unemployment was the initial price to be paid for streamlining industry and labour markets in preparation for the new challenges of global market competition (see Hutton 1996). As competition for work grew, forward-thinking employers would be able to pick the best – in the sense of the most functionally educated, skilled, innovative, enthusiastic and compliant – for the challenges that lay ahead. The British economy would now rise or fall as a result of its ability to offer new and improved ideas, designs, goods and services as cheaply as possible to consuming populations seeking value for money and global corporations concerned solely with the financial interests of shareholders. As Britain stumbled into the 1990s, the high rates of unemployment and urban unrest that typified the 1980s at first glance appeared to have passed. As the City of London established itself as a global financial centre and the unemployment rate seemed to decrease, house prices rose swiftly, prompting an upsurge in consumer confidence that buoyed the national economy.

However, despite the apparent economic success of Blair and Brown's 'New Labour' administration (see Toynbee and Walker 2005; Giddens 2007), which brought on the temporary 'feel-good factor' before the realisation that it was a mirage appearing in a fragile bubble of expanding credit started to dawn on traditionally slow-on-the-uptake British political pundits, the affluence of the late 1990s and the early years of the twenty-first century only partially masked the continuity of a sector of British society now commonly cast as an urban 'underclass': a marginalised, depoliticised and redundant rump permanently at the bottom of Britain's supposedly fluid social hierarchy. Even the ranks of casual workers that endured throughout the industrial period in the larger cities usually maintained some contact with the formal economy and functioned as a reserve army of labour, putting downward pressure on wage levels and serving as a subtle reminder to those in work that everybody was expendable (Stedman-Jones 1976; Byrne 2007). The new consumer economy simply did not require such high levels of employment, partly as a result of the development of new technologies and the streamlined, downsized forms of work and industry that tended to predominate in the post-1980 western world. As working-class fathers gave way to underclass sons (Lash 1994), some previously functional and socially ordered working communities began to degenerate into turbulent and deeply problematic locales often typified by high levels of violence, crime, and a range of other social ills (*ibid.*; Wilson 1987, 1997). The locales in which we conducted our research were just such places. Carville in Newcastle and the North River and Southfield estates in Sunderland already had established criminal traditions, but up to the 1980s they were relatively small, problematic aspects of what were once well-ordered and reasonably politicised dormitories for the modern industrial workforce, which appeared after the slum clearances of the early and mid twentieth century. The shipbuilding industries in both cities were major employers of men on these estates until the late 1970s, and by the time the shipyards finally closed for good in the late 1980s, these places were firmly established as areas of permanent recession (Taylor 1999). These neighbourhoods now suffer high crime rates and all the other social problems usually associated with areas of concentrated relative deprivation and marginal cultural and economic significance, and it was in these places that we began to develop the research contacts that would help us to formulate our central thesis (see Hall *et al.* 2005).

From the outset it was clear that those with whom we sought to speak were very different from older generations on these same estates. Our previous research, commencing in the late 1990s and continuing into the early twenty-first century (*ibid.*; Winlow 2001; Hall 1997, 2000), produced accounts of economic and social transitions within working class cultures, but by the time we took to the streets again for this project, those transitions were complete; only the vague, mutated remnants of the previous cultural order lingered on as an almost spectral background hue. Most strikingly, there are parts of the Southfield estate in which no one works. Older generations no longer populate the small cluster of streets in which we conducted the majority of our research, and the lively cultural activity occurring here tended to centre on a large and shifting population of young men. There were groups of young women, occasionally pushing prams or accompanying toddlers to school or to the local store, but for the most part these were masculine domains. As we moved a little further into the estate, demographics changed slightly. There were older generations out in public space, especially women who appeared to be aged between 30 and 50. Very few middle aged or older men were out on the street during the day. This is not an estate populated solely by young unemployed men, but there are certain times and places where they were quite clearly the most visible section of the population.

What became the main focus of concern was the palpable shift in criminal cultures that had occurred on estates such as this. Violence has throughout the industrial era been a part of working-class culture, but what was once heavily restrained and ritualised by traditional masculine codes now appeared to be both ubiquitous and increasingly random in occurrence, and often cast outside or in opposition to the prevailing criminal hierarchies on the estate. The buying and selling of illegal substances now constituted a veritable shadow economy, and we quickly discovered that the adaptable and multi-skilled criminals of our previous research had for the most part evolved into a new cohort of committed drug-dealers and occasional criminal opportunists. As we investigated further it became clear that, as the links with industrial work and the politics and ethico-cultural tradition of the industrial working class had been entirely severed, consumerism – and the individual struggle for the acquisition of status within its circuits – had become entwined with the broader and more traditional form of social competition to produce a new and decidedly fractious criminal culture deeply indicative of the cultural logic of advanced market capitalism (see Sennett 2006). We explore the fine details of this in later chapters.

As hedonism, instrumentality, individualisation and risk increasingly came to characterise the whole of Western culture, so these places became less stable, more competitive and increasingly devoid of the community cohesion that typified these very streets in the not too distant past. Criminal traditions and hierarchies of violence and criminal competence had evolved from the toughness, physicality and endurance that were masculine characteristics once systematically cultivated to service the needs of heavy labour, nationalism, military expansion and methods of internal social control in the modern era, but now they seemed to be merging in strange hybrids with the new disciplinary demands of entrepreneurship, lifestyle enhancement and ornamental consumerism. Similarly, the dependable structures of gendered identity that ordered these communities during the industrial modern period had been transformed into a tangled web of narcissism, egoism, uncertainty and anxiety, framed against an imposing background of advanced consumer symbolism. Immediately striking here was the number of young adult men who had powerful bodies and brutal attitudes towards others, yet who also displayed an almost childlike fascination with youth-oriented clothes, gadgets and media productions. For those we spoke to, life was understood as a constant battle for cultural significance in the locale and in a fantasised version of the broader culture, a battle that could be fought only with an armoury well stocked with the weapons of consumer symbolism, a battle in which involvement was compulsory and the perceived benefits of triumph massively out-weighed the potential pitfalls. In the vast majority of cases the lives of our respondents were dominated by the constant scramble to accumulate and display, and many had become enchanted by an idealised image of themselves that bore no relationship at all to the actual material and socio-political realities of their lives. Despite existing on a precipice beyond which there was nothing but total insignificance, they believed that some day soon things would change, and change radically. A magical reversal of (mis)fortune, a classic Heraclitian *enantiodromia*, awaited just around the corner, after which they would experience a meteoric rise and take their place among the lucky ones who were able to indulge in the most grandiose consumer fantasies of excess and gilded opulence, which would distinguish them from the bovine 'herd' of losers who might once have been regarded by their ancestors as comrades in a political struggle to improve a common position. Below we want to commence what will become a more detailed exploration of life on this precipice by offering some data that provide an insight into how its largely hard-bitten inhabitants make sense of and engage with the consumer-driven world around them.

Living on the precipice

The majority of those we spoke to have experienced quite stark forms of relative material deprivation, humiliation and emotional hardship throughout their lives, and most are currently getting by on welfare and what they can scrape together from the illegitimate sectors of the economy. Many also spoke of turbulent childhoods blighted by family break-up, physical abuse, the death of close family members, and spells in local authority care. Stevie, one of our oldest respondents at 33, tells us that:

> I was brought up by my two older sisters really, me and me younger brother, she [mother] was always out, you've got no idea. I haven't got a clue who me old man is, I don't think she even knows herself. Couldn't give a fuck to be honest with you.

Stevie's mother frequently abandoned her four children and often failed to provide for even their most basic needs:

> I can remember having to go and pinch food from the Spar [a local store] coz she would leave us with nowt. Me sisters used to make

me do it but I suppose they had no choice. Most of the time we would knock on the neighbours' [door] and bum tins of soup and that off them. Even at Christmas and that we used to get next to nowt, there was never any special dinners and hardly any presents, nowt good that's for sure. She would tell us that we'd get stuff in the sales in January but obviously it was just to keep us quiet.

Eventually Stevie's family came to the attention of social services and at the age of nine he experienced the first of what was to be several spells in local authority care. Stevie explains that this was not at all an unpleasant time; he was well fed, well cared for and quite happy:

It was canny to be honest. The only real bad part was that me sisters weren't with me, they were older so stayed at home but wor kid [meaning 'our kid', his younger brother] was with me. They bought you decent clothes as well. I got me first decent trainers off them, a pair of Adidas, I always remember that.

Growing up during the 1980s in the Carville area of Newcastle and with a strong dislike of school, Stevie quickly found himself in the company of a ready cast of criminal associates. He regularly truanted from school and then found himself embroiled in car theft, shoplifting and burglary. He isn't keen on exploring the more intricate dynamics of this process, but believes 'falling in with the wrong crowd' sealed his fate:

I was doing houses [meaning burglaries] at the age of 12. Clemmy [a friend], he was 15 at the time and a few of his pals got me into it. I had no fear so they thought I was cush. Getting locked up or the threat of it was nowt to fear in my little mind at the time. As far as I was bothered you got well looked after if you got locked up. Even in the bizzy station they were always nice to you, you got cups of tea and sarnies and that. It was certainly nowt to be scared of.

Stevie's association with Clemmy also led him into the world of organised football hooliganism, but what interested Stevie about this particular social setting was not the prospect of violence or some suppositious hankering after mock anthropological rituals, but the criminal opportunities provided by the cover of the 'mob' and his expanding circle of contacts:

It was Clemmy again, he got me into it. I used to go [to] home and away [games] all the time. I used to love it. Not so much the fighting, I did get stuck in, but that wasn't the best bit. It was going away and terrorising people, everybody used to shit themselves, the locals, and we used to go mental in the shops, that was the bit I liked, just steaming in the shops and blagging loads of gear. Fuck the match, get the gear. It was all designer swag at the time, Fila, Lacoste, Tacchini, Fred Perry was popular then as well as smart trousers, Farah and that, Diesel jeans, Nike Air Max or Kickers. You had to have the proper gear as well. We used to make fucking fortunes at the time. You know Fenwicks [department store]? In Newcastle? We used to rake fortunes in from there, everyone was wearing Barbour stuff, wax jackets and that, and we used to travel all over in Clemmy's car. Used to sell all the swag on a match day. Fucking great times they were.

Stevie's growing love of hedonism immediately led him towards the rapidly developing rave scene, and while he claims to have been a dedicated raver, the rediscovery of the 'luvved up' (Collin and Godfrey 1997) hippy ethic of early British dance music or the so-called 'new communities' evolving in this scene did not persuade him to put aside his ongoing preoccupation with the bottom line. Neatly avoiding perilous run-ins with the organised criminals who attempted to dominate the huge market for recreational drugs at raves and nightclubs, Stevie prospered:

I used to sell Es and speed, trips as well when I could get them. I always got them on bail as well. It was naughty with the likes of ***** and them trying to run everything but the places, where the raves were on, they were fucking massive, fucking hundreds and hundreds of people, no one can control everything on that big a fucking level. I used to just be careful; people used to pull you for to sort them out, you didn't really have to advertise. I got away with it every time, fuck them, plastic fucking gangsters trying to run the show. To be honest, half the time I was too off me own head to care about them.

Since these heady days, Stevie has had an ongoing involvement in Carville's drug trade. Despite experiencing the ups and downs that come with prolonged involvement in relatively low-level drug sales, Stevie has been able to provide his girlfriend and newborn daughter with a reasonable standard of living by manipulating the benefits system and profiting from the estate's voracious appetite for weed and coke.

Stevie is quite clear about the abiding rationale that underlies his criminal dealings: money. He suggests that he's always been preoccupied with accumulating enough cash to go out and buy the material/ symbolic possessions that were denied him throughout his childhood and adolescence. His current abode, a mere stone's throw from the house in which he grew up, is a world away from his traumatic former life. Both he and his partner spend much of their disposable cash on elaborately furnishing this modest terraced house on the edge of Carville, and as we stroll through his home he identifies new purchases and mentally tabulates their combined expenditure before sharing the information with our researcher. He immediately recalls how much each item cost and from where it was purchased, and he is very keen to impress upon us that all of the branded items are authentic and were bought in respectable stores.

Stevie has an ongoing attachment to gadgets and gizmos, and as we enter an upstairs room he lovingly displays his collection of 'boys' toys'. For the most part, what we see laid out before us, like most of the other expensive consumer items that occupy his home, have been purchased with the proceeds of crime. A top of the range racing bike with all the accessories, an expensive crossbow, Xbox 360, PlayStation 2, PSP, plasma TVs, home cinema systems, paintball equipment, a laptop computer, a huge Bose music system, a jet-ski parked in the yard, every item momentarily captivating but ultimately unfulfilling. As we work our way around the house, it becomes abundantly clear that this is not merely an informative tour, but rather a calculated tactic aimed at convincing our researcher that things are going well for Stevie, that his life is a success, and that we should in fact envy his accomplishments, his innate talent and entrepreneurial flair. Above all, we must not see Stevie as a loser, an undistinguished member of the herd. As we shall see later, this is not simply born of a self-satisfied, grandiose perception of his own criminal success, but rather a telling indication of the unavoidable anxiety deliberately cultivated by consumer culture and the symbolic violence that is a crucial component in its mode of operation.

As a dedicated consumer deeply concerned with presentation, Stevie has wardrobes full of designer clothes and a staggering assortment of pairs of expensive, fashionable trainers, many of which are in such pristine condition that they appear to have been worn very infrequently, if at all. He attends the gym regularly and sports a year-round sunbed tan. In order to maintain this enviable lifestyle, albeit on one of the most deprived and crime-ridden estates in the country, Stevie must continue to stay afloat in the choppy waters of the local drug trade. For the moment his main trade is in 'nine bar' blocks of cannabis resin, but he also has a growing interest in cocaine:

Most people sell shit Charlie for forty quid a gram. It really is shit as well. They pay eight hundred quid an ounce. But it is proper stamped on to fuck. They stamp on it a bit more so it's even worse when people get it. I pay eleven hundred quid for proper swag. I take my bit out so I get good stuff, then bosh it into two and it's still better than the crap they put out. You have to pay more for owt that's good. People would rather pay fifty quid a gram for my stuff coz they know it's always quality. Same with dope. Crappy normal solids is cheap as fuck but it's shit. Skunk's dear as fuck coz it's good. You get what you pay for, clothes, everything, good gear always costs.

Stevie's inexhaustible desire to indulge his innermost consumer fantasies continues unabated, and while he is now less inclined to blow his money partying in the city's nightclubs, he remains wide-eyed and awestruck by the inexhaustible array of items that, he believes, possess the magical qualities necessary to transform his life into a continual, deeply indulgent and richly rewarding excursion in which the thorny memories of his childhood can be progressively left behind; he is pushed as much as he is pulled, driven by his individual escape from the gaping absences and disturbing presences that constitute the memory of his former life, not simply by an attraction to any collective terminus in the future. While Stevie is painfully aware that his current life can be thrown into turmoil by the powerful vortices and riptides that lurk beneath the neighbourhood's drug economy, and which could rapidly pull him down and sweep him along into all sorts of trouble, he cannot picture a life without continual involvement in what to him are the upper echelons of consumer culture, and, as a direct consequence, he cannot picture a life without crime.

Other interviewees linked consumer culture to criminal activity in an even more direct fashion. Karen, 24, is a sex worker living in the north-east of England. She explains her present situation in the following needlepoint way:

Look, it's like this: I want nice clothes, I want to get my hair done, I want nice bags and all the other shit. I've got no qualifications, I don't know anyone who works and gets real cash, and I wanted to live in a nice place. How the fuck else was I gonna get all that?

Karen uses drugs, but scorns the basic presumption that being a sex worker is a direct result of drug addiction:

At the end of the day, I'm a fucking 'sex worker' [heavy irony here] because I want the money, and I take drugs because it means I don't have to think about what smelly man I'm going down on. These mugs [probation officers, youth workers, etc.] just want to hear that I'm addicted to drugs, and so somehow need to go out on the beat. It's easier for them than just having to accept that I choose to do this shit.

Karen is now adept at proffering a basic utilitarian explanation for her continued involvement in prostitution. Like so many other workers in the new economy, hers is a job to be done and then blocked from the mind, its function being nothing more than a means of acquiring the cash to fund another consumer binge. Tellingly, Karen can see no other option, no other defining rationale, no other way of forming or fulfilling her desires. For the moment, she appears relatively sanguine about her lot and happy to revel in the spectacle of competitive acquisition. She has identified what is important to her, and she is willing to commit herself to what she perceives as the sole options available to get it:

> The right shampoo, the right shoes, the right fucking name on your T-shirt: it's life, it's all there is. Show me a way to get that shit without pimping myself out and I'll do it. So what, I suck dick for a living. But I live in a great flat; I've got a 42-inch TV and a wardrobe to die for. Every girl that passes me wishes they could have what I've got . . . It's just a job at the end of the day. I wouldn't give it up; I want it all too much. I'd just be some little mug living in a shitty flat on a stinking council estate, probably with a few kids to boost my benefits on a Monday if I hadn't made this choice. My worker can rattle off all the bull she wants about what I do, at the same time as staring at my Gucci boots and hungering for them (laughs).

Paul is 26 years old and lives in one of the most deprived sections of the Carville. His childhood was very similar to that of Stevie, who we met above. His home life was far from supportive, and he endured quite severe material deprivation and a deeply problematic relationship with his parents. From a very early age he began spending a great deal of time out on the streets and quickly became involved in crime. He identifies consumer symbolism as the key to social acceptance:

> I got picked on at school coz I had shitty trainers. I was a proper bamp [meaning tramp]. I was 12 and was at town with a few of my mates and I saw this kid with these brand-new Air Max, so I just went over and hit him a few times and took them off him. Fucking street robbery at 12, man. They were two sizes too small but I still wore 'em, and things changed at school coz of them new trainers, so I just kept doing it, taking what I wanted. You get noticed, you're one of the cool ones.

Paul's desire to 'fit in yet stand out' (see Miles *et al.* 1998) drew him to conspicuous consumption, and from there into progressively more serious crimes, but his unfolding and deeply turbulent biography veered

35

sharply in a more problematic direction with the introduction of drugs. Once an up-and-coming criminal, highly attuned to the estate's post-proletarian and post-political entrepreneurial culture, he was now a drug addict with little or no disposable cash to indulge his penchant for designer clothes. Paul's retrospective explanations remain remarkably clear:

> Before I was on the rock [meaning crack cocaine], I used to make good money. I've been a grafter since I was about 10, always looking for the fast cash, the easy option. Everyone on my estate's like that ... Come on, you know the shit, it comes down to whether you're a 'have' or a 'have not'. Who notices the 'have nots'? You ain't got the best, then you just don't cut it, simple as that ...

Graham is 40 years old and is one of the most successful criminals we interviewed. Graham's start in life was quite similar to that experienced by Paul. His mother died while he was still a young child, leaving Graham's father to raise and provide for his five sons. Graham's youth was spent on one of the most notorious housing estates in the north-east, and his recollections of childhood poverty are quite stark. He is, however, quick to point out that the strict rule of his father kept him away from serious crime. He explains:

> Me old man used to work down the shipyards; he had to pack it in to look after us. He made sure we had enough to eat and he did his best for us. He used to work in the mornings, a fiddle job, then come home and get all of us ready for school and that. We never had fuck all, clothes or nowt. I used to get called a tramp at school. But it wasn't his fault, there was loads of kids whose mam and dad didn't give a fuck about them. He brought us up to have manners and he was a strict fucker.

Graham credits his father for instilling in him the work ethic that would ensure he steered clear of the abundant hazards strewn around his estate and found his way into a solid, legitimate job once he'd left school. He became a trainee chef and enjoyed the work immensely, but the lure of money and all that it brings eventually drew his attention:

> A lot of the lads were getting into bits and pieces of graft. A couple of my close pals were doing bits of burglary, newsagents, small Co-ops and that. I used to watch them going out every weekend, lovely new clothes on, plenty of wedge in their pockets, they always had girls after them. I thought, hold on a minute, I'm doing the wrong thing here ... To cut a long story short, I pestered them to

take me on the graft with them and that was that, never looked back. I went straight from doing nowt criminal at all to commercial burglary.

Graham's increasing involvement in crime gradually allowed him to taste the lifestyle he desired, replete with designer clothes, flash cars and expensive nights out with friends, but soon the financial reward of being part of a successful team of commercial burglars was judged to be inadequate. Graham had already become involved in ram-raids as a sideline, and he came to the conclusion that he may as well seek out serious money if he was running the risk of a significant jail sentence:

Me old man used to say, 'Rather be hung for a sheep as a lamb'. I was making all right money but it wasn't enough for me. Then I thought about it properly: people were getting four, five-year stretches, just for commercial burglary. I was on the ram-raids at the time and the bizzies and the courts were going off about it. It was in the papers every week. It was a knocking bet that someone was going to be made an example of. So it made sense to go on the naughty graft [meaning armed robbery].

For a long time, Graham prospered. He proved himself to be a particularly astute criminal and quickly established himself as a key figure within the region's serious crime networks. Then one day his luck changed. He and his compatriots appeared to have pulled off a particularly audacious robbery at a security depot, netting a huge sum of money. However, when it came time to dispose of the getaway car, they were observed by an off-duty policeman who raised the alarm and summoned assistance. Graham wistfully explains that:

I was a millionaire for about five minutes (laughs). We thought we'd pulled it off, I was fucking spending the money in me head when it came on top. One daft off-duty bizzy fucks the whole thing up. Cunt.

Graham received a nine-year prison sentence, and is now back on the streets of the north-east. He is not willing to discuss his current means of making a living, but he drives a top of the range BMW, holidays regularly and is always impeccably turned out. Graham's chequered but often very successful criminal background ensures he remains firmly established in local folklore and the region's ivy league of crime. (He turned up for one of our interviews wearing one of the luminous vests often worn by council workers, apparently direct from a stint 'observing' some place of business or other.)

Graham's four younger brothers eventually followed him into crime, but they have not even come close to replicating his financial success or his criminal status. His youngest brother is currently serving a seven-year sentence for supplying heroin, and two others are now heroin addicts. Graham comments:

> It's a shame but what can you do? It's the estate, they came after me and got into the brown, it wasn't really there when I was younger. It's a fucking hopeless place . . . [there's] fuck all there for you if you live in that estate.

When asked to offer further insight into his involvement in crime, Graham's assessment is remarkably similar to those offered by the other respondents throughout this book:

> Everybody likes doing nice things, money gets you them things: car, house, holiday, whatever. If you've got fuck all you're limited in what you can do, you get left out. There's nothing worse than everybody going somewhere, weekend in the Dam or whatever, and you have to miss out coz you're skint.

Graham's involvement in crime appears to be a direct result of his desire to be continually immersed in a world of consumer indulgence, and this 'pull factor' seems to outweigh 'push factors' – apart, that is, from his relative material impoverishment; his early home life seemed to have been ordered, disciplined and, in a firm sort of way, quite caring. What were significant, of course, were the mediated meanings he bought into and ascribed to underlying values and experiences, and the normative strategies these meanings suggested. Like all good entrepreneurs, he has been hoodwinked into believing that freedom and enduring satisfaction are available to all those who desire success badly enough to make the required sacrifices. A life truly of one's own, free from the anxieties and stresses of the hoi polloi, free from the petty restrictions of what remains of the social and moral order, awaits those who recognise the dourness of the mediocre herd and display the fortitude to strive, really strive, for something better. This sacred, mythical place is believed to await all those who manage to acquire the money necessary to gain access, but even a successful criminal like Graham, whose presence causes a sharp intake of breath from the assembled masses as we walk into the local pub, is destined to a life of perpetual struggle. He is condemned to continually appraise his current position as 'not quite good enough' or 'almost there', forever just out of reach of this vividly idealised state of nirvana that will one day wash away his considerable pressures and ongoing tribulations, rendering what he had to do on the long and winding road to this place unimportant, nothing more than a ghostly memory of what he was once willing to do to succeed. As a direct result of this complex process, Graham is attempting to explore other avenues, other ways of making the money he so desperately seeks. He is reflexive enough to recognise that he is unable to continually recreate his present financial success legitimately, despite his growing interest in the local housing market:

> No doubt I'll always get me hands dirty in some way, but if I had real money, that's what I would be doing, buying places, doing them up and selling them. I could make money from drugs as well but it's not really my thing, too many cunts that I wouldn't want to have to trust.

What is important in this account is the essential similarity in orientation and motivation of all the criminals we talked to. It appears that in our thoroughly depoliticised and consumerised times, the fundamental appeal of crime has less to do with excitement or parochial criminal status, and more to do with acquiring the money necessary to make one's way up the mountainside to a place that represents the impossible paradox where social escape and social distinction converge. Unlike so many of our respondents, Graham's crimes are professionally conceived and planned, and painstakingly thought through. He shrewdly assesses the chances of success, and is willing to bide his time if needs be. However, if we unpack and critically appraise his motivations they appear remarkably similar to the low-level street thieves and drug-dealers who make up the majority of our sample. Furthermore, Graham's success and skill at playing this complex and very serious game appears to reinvigorate the perverse system of incentives that drives many young men from these estates towards crime. Graham has reached the elevated criminal position that so many of our younger respondents strive for, and as a direct consequence he has unwittingly become a locally iconic representative of the *ego ideal*, stimulating the desire in others to achieve social success through crime.

Diana proved to be a key research contact, and one of our most informed and articulate observers of evolving criminal cultures in the north-east of England. Reflecting on a long and varied criminal career, she comments thus:

> We never had any money growing up, I never did without, I just never had the best. School was all about what you had, not who you were. I wanted to be a 'somebody' and really thought if I had the right things I would be. I was 13 the day I promised myself I would do whatever I had to to get what I wanted, the day I chose to

become the best criminal I could be. I meant it. I spent the next five years doing masses of fraud, not to survive, not for food or for a home, not for drugs, just so I could be someone, be like those people on the telly. Live the dream. I had it all, the best clothes, the most expensive make-up, the newest trainers, the named jeans, I had everything . . . right down to designer fucking soap in my bathroom.

But the satisfaction and contentment Diana associated with conspicuous consumption somehow failed to materialise, and the acceptance, status and envious position she had managed to attain proved to be of only passing comfort:

I still didn't feel like I was 'somebody'. On the outside, though, people thought I was something, someone special, someone good . . . the more you have, the better people seem to think you are. My mass history of crimes come down to one thing and one thing only: materialism. [I was] buying into this notion that having all the right things would mean I would have a good life. The endless search for that something that would make me feel a 'somebody' in other people's eyes . . . I'm still fighting that particular addiction today even, because it's the hardest, most intense addiction, to fight this image that's been planted into you, that what you have is who you are. It hits from all sides, no escape, it's subliminal, covert and more dangerous than any drug I've ever injected.

In contrast, Taz is not prone to this kind of self-analysis and not yet capable of this level of insight and articulation. Since a very early age, Taz has carried with him the significant cultural power that accompanies a violent reputation. He is not simply skilled at violence; he has deliberately cultivated an image of extreme unpredictability coupled with the excessive use of force, and has already proven himself willing to use weapons with potentially lethal consequences. In an area populated by many violent and occasionally desperate men, it is this combination of skills that has enabled Taz to rise rapidly to the very top of the estate's criminal hierarchy. He might be only 20 years old, but he has already accumulated crucial knowledge about the drugs business and clearly knows how to impose his will upon suppliants involved in the street-level drug traffic. Unwilling to follow the painstaking route to the top, Taz dove straight in and let the chips fall wherever they may:

There's no point in grafting for somebody else, whatever you're into you have to be your own boss, get rich by letting the divvies do all the work and take all the risks.

Driven and ruthlessly ambitious, Taz's business strategy was rather basic but highly effective; all drug-dealers who wanted to operate on the estate would have to buy their drugs from him or they would be permanently put out of business:

> I get dafties to deal for ez, I lay it on bail for them and they only get so long to sell it and hand the wedge over ... I just tell them, sell for me or don't sell at all; if they're sensible they do what they're told, if not, they know the score.

In this way Taz has managed to get a lot of street-level dealers to sell his products, and his fearsome reputation has so far ensured that the recalcitrant debtors that are endemic in local drug scenes have yet to impinge upon his meteoric rise to the pinnacle of the region's criminal networks. At 20 years of age, Taz has achieved far more criminal success than most of his peers combined. He is rich, and revels in his success. His concern for the established Godfathers of the area appears negligible, but he seems aware that at some point conflict will be inevitable:

> There's fuck all they can do. If any fucker says owt it's not just me they have to worry about, the people I get my gear off are proper dangerous, into robbery and all that as well, they'd blow their fucking legs off, no messing.

The abundant pleasures of hedonistic leisure and consumerism are the pay-off for the real dangers of his occupation. Most weekends you can find Taz strutting from nightclub to nightclub and from bar to bar, followed by an entourage of subordinates, squandering rolls of money, seemingly without a care in the world. For the time being, his is a bountiful world of champagne, designer clothes and high-strength cocaine, a world saturated by the respect, fear and terror-driven obsequiousness shown by his subordinates. The position he has attained acts as a beacon of social distinction to others awestruck by its power, an idealised state of encultured manliness, unremitting brutality, ruthless enterprise and hard-won success. Around Carville there are muttered oaths of revenge and imminent doom, quickly covered up with a thin veneer of smiles and friendly conversation. But despite the snares and hazards that lie in store for Taz, there are few men in this neighbourhood who would turn their back on a chance to gain even a part of what he has; he is what passes here today for the entrepreneurial *Übermensch* – although we are well aware that this is not what Nietzsche meant by the term but a thoughtless Randian perversion of his original meaning – who sits atop the herd of divvies, dafties, losers and punters on a crest of barbaric distinction.

Today Taz is patrolling the streets in his brand new Lexus, enjoying the envious glances he receives from old and young alike. His car embodies his material success, an indulgent reward for all his hard work, and he 'wears' it rather than drives it. He is also keenly aware of the power of its image:

It's a rapper's car, isn't it (laughs)? All the rappers drive Lex's. It's a symbol thing, isn't it?

Although Taz's childhood was far from idyllic, he did not suffer the material deprivations experienced by Stevie and Paul. He remains in regular contact with his mother, and he is proud that he now has the money to indulge her a little:

See the telly, DVD, hi-fi, I got all them for me mam, that ornament there [a large ceramic leopard] I got her that this Christmas, four hundred fucking quid that was, from Collectables [a local store specialising in faux-exotic ceramics and cutlery]. I'm going to get her the matching one for her birthday.

In a way similar to many of our other respondents, Taz believes he has fully appraised the blunt realities of his social world and made a calculated decision to take on the challenges of a life totally committed to crime. For him the prospect of total cultural irrelevance is far more terrifying than prison or even a sudden hail of bullets, and for a young man like Taz the answer appears straightforward:

What's that Fifty Cent album, *Get Rich or Die Trying* (laughs)? That'll be fucking me that, I'll either be fucking loaded or some cunt'll end up topping ez. Why worry, eh? You've got to have a try, either that or live like a divvie.

While Taz was making his ascent up the organic hierarchy of the area's criminal culture, he might well have passed another of our respondents heading in the opposite direction. Craig has been an active criminal for many years and was once enmeshed within one of the region's most successful criminal crews. Once respected for his steadfastness and criminal entrepreneurship, events have conspired against him and his life has become increasingly perilous. Recognised by all as a skilful grower of cannabis, Craig's bad luck story is common to many men who populate this estate. After successive prison sentences, creeping drug addiction and spiralling debts, the expansive vista of possibilities he once surveyed during his youth has disappeared, and he is now exiled in a run-down flat attempting to avoid those who would do him harm.

Craig was once a man with a pocket full of money, convinced of his own criminal skill and certain of his continuing ability to generate money by illegal means. The succession of criminal scores that came his way led to bouts of excessive consumption and a penchant for cocaine. In the intervening period between scores, in keeping with one of the risky principles behind Western capitalism's bubble economies, he overvalued and speculated too hard on his future prospects, running up drug debts in the belief that they would be paid off in due course, as soon as his pockets filled up again. Craig overplayed the local futures market, and the run of bad luck that increasingly appeared to be shaping his life came as a shock, and then things became worse, and then worse still. One of his growing operations was busted by the police and another planned centre of horticultural productivity failed to materialise because of the negligence of one of his less industrious partners. Craig then found himself in prison once again for a theft that he would have once regarded as beneath a criminal of his stature. Throughout all of this, he bought cocaine and amphetamines on credit, desperately trying to feed his addiction and financially keep his head above water. Inevitably, a disgruntled former colleague caught up with him and the tumult of his life momentarily receded as he found himself in hospital nursing numerous stab wounds. During his spell in hospital Craig was visited by a benevolent apparition in the form of an old friend and occasional criminal colleague who had managed to hold on to his reputation and his grip on the criminal markets in which he prospered:

> I think I would have been done in by now if Wayne hadn't stepped in. He paid a couple of people off and the rest know him though so they haven't done nowt. He doesn't know every fucker well enough to keep them at bay. Me old doll [his mother] helped out and all. I owe her fucking fortunes, all me dad's insurance money just about [his father had died of heart disease two years ago].

In order to fuel his speculation, Craig had also become involved in the magic process of fractional reserve lending, except that, of course, he was borrowing from what he himself did not have. As he explains:

> I had a canny run (laughs). I was just robbing Peter to pay Paul at first, paying them a bit here and a bit there, putting them off. I'd sold gear for ages, I used to make good money for them, it just went tits up. The money just used to disappear, then you have all them cunts that won't pay their chuckie and I was doing [meaning taking] loads in meself. I was smoking the rocks, that's what went wrong. I didn't know what fucking day it was half the time, never mind getting debt money in. I was handing out Es like fucking Smarties as well,

especially to rammy lasses. Clubbing, smoking loads of skunk, I had a try at the dirty brown stuff but it's not for me that, I get daft enough as it is, just going mental, doing everything all at once. Before you know it you owe fortunes and then you can't get any more gear to sell and you're fucked.

As Craig suggests above, his desire to display his success to members of the opposite sex often depleted his reserves. A succession of women came and went, and with them a significant proportion of the money he earned from drug sales:

They want every fucking thing top notch, when you live with them it's all the best fucking gear, two grand settees, mahogany fucking coffee tables, fucking expensive blinds, wood floors. We had a bastard eight hundred quid cooker and she never even used to fucking use it. Then they want money for clothes all the time, jewellery, it never stops. The kiddies have got to have all the best swag and that as well, fucking designer stuff, fifty quid a pop for shoes for fucking two year olds and that. She spent fortunes on tanning herself, fucking holidays in Ibiza, Tenerife, it's mental, that's where money goes, stuff . . . and drugs like (laughs)!

Craig is, however, magnanimous enough to acknowledge his own role in his downfall. His party lifestyle inevitably drained his finances:

Everything you do now, well good stuff, it all costs a fucking fortune. A night out, a proper night out, for a kick-off you want a Henry, there's a hundred and twenty five quid before you even buy a drink. Even if you sell a gram you only get forty quid back, then paying into places, taxis, drink, every fucker's into buying fucking jugs of vodka and Red Bull, tabs, maybe a couple of Es, a smoke for when you get home, it all adds up. That's without buying owt new to wear or fuck all. No wonder I'm in debt.

Trapped in a prison cell for a while and now in a decaying flat on one of the worst stretches of Carville, Craig has had plenty of time to reflect on where it all went wrong. In a painfully accurate and reflexive analysis, Craig suggests:

You've got a choice, either manage to get the money or miss out. It's simple. But why should you miss out? I can't help myself. I never could. If there's a way I can get to the stuff I want, I'll do it. That's why I'm in bother. I'm not a bad laddie, I'm just weak. I know when I'm spending other people's money, money I should be paying back to them for gear especially. I know I shouldn't do it but I can't stop meself. I can't sit in the house or not have any Charlie when there is money there, can't walk about in shit clothes. I just can't be trusted; I fuck up all the time.

In the places in which we conducted our research, we saw in the initial data outlined here that the lives of most young criminals – despite their different backgrounds, biographies and trajectories through the social hierarchy – revolve around the acquisition and display of consumer symbolism; the 'pull factor' of consumerism tends to outweigh all 'push factors', although in many cases the latter are still significant, and this obsession with consumer symbolism requires an explanation far more sophisticated than the materialist concept of relative deprivation. Our interviewees were all keenly aware of the general ethos of ornamental consumerism, and located this complex concatenation of values, norms and meanings – which we explore in more detail in the theoretical chapters later in the book – in a position central to their construction of identity. Despite the fact that many had had a distinctly inauspicious start in life, all had become acutely attuned to the cultural logic of the current phase of market capitalism. Consumerism was very much a part of their day-to-day lives, and above all they were not willing to condemn themselves to the drudgeries of welfare, job-seeking and 'just getting by', an undistinguished position in the herd of losers with whom they now felt no sense of common identity or fate. They understood crime primarily as a means to a personal end, a way of generating the cash necessary to indulge in their attachment to hedonism and conspicuous consumption. Crime had no other symbolic meaning whatsoever, and there was not even the slightest hint of subversion, transgression or budding radical subjectivity. Of course, some crimes were judged to be exciting in themselves, and most interviewees demonstrated an awareness of status via demonstrations of criminal expertise, but both these concerns were judged to be far less important than the seductive pleasures attained by acquiring and displaying the symbols of social distinction that were on offer to those who managed to accumulate a significant disposable income by whatever means necessary.

Our interviewees often implied an element of cultural competition with peers, although few discussed this directly. Many felt that they had to get new trainers, they had to get other designer items, not simply to remain an active constituent of the culture, but as a means of triumphing in the continual battle to acquire, display and experience all that the consumer universe has to offer. They wanted to be part of the local culture, but at the same time they wanted to use consumer symbolism to ascend its hierarchy to a faux-aristocratic position above it. Better to be a fallen local aristocrat than never to have been one at all, or to have never tried to elevate the self to these imaginary heights. If their lives were to count for anything, they must avoid joining the ranks of the dispossessed poor who also populated the estate, they must continue to believe that one day they will find their way to a socially elevated plateau – a glittering promised land of consumer indulgence in full view of the herd below – and they must never cease battling to win the entitlement to display the exalted symbolism of the consumer market before the lower castes. It's this relationship with consumer symbolism and its criminological implications that we want to explore in more detail in the following two data-based chapters.

Chapter 3

Consumption and identification: some insights into desires and motivations

Look, it takes a certain type of stupid cunt to work for the council and other socialist shite like that. I think that those cunts should be fucking sacked and the fucking commies who employ them should be fucking shot. And the same goes for that fucking university across the road. I'm not one of those stupid cunts, I'm a successful businessman, and I make my own way in life. If any of the useless cunts I employ complains about anything, they can fuck right off, they're two-a-penny. (30-year-old self-employed mobile carpet cleaner, who turned to petty crime when his business collapsed after three months)

The data in the last chapter clearly indicated the extent to which the lives of committed criminals in economically marginalised neighbourhoods are framed in relation to the dominant ethos of ornamental consumerism. In the following pages we begin to expand upon this central concern and attempt to situate the role of desire more directly within the lives of our respondents. The criminal lives of the vast majority of those we spoke to were not characterised by dazzling criminal successes, advanced criminal ingenuity or the deadly internal politics of today's loosely organised 'flexible' criminal networks; rather, they tended to be defined by the effort to escape real material disadvantage, welfare dependency and social insignificance, and low-level criminal scores followed by drinking, drug-taking and consumer spending. Our respondents were, however, keenly aware of the multitude of criminal success stories that litter the conversations of the young men in the pubs and on the street corners of the estate. These big-time criminals serve as a constant reminder that real money is on offer for those who appear to possess the necessary skill and desire; that the game does actually produce one or two winners from time to time. And what's more, these men often continue to be right in the middle of it all: a dazzling example of the image and lifestyle that must surely await all those committed to a life of crime. Many of our interviewees who were involved in drug-dealing were of the opinion that a lucky break would come along and allow them to distance themselves from the workaday cycle of bagging up coke and chasing down debts, and ascend to the stratospheric heights of an international jet-set lifestyle, clandestine meetings with Colombian drug lords, and industrial-scale drug and alcohol abuse. They knew this kind of success was actually being enjoyed by the select few and this tended to perpetuate their barely conscious acquiescence to their present way of being-in-the-world. Watching the successful criminals circumnavigate the estate in a flash motor, reading about their feats of derring-do in the local press, watching them drink champagne in a late-night bar, maybe even having them acknowledge your presence, all of this tended to act as a continuous motivator, a clarification of values and goals and the normative and practical strategies required to achieve them. Despite being petty drug-dealers with only lint in their pockets, it appeared to them as if they were on the right path and heading in the right direction; sooner or later they were bound to arrive at the dream destination where all of their bad memories, fears and dissatisfactions would melt away. Of course, only a very small proportion of the overall population of committed and sometime criminals would manage to create a lifestyle roughly equivalent to the median British standard of living and a minuscule percentage would actually 'live the dream'. While this fact appeared to be nestling in the back of the minds of many, its painful reality could not be faced directly. Most appeared to have promised themselves that they would keep striving, even if their efforts became increasingly half-hearted. Eventually a break must surely come their way.

In the meantime, they had the vivid pleasures of consumer excess to distract them from the oppressive realities of their social position. Some sort of consumer fetishism was clearly displayed across the whole sample: every street criminal we spoke to appeared to believe wholeheartedly that the good life should be understood in terms of the acquisition and conspicuous display of commodities and services that signified cultural achievement in the most shallow of terms. To be wealthy was to be happy. To be happy was to indulge, to buy, to squander, to be released from the normal restrictions of everyday life on estates like these. This was more than an opinion; this was something they knew to be true. Carl, 26, suggests:

You hear these people, on the box and that, and it's 'money doesn't make you happy' and that. Fucking money doesn't make you happy!? Give me some money, give me some fucking money, see how happy it makes me. Fucking wankers. If you've got nowt, money's fucking, well, *money's fucking IT, isn't it?*

Within such a cultural system commodities indeed appear to take on 'magic powers', not just in the Marxian sense as reified objects with their own inclinations outside of human control, but also as reflective mirrors of identity and distinction and providers of happiness, merged *imagos* and *ego ideals* in a Lacanian (see Lacan 2006: 75–81, 671–702) fundamental narcissistic fantasy, which act as a means of temporarily confirming existence and identity. All the hurt and hardship of their everyday lives would be banished for ever if, if, they could just manage to acquire a flash new car, a dazzling collection of designer clothes, or a kilo of cocaine. In the same vein, there were some cultural signifiers that needed to be displayed simply to maintain some viable sense of self and to remain connected to everyday culture as they knew it. For example, our researchers simply had to get used to the fact that they were spending an inordinate amount of time discussing training shoes, or 'trainers'. The *lingua franca* of the trainer aficionado can be quite complex and tends to be framed by aspects of localised masculine street cultures. For many, trainers were the first thing they needed to buy when their welfare money arrived or they managed to earn some cash from crime. A great deal of attention was paid to brand, colour, how they were worn and with what they were to be worn. To have a box-fresh pair of Nikes meant a significant boost to self-esteem, especially if the wearer was the first on the estate to display a particular style. But as we have stressed elsewhere, this prized feeling is fleeting and accompanied by an obscure but acute sense of anxiety: leaving your trainers to wear and become dirty can only be allowed for so long. Eventually, if your trainers become too dirty, you will become a figure of mockery, dismissed as a pathetic waster with no self-respect, and this appears to lead to intense forms of depression and self-loathing. Failure to maintain an image that draws upon the standard cultural signifiers means gradual degeneration into abject failure and cultural insignificance. A young man who cannot even acquire a good pair of trainers only exists as a cautionary tale, a wasted life (Bauman 2004), a constituent of the faceless mass of politically and existentially inconsequential urban poor. As we shall see, the threat of falling into this particular social grouping is very potent in the lives of a significant proportion of our respondents, and the barely conscious insecurity this threat breeds – that their lives may be gradually washed away by the failure to engage in ornamental consumerism – unavoidably impacts in a corrosive and reconstitutive way upon their behavioural norms and practices.

It's perhaps worth reiterating that all of this tends to be played out under a cloud of potential violence and looming imprisonment, and in some cases rather bleak desperation and emotional isolation. Most of our respondents showed no traditional sentimental attachment to the neighbourhood in which they lived, and often blamed their immediate environment and the people within it for the way their lives had turned out. As Ames (2007) notes about the failure of slave rebellions in *antebellum* America, it was far more common for those in a position of subordination and insignificance to blame each other in a hostile manner than to blame the master and the culture, society and politico-economic system he represented. This negative assessment of their real environments and the people who constitute their regular circle of associates provides a crucial contextual framework for understanding the nature of desire and acquisition within our sample of young criminals. This dissatisfaction and discomfort appeared to find form in virtually every aspect of their lives. For many of our respondents there was no consolation of a loving family environment, a committed relationship, a fraternal bond among peers or membership of a mythological and political collective. Most recognised that their regular associates were in fact criminals, and therefore not to be trusted, and radical or sociable subjectivities did not exist; everyone was a potential thief, grass or cheat. Their sexual relationships tended to devolve into a perpetual cycle of crisis and resolution, or were simply fleeting couplings or passing alliances. As our researchers immersed themselves in their respondents' lives, they were left with the impression that many of their respondents rarely experienced any real sense of repose or relaxation; when satisfaction did intrude upon the monotonous turmoil of consumer dreams, petty crime, welfare machinations and soap-opera relationships, it was short-lived and usually linked to bouts of bacchanalian excess brought on by the sudden arrival of money into their pockets. Their primary goals tended to be set by the symbols carried by material goods, and the first step on this impossible journey to spectacular material prosperity was to move away – physically, socially or both – from their immediate environment.

Niall, Roy and Tom

Niall, Roy and Tom all live on a large estate in the north-east of England. They are 21, 19 and 18 respectively, and they're all out of work. Today they are earning a little bit of extra cash by dropping off small amounts of drugs for a local dealer. Niall wears a Hackett T-shirt, a pair of light blue jeans, and Reebok Classics trainers with the laces worn loose and tucked into the shoes. On the middle finger of his left hand is a gigantic sovereign ring. Roy has a baseball cap fixed to the very back of his head, and wears a plain black T-shirt and a pair of nylon track-pants that he has tucked into his white sports socks. On his feet are an expensive-looking pair of Nike Shox. Tom has on a Burberry polo shirt, worn with the collar standing up, a very thick gold chain on the outside, a pair of well-worn jeans and the same kind of Nike trainers as Roy, but in a different combination of colours. These young men are not committed criminals, although all admit to committing crimes recently. Tom has been involved in a few late-night fights outside bars and nightclubs, but doesn't have a criminal record. He's also 'stolen stuff, like from cars and that', and 'just done daft things, like whatever comes up really, [just trying] to make some money'. Niall has no record of violence but has been caught shoplifting on a couple of occasions, and the only crime on Roy's sheet is a 'going equipped' charge from a couple of years ago. They form part of a significant population of young men in this neighbour-hood who have no moral compunction about criminal behaviour, and may suddenly find themselves embroiled in a crime if there appears to be a reasonable chance of success and the crime doesn't require too much planning or commitment. For the most part they are welfare dependent and continue to be heavily reliant upon their parents. All three express a desire to find legitimate employment, but they are all agreed they'll only work if they're adequately paid. Otherwise what's the point? For them, work is simply a means of getting money, and they make a simple calculation weighing remuneration against the perceived terrors of time management and the indignities of being told what to do by a boss. They've had jobs in the past, and appear to accept they'll have jobs again in the future, but for the moment they appear happy enough to be unemployed, lounging around in the sun, daydreaming about what they'll do when they manage to accumulate the huge stack of money that apparently awaits them in the not too distant future.

As with many of our interviews, money and all that it brings allows us to fall easily into the parameters of established conversation in these locales. All three are immediately dismissive of the ranks of urban poor who live on this estate. Niall calls them 'dog's lives'; he appears to mean they live like dogs; that their lives are worthless because they have never and will never experience the acute pleasures of material indulgence and the social symbolism it carries. Niall says you might as well kill yourself, living like that, never having any money, saving up to get a bit of shopping in at the local discount supermarket. What's the point? Despite readily admitting to having no money, Niall, Roy and Tom do not see themselves as part of this surplus population that clogs up their streets. Although it is difficult for a third-party observer to distinguish them from the rest, they are always in their own minds separate from these depressing figures, as if their youth and acquisitive desire will somehow forestall the onset of long-term welfare dependency and eventual cultural insignificance. Tom asks his friends if they've noticed now all the 'dirt-poor people' are always fat. They've always got money for food, haven't they? That's it! They spend their money on food instead of getting some decent clothes. Roy says the dealers are the ones with the cash, everyone knows that, everyone knows who they are around here. Walk around that corner there and have a look at the house, he tells us. We do: there's a council house, externally like all the others on the street, but with elaborately double-glazed windows and an impressive assortment of potted conifers dotted around the partially paved garden. On the driveway sits a huge luxury caravan, and parked at the kerb is a new Audi A4. On one of the most dispossessed estates in the country lies a tiny oasis of *petit-bourgeois* affluence, enough to convince these young men that all the prizes of the consumer economy are readily available to those with the requisite desire and fortitude.

Tom says he can't see the point in being a dealer unless you're going to be right at the top, earning big money out of it. There's no money in it unless you're big-time. Then you can move away from here, live somewhere 'proper'. Niall wants to move to Spain, where a friend of his dad could get him a job selling timeshares. He hates it round here. It's fucking minging, innit? No one's got any money, it's fucking total shite. He wants one of them proper top-notch houses, swimming pool and that. Get a nice car, top-class bird, and never come back. No, wait a minute, *do* come back and drive around in a flash motor, tell all the skip-rats to fuck off. The boys see drug-dealing as a foundational occupation on the estate and talk about it in terms that appear to indicate the total irrelevance of distinctions between 'legal' and 'illegal'. They hold the belief that everyone who has money on this estate must have earned that money from the burgeoning, recession-proof and tax-free drug market. Drugs themselves are also discussed in a disarmingly matter-of-fact tone. Niall says he isn't particularly interested in drugs; he smokes some weed but that's it. Some of the lads he went to school with are into heroin and some are still sniffing glue and boffing petrol, proper no-marks, wasters, dog's lives. He'll never end up like that. He wants to be a top drug-dealer, suitcases full of coke, like Scarface; have everyone shit-scared whenever he walks in the pub.

Roy says he's not bothered about moving away, he just wants the money to get a flash house and a top motor. He wants a top-class motorcross bike, and 'them massive plasma screen TVs all over the place . . . live in a proper mansion and that, big gates and CCTV cameras, coz the fucker's around here can't let you have anything'. 'Flying in [meaning importing] aeroplanes full of coke' and experiencing the extreme indulgence that the drugs profits would bring was at the forefront of his most grandiose fantasies. But for now more mundane concerns appear to preoccupy him: he needs new trainers. Roy picks at the soles of an expensive but worn pair of Nike Shox. When he gets some money he's going to get loads of pairs and keep them all in perfect nick. He also suggests that he wants to get enough money together so he can tell his 'Ma that she doesn't have to work no more'; a magnanimous suggestion that appears to make his friends a little uneasy about what to say and how to react. He also wants some Sketchers trainers, 'the white ones off the TV advert'. Everyone wears Nike or Reebok, and he wants to get himself 'a pair of something different'. Now, he says, whenever he gets new trainers 'people around here just copy off him'. His friends mock his boastful claim, but Roy is not to be distracted from the list of things he must acquire: a new pair of jeans, a top-class Stone Island coat, a season ticket for the match. Top of his list, what he really appears moved by, is the fanciful prospect of getting a driving licence and buying a black Hummer jeep with massive silver wheels. His conversation drifts off and he momentarily appears distant, almost misty-eyed, lost in a daydream in which he presumably imagines himself cruising around the estate in an enormous jeep with the sound system turned up full. Tom, on the other hand, wants to go to the Olympics and box for his country, then go to America. 'It'll be like MTV Cribs, top-class bint in the swimming pool . . . and a top of the range motorcross bike and a big van to keep all the gear in; go rallying all over the place.'

These stratospheric daydreams are interspersed with more achievable goals. Niall, Roy and Tom are currently experiencing the first flush of romantic attachment to the city's night-time drinking circuits, constantly trying to make enough money to make it out 'down the town'. They're happy to acknowledge just what an expensive business this is, with all the hidden extras of taxis, clothes and nightclub entrance fees. Tom doesn't drink unless he's going out because drinking in the house or around the doors is for alcoholics and wasters. He doesn't touch drugs: he's seen what it does to people and he can't be doing with that. Our conversation peters out when the man for whom they're running errands today emerges from the house behind us and motions for Niall, Roy and Tom to join him. There's a short discussion before the lads move off with only a nod as a farewell gesture.

Negative appraisals of current ways of life

The material/symbolic desires expressed by Niall, Roy and Tom were very similar to those of many other young men we spoke to. The fact that most of our respondents had not immediately dismissed legitimate paid labour as a route away from their present circumstances – and would gladly return to it if it once again became available in highly remunerated forms – is, of course, a notable refutation of New Right interpretations of 'the underclass' based on dependency culture and the erosion of the 'work ethic' to a condition of near total absence. If anything, our respondents' attitude suggests a lack of understanding of the normative insulation that is supposed to surround the brutality of basic neo-liberal economic principles rather than a set of cultural values demarcated from the mainstream. They seem like disarmingly guileless and resource-poor beginners playing the game of getting rich by entrepreneurial means but acting without the required social network or cultural capital, on the outside trying to get in. However, the attitudes of most of our sample towards paid work was decidedly instrumental and the expected rewards they believed lay in store for those who managed to drag themselves through the pride-swallowing drudge of legitimate work were far from realistic. John is 17 and lives on a large estate just north of one of the north-east's largest conurbations. He forms part of a group of around fifteen young men who hang around and smoke weed and drink together on a patch of waste ground close to the centre of the estate. John is actively seeking work, and his motivations in doing so are quite clear:

> If I get me trade, I'll have a nice house, nice car and that, have me own house not council . . . I'd love to be rich, proper rich, like the rappers and that . . . that's never going to happen unless I win the lottery. I know some get loads of money doing the drugs, coke, skunk and that, not many but some do. Loads of people do all right from it, though, have lush cars and all good tom and that. Everyone knows who the dealers are, everyone.

John's pal Robbie, also 17, expands on this train of thought:

> It would be cush being a fuck-off top-class dealer; me dad's mate's got a BM X5, loads of money and that. He's been doing it for years, used to be into robberies and all that and all. You have to know the right people, you can't just fucking apply to be a dealer like getting a job. It would be cush though.

Dwayne, now a committed and reasonably successful drug-dealer, has tried the world of work and has no desire to go back:

> I tried all that, but I couldn't get out of bed on a Monday, drag yourself into some fucking job pays you a hundred and fifty quid a week. Most of the jobs they put me in for was even less than that, part-time or nights or whatever. I couldn't see the point, you're better off claiming your fifty quid a week down the town [a

reference to Jobseeker's Allowance]. At least then your life's your own a bit.

The distinction between legitimate and illegitimate sources of money appears to be significant only in relation to the potential downsides of both. Working in a legitimate job means surrendering the autonomy that is one of the few benefits of joblessness, while working in an illegitimate job requires avoidance of the gaping pitfalls of violence and potential imprisonment. It's significant that John directly expresses a sense of fatalism about his ability to manifest his consumer dreams in reality. This nagging sense that their pronounced consumer desires might well come to naught tended to lurk in the background in our discussions, always there but rarely acknowledged. For most, it appeared that if just for once they would point their cynicism in the right direction, turn and look the beast square in the face, then the great neo-liberal deception that sustains their false hopes for future prosperity might evaporate before their very eyes; but they never did.

At 24, Foz is a veteran drug-dealer who lives in a neighbouring city. At the moment his operation is very small indeed, and he is keen to avoid any discussion of his fall from grace from the middle rankings of the local drug scene to the relegation zone. For Foz, drug-dealing is a means of generating cash and nothing more. Once, in his brief glory days, the cash it generated afforded him an enviable lifestyle of indulgent hedonism on the local leisure scene, but now it allows him to maintain a basically acceptable appearance and nothing more:

With the coke and that, there's no way I'd be doing it if I didn't need the money. Simple as that, really. You'd have to be daft to do it otherwise. You can get locked up even for doing what I'm doing, so it's got to be about money, otherwise why bother, you know?

Q: Long term, what are you after out of this?

Fuck knows. I'm just about trying to get some cash together to go out on the piss and that, keep ez in trainers.

Foz still has hopes of climbing back up the league table and recreating his dream life of champagne and Armani, but he appears to realise that this may be some way off:

I'm not bothered with all that gangster stuff, treating it like a job and that ... [obviously] I'd be over the moon to be in that position, thousands coming in every week, fucking people running about for you and that. Just think what you could do with that kind of money, man. Just think, going to the town, all the flash shops and that,

55

money no object. No worries about money, how am I going to pay for this, how am I going to pay for that. You go out, you've got women all over the place, it's just the dream isn't it ... There's people round here that are making fortunes, but they're putting themselves up aren't they, putting themselves up for all sorts, not just prison. It's hard to say. Obviously for more risks you get more money. What you want is something safe but something that brings in the wedge, but how do you do that? If I could see more money at the end of it, I mean proper money, thousands and thousands, you've got to have a go because, well, what other chance have you got [of getting that type of money]?

For Foz, drug-dealing appears to represent the only conceivable means of recreating the prosperity of his past, but for now he has been cast adrift from the local drug-dealing networks and forced to engage in the kind of petty dealing once delegated to his minions. This fact is hidden between the lines of the conversation, known to both interviewer and interviewee but destined to remain unacknowledged. It appears that, for Foz, the pain of not being able to consume is all the more acute because the indulgent shopping excursions to which he refers were once the main reward of his drug-dealing enterprise. Now his memories of how it used to be appear to haunt his assessments of his current circumstances. He wants that lifestyle back, but recognises that it may well be beyond him. Now he lives in the shadow of a former life that has long since crumbled. At 24 years old, there appears to be nothing positive on the horizon:

Q – Where do you want to be in ten years?

I'd want to be living somewhere flash, nice car on the drive. I'd want holidays all over, money there when I need it and all that.

Q – Where do you think you're going to be in ten years?

Ha! I'll be right here, won't I? ... You want to get more stuff and that, you want to move away, but the chances are most of the lads from around here are going to end up like their fathas, sitting around the house or down the club or just trying to scrap up some web. But I'll tell you what, I'll never be one of those waiting on the dole and saving pennies and never having nowt. I've got a bit about ez, I'll always have money for this and that. You'll never see me in dodgy trainers or manky gear, looking fucking scruffy or nowt like that, I tell ya ... look, the truth is no one knows [where he'll be], you don't, I don't, no one, because owt could happen. I could get a decent job, making money and that, I could be making more money other ways, I could be banged up, I could be fucking dead. I might win the lottery for all anybody knows. It's impossible to answer that question isn't it?

Foz is clearly of the belief that he has very little influence over his unfolding biography. Life is something that happens to him, good or bad, and as a direct consequence of this his response is to wait, hope and believe that eventually things must change for the better. He also appears to consider the possibility of ending up like the older generation of men on the estate to be the clear embodiment of abject failure. In all likelihood, these are also men whose response to their material circumstances is to wait, hope and believe. At some stage circumstances will create an opportunity that will be grabbed with both hands and nurtured to fruition. While there is a great deal of vacillation in spoken accounts of success and failure, in order to maintain the pretence of impending future prosperity individuals must not abandon all faith in their ability to create something better. Most appear committed to the entirely understandable belief that individual success is a reflection of individual talent and determination, while individual failure is a result of bad luck. Life is not really a meritocracy but a strange combination of struggling and waiting for a break, and the social and political dimensions have simply evaporated.

Foz will not be allowing his guard to drop for a minute and continues to maintain that, by hook or by crook, material prosperity can be his. Like many others we consulted, Foz appears to believe with unshakeable fervour that something inside him will save him from the fate he fears most: disreputable poverty, material hardship and total lack of distinction in social and cultural terms. This deep-seated fear, coupled with a broad array of other forms of insecurity and the keenly felt competitive and instrumental ethos of his cultural world, is palpable as he resists his fatalism and once again mouths the prescribed script of certain and imminent future prosperity. This oscillation between highly individualised and paradoxical forms of fatalism and optimism was a characteristic of many among this group of interviewees.

The fundamental issue that appears to unite the various social understandings of Foz, Niall, Roy, Tom, Robbie and John is a clear sense that their present social reality is simply not good enough. Nobody thought that the location – both geographical and social – was a bit run-down but could be improved with a bit of collective effort. Out there, somewhere, is something profoundly better, and one is condemned to a powerful sense of dissatisfaction and discontent, a kind of emotional unease, until the dreamlike state suddenly manifests itself. It is important to note that many of our respondents appeared to truly believe that this personal transformation was imminent, or at least were subconsciously required to parrot ultimately meaningless scripts of impending wealth and hyper-indulgence. Beneath this bluster lurk quite advanced forms of anxiety and sentiments of lack, inadequacy and failure, but the façade must be maintained if the individual is to retain some semblance of cultural normality and forward motion.

Negative perceptions of the other

For many of our respondents, poverty is more to do with a lack of self-respect than a lack of material resources. Most had very little money, but wouldn't think of describing their situation as one of 'poverty'. They were happy to acknowledge that they had no money, but 'poverty' was not a topic that ever encroached on our conversations. Our respondents had clearly positioned themselves in a social sphere very different from that of those for whom they had constructed a range of imaginative but aggressively disparaging monikers. The disreputable poor, or, more aptly, the poor who appeared not to be concerned with displaying the outward signs of material wealth, were termed 'dog's lives', 'no-marks', 'wasters', 'black' [apparently a reference to being unclean rather than having black skin], 'minging', 'Aldi-bashers', 'scum', 'skip-rats', 'window-lickers', and so on. Every conversational reference to this group created an opportunity to recall or construct some new label that might entertain those gathered in conversation. What was striking about this division is its general artificiality. All that divided one group from the other was age and the ability to get hold of a few basic signifiers of consumer engagement. An outsider might also add a sense of threat, relative to gender, size and number, but these young men certainly did not exude a sense of affluence. They may be adorned with a little bit of gold jewellery and a pair of expensive trainers, but in many cases they had been born into and continued to be in the grip of relatively advanced material/symbolic deprivation. Yet despite this, they continued to express the belief that various biographical contingencies, personal skill, innate desire or just plain luck would allow them to rise to a different plane from those with whom they currently shared the estate. They would become successful criminals, they would get well-paying jobs, they would win the lottery, but they would not grow old and submissively accept their fateful place within the ranks of the dispossessed. Life for them would be different, better in every way. They had the self-respect necessary to create a meaningful life. They would not meekly submit to this shadow life of 'just getting by' that they saw unfolding before their very eyes. They believed they understood what was simply beyond the ranks of dispossessed that surrounded them: to be alive meant dedicating oneself totally to a version of 'success' filtered through the lens of consumer culture. A life without extremes of pleasure, without a portal to the plane of *jouissance*, was a life of living death, of the cultural 'undead'. The indulgence that they occasionally experienced and constantly dreamt of was to live life where the air was at its purest, an existence unfettered by the banalities of the real. This was the world they had come to believe was on offer to anybody with a modicum of desire and wherewithal, and their lives could never be considered whole until they had found their way to this place. The dismal existence of those who appeared to have given up this battle for symbolic prosperity merely served as a reminder of what lay in store for those who 'failed'. Even those who had achieved an element of material success were not spared the critical eye of our respondents. Some believed that those with jobs just didn't get it. Jonathan, 18, belongs to the same loose group as John and Robbie, who we met earlier. He comments:

> It would be shit being one of them normal fuckers that never does nowt. Just going to graft all day then sitting bored off your tits watching the telly or fucking going playing golf and shit. Life's meant to be a laugh, isn't it? Fucking do everything I say, take loads of drugs, shag loads of birds. I should be a fucking rap star me (laughs). Naw, it would be shit, I just want all the fucking good stuff.

Jonathan's mate, Robbie, appears to particularly dislike those who utilise the local discount superstores that are often situated close to local council estates. He derides all who enter one particular store as 'Aldi-bashers' and complains: 'It's a fucking asylum-seekers' shop; the tills are full of fucking vouchers, they don't take any money.' For Robbie, even something as mundane as shopping for a tin of beans and some toilet paper needs to be done in a particular style. He wouldn't dream of being seen in such a store, no matter how cheap, reliable and good quality the products are. The mere fact that particular items are stocked in this store immediately reduces their currency, a problem to which some designer labels appear to have become alert, refusing to allow their products to be stocked. Robbie once again explains these attitudes in terms of 'respect'; he has too much of it to be seen in such a store, and those who frequent it have none at all. All of this belies the orthodox notion that young criminals suffer from 'lack of self-esteem', although it's possible to suggest that, rather than being in deficit, this form of narcissistic caste-like self-esteem is inflated to a condition of extreme and potentially explosive fragility. More about narcissism later in the book, but for now it's sufficient to note that for Robbie and the rest of his group even the mundane act of purchasing everyday items is loaded with symbolic meaning. He will be the man who shops at expensive stores or not at all. He will not trade in his self-respect for a short-term bargain in some 'minging' store populated by shoppers waiting around till closing to see if the management further reduce the price of food about to pass its 'sell-by date'.

Dwayne is a 23-year-old drug-dealer from a neighbouring city who expresses similar sentiments:

> When you're out buying it's not just the stuff you buy, it's the shop, innit? If you're going to be a flash cunt then be a flash cunt, it's no use having, like say Armani gear, if it's snide. Like if I walk in some shop down the town, flash shop right, they're fucking looking thinking, 'Who the fuck's this cunt?', and I walk in an drop a couple of hundred quid, it's like 'Fuck you', innit, 'Fuck you, you fucking tit' . . . Round here, for fuck's sake, what a fucking depressing place, fucking queuing up down the pub waiting to buy the gear off the shoplifters. Honest, it does me in, man. Get yourself together for fuck's sake! Show a bit respect man, fucking get a fucking job or something.

And on his own attire:

> See that [points at a large gold ring], fucking two hundred quid. None of that fucking Argos shit, that, you know. Chain? That's kicking on for two hundred quid. Trainers? What, another hundred? See this top right, that's real Armani that right, can't remember, hundred quid say. Look at that. Armani socks. Armani belt. Maybe's fifty, hundred quid. These jeans is only Replay, but I've got a pair of Evisu jeans in the house cost three hundred quid. Fucking three hundred, man. It's fucking mad. I bought a bottle of champagne down the town Saturday, fifty, sixty quid, innit, something like that. Fuck it, that's what I say. What's it for if it's not to enjoy yourself? It's what it's all about, man, innit?

Dwayne's drug-dealing business seems to be going quite well for the time being and he appears to be in a position to indulge in the occasional buying binge, but his dismissal of others on the estate is not simply associated with their fashion choices. Dwayne is absolutely certain that all individuals on the face of the planet are out for themselves:

> It's just the way it is, everywhere, everyone, especially round here. It's happened to me loads of times, you trust someone you get fucked over, simple as.

His bleak but perceptive thesis is clearly related to life in the business world:

In this business you've got to be wide awake twenty-four hours a day coz everyone is trying to rob you. You've got to be a bit nasty as well otherwise people's not going to pay you what's owed. It's a nasty, nasty business that way because you've got criminals as mates, you know what I mean? So you've got to be nastier and that's it.

The expectation of instrumental social action by the other was, of course, a common feature across our whole sample, and this reading of their own cultural environment was tinged with the dread of impending and unavoidable violence that is woven so deeply into the fabric of their everyday existence. Interviewee after interviewee would recount in detail their willingness to hurt, maim or kill anyone who threatened their own personal interests either directly or indirectly. Much of this was meaningless bluster as young men attempted to portray themselves as bestial, scary hard men devoid of compassion and with a propensity for extreme and random violence. Very few of our sample could realistically claim to have accessed the hallowed halls of local fistic folklore and in all probability most never would, but we were repeatedly left with the impression that some of these young men could no longer be held in check by the established hierarchy of primitive gangsterdom that continues to exert its influence in a variety of forms on these estates. Most of our sample was far from the stereotype of the northern gangster, but virtually all of them expressed a willingness to use potentially lethal weapons to overcome a foe. This is a marked shift away from the established local protocols of violent action that forbade weapons or dismissed them as unmanly (see Winlow 2001). This meant that minor incidents could and would escalate rapidly as the local criminal cultures became increasingly aware that nothing was over until it was over. A fight would no longer end with the throwing of the final punch, and some of our respondents actually spoke of being actively embroiled in ongoing conflicts that could immediately reignite if they found themselves in the wrong place at the wrong time. Foz, who we met earlier, has no great reputation for violence, but he is still not someone to be crossed lightly:

I've done lots of daft things. When I was young and that I was a bit of a nutter me. Fighting and getting into bother . . . [I'm not like that] now. I'm sick of all that. People still know me and they know what I'll do, but if I do anything now it's coz I need the cash not coz I'm fucking bored or something.

One particular conversation with Foz started with our usual enquiry about clothes and money, but rapidly shifted track to reveal just how dangerous these streets can be:

That ring, three hundred [pounds]. I've got a chain here and it's proper top-notch, paid about eight hundred for it years ago . . .

Q: Someone's going to have that away . . .

I hope they fucking try it, mate. I'll cut them up proper. My mate, coming out of the chippy ower yon, [they] fucking took all his gelt, fucking money, the lot. Even took his belt off him, bust his nose. Fucking scum, man, I'm not kidding. Fucking once, it fucking happens, just once, I'll stab them up proper, honest. I've fucking had it, man, with all that shit, I'll do time, I'm not bothered. It's fucking out of order, man. Little shit-heads hanging around the shops, like little fucking rats, turning over old women and that, it's mental I'm not kidding, you've got fucking no idea, mate.

Q: They'll have those trainers as well . . .

Ooo! It's 'goodnight' [meaning he'll kill them], [if you] fuck with a man's trainers!

The game's the thing

To sum up what we have so far, what is notable about these quotes is the extent to which low-level criminals believe that future material prosperity is soon to result from their criminal activities or some other quirk of fate. In order to remain connected to the dominant form of consumer culture as it was played out on the estate, it was necessary to acquire and display key consumer artefacts and regularly indulge in regular bouts of hedonistic excess. This tendency is not an ethical or proto-political response to a life lived under harsh social circumstances, or a hybrid 'sub-cultural' reworking of mainstream 'values', but rather a general cultural injunction created by the market economy and filtered through the ideological apparatus that supports advanced capitalism and its liberal democratic system; the reworking is being done in the strategic normative practices, not the meanings, values and goals. The actual means of getting the money to engage in this spectacle are, of course, closely tied to the realities of this particular cultural environment. However, once that money is acquired, the vivid symbolism of the mainstream consumer lifestyle exerts its powerful allure and presents a seemingly inexhaustible supply of consumer products and services, all apparently imbued with mysterious and magical qualities, for the personal delectation of each individual and as the imaginary means of social distinction, at least until the next wave of fashionable symbolism is unleashed by the marketing industry. Each single respondent could recount details of recent bouts of hedonism and excess, the indulgence in spectacular 'waste' that signifies the privileged entitlement of a barbarian leisure class (Veblen 1994), a group of individuals who have made it simply by pulling themselves above the bovine herd by means of their own wits and violence. Even those in the grip of advanced material hardship happily slipped into tales of drug and drink-fuelled party extravaganzas that they perpetually endeavoured to relive. For the vast majority of those we spoke to, when crime eventually began to pay, the money would not remain in their hands for too long. There would never again be abstinence, parsimony or gratification postponed; life was for living, and the only conceivable style of living was that which signified the social distinction of the individual in a position above the social, the high life of the dedicated consumer.

For many, this clearly identifiable trend to live in the worlds of imagination and excess at least partially ensured that real material hardship would continue to cloud most of their days, but all our respondents were sure that things could, and indeed would, rapidly change for the better. The glittering presence of successful criminals on these very streets clearly reinforced the message that material success through criminal action was not only a possibility, but the best possibility open to them. The dismal realisation that crime would propel very few to the apex of the local criminal hierarchy was often too painful to contemplate; instead, the intricacies of the game tended to preoccupy them, along with quixotic dreams of what they would do once their success was assured. It was also striking the lengths to which some would go to present successful images to themselves and others despite clear indications to the contrary. To us this tended to reflect the deep-seated sense of insecurity and lack that typified almost every facet of their everyday lives. They had to believe that they would eventually become skilled enough to win the prize they knew to be on offer. They would be the ones, it would be them who beat the odds and washed away all the travails of life suffered thus far with a spectacular display of toughness, daring and criminal acumen to secure the dream life of unrestrained consumer indulgence. Any other option was inconceivable; they must experience the vivid spectacle if their lives were to count for anything, and a reality characterised by the lack of such opportunities and prizes, as Eliot once reminded us, was far too dismal a prospect to contemplate.

In many cases their reverence for particular consumer artefacts was palpable. These were not mere superficialities or a one-dimensional means of making status claims. The powerful allure of such artefacts penetrated to the very heart of our respondents, defining them as individuals, clarifying and justifying continued involvement in the cultural life of the estate to its criminal and quasi-criminal inhabitants. Many of our respondents appeared to elevate these objects into untouchable, sacred yet ephemeral things that can only be observed and displayed without ever really being enjoyed. The satisfaction of ownership was always fleeting and related to the artefact's suitability for conspicuous display rather than the subject's desire for the thing itself, which was often rather lukewarm. For us, the attitudes expressed by our respondents in this chapter clearly indicate the extent to which they are bonded to the ideology of our present system: put pleasure before sacrifice, accumulate and display to create an identity beyond the social yet which is recognised by it, and give blind obedience to the iron laws of raw utilitarianism. As we shall see later, this form of criminality should therefore be clearly understood as an outward expression of narcissism shorn of many of the minimal ethical norms demanded as insulation by the agents of the traditional capitalist system.

Chapter 4

Criminal biographies: two case studies

In this chapter we want to explore in a little more depth the realities of criminal life in locales of permanent recession. Below we present case studies of two very different criminals, who, despite living in different cities, inhabit the same cultural and economic life-world characterised by a rapid withdrawal of meaningful legitimate employment, a pervasive cultural norm based on minimally restrained self-interest, and the adoption of identities that are constituted and reproduced largely by consumer culture rather than any traditional cultural form. These men exhibit similar attitudes towards crime and punishment and, despite occupying very different positions in the vague hierarchy that continues to exert its influence within the north-east's criminal cultures, both are preoccupied with the symbolism attached to the consumer objects that now permeate Western culture.

Billy, who we will meet very shortly, wants desperately to achieve some semblance of consumer success but is quite fatalistic about his chances of ever attaining anything more than a few basic consumer items that he can use to wrest some acknowledgement from the world around him. He feels compelled to enter the battle for consumer significance, making a paradoxically half-hearted yet compulsory attempt to stake his claim for criminal success and affluence, but underneath the bluster he clearly displays a rather pessimistic view of his unfolding biography and his chances of ever making it as a successful drug-dealer. Tony, who we will discuss later in the chapter, is considerably older than Billy and has already achieved a modicum of the criminal success that might not come Billy's way. Importantly, both men express a rather dystopian interpretation of the world they inhabit, talking at length about the nakedly instrumental and brutally aggressive criminal cultures in which they move. Despite the resignation that their lives are forever likely to be typified by the ceaseless scramble for criminal and consumer achievement – a desperate fight for an individualised form of social distinction that will occur in the absence of meaningful emotional bonds or any realistic alternative associated with 'authentic solidarity' with other human beings (see Žižek 2008) – both of these men feel compelled to simply keep going as they are. While Billy sees no realistic alternative to his present way of life and holds out little hope of any meaningful success, Tony sees every new day as an opportunity to change his personal lot for the better and re-establish his position among the north-east's criminal elite. Active pessimism about the social and the political, alongside active optimism about personal entrepreneurialism, have both been box-pressed and contained within the narrowest of ethico-cultural parameters in an entirely depoliticised and aphadiorised culture, with differing modes of expression according to the individuals and their situations. Both of these men are indicative of criminal cultures at this point in British history. As both Tony and Billy are quick to point out, modernism's social, cultural and legal forms of behavioural regulation have, for the most part, broken down in their neighbourhoods. Both expect other inhabitants of these blighted areas to be just as unequivocally self-interested in every aspect of their lives as they are, and this climate of cynicism and suspicion, which motivates and justifies criminal competition, appears to exacerbate their nihilistic outlook and their general sense of insecurity.

Billy

Billy is 21 and lives on one of the country's most deprived estates. He stands slightly less than six feet in height and is broad-shouldered despite otherwise being quite thin. He is a slave to sport-casual wear, a topic upon which he can become quite animated. On his feet are an almost new pair of Reebok trainers, still dazzling white, matched with an Adidas tracksuit top and a pair of Levi jeans. On his right hand are two fat gold rings. At the time of our first interview he was living mostly at the home of the sister of the mother of his child. Billy moves around a lot. He still spends time at his grandmother's home, just a few streets away from his current location, and in the last year or so he has also lodged with the mother of the mother of his child, a girlfriend and an assortment of friends and acquaintances. Our interviewer has met Billy just once before, in the company of Billy's cousin, who made the introduction and helped to set up this meeting.

Billy's life and his present living environment appear rather chaotic, but for him things have always been this way. His childhood was blighted by spells in local authority care, and the suicide of his mother. Throughout all our meetings he was unwilling to talk about his childhood and his family. Our initial enquiry produced a response of 'Bollocks, I'm not talking about any of that. Fuck it', so we skirted around issues which are clearly very important to further our insight into Billy's life. He does, however, reveal that he too has attempted suicide. In a dramatic gesture, he pulls up his sleeve to reveal deep scars running down his forearm. This gesture, rather than anything he can muster with the spoken word, is his response to questions about his childhood.

Billy can conjure up crime tales with very little effort. He lapses easily into the habitual frameworks of justification and meaning, voicing a stock of responses that require minimal engagement with the question and neatly sidestep any meaningful form of self-analysis. Our initial meeting found him in expansive mood when asked about crime and money, and much of our discussion remained rooted in these areas. He clearly wanted to be of some help to our interviewer, but some issues were out of bounds, not because he felt uncomfortable discussing them with a partial outsider, but because he discussed them with nobody, and in all likelihood avoided reflecting on them as much as possible.

The environment in which our first interview took place was far from ideal. Around half a dozen of Billy's friends are sitting around on the front garden wall drinking cans of lager and talking loudly. The mother of Billy's child and two of her friends are in the kitchen chatting, smoking dope and listening to music. Billy perches on the edge of an old two-seater sofa, while our interviewer is directed towards a matching chair. The room is a mess. A large pile of clothes lies in the corner of the room next to an ironing board, and there's a half-full pet's bowl lying in the middle of the carpet. Billy has a small table next to him upon which sits a full ashtray, a packet of fags, some cigarette papers and the torn-up remnants of cigarettes, the tobacco from which has been used to make a steady cycle of joints. In addition, scattered on the floor, there are two large pizza boxes – one of which lies open and is also being used as an ashtray – a few discarded cans of lager, a plastic bong and some children's toys. The pungent smells of dog food, dope, stale beer and cigarette smoke combine to permeate the house.

Billy's criminal biography is painfully predictable. He started out shoplifting, first in local newsagents and general stores and then in the major shopping areas in the city centre. He grew to favour larger chain and department stores because they were always busy and their security was lax. After his childhood concerns to acquire sweets, chocolate and toys faded, he targeted aftershave, cameras and small electrical items, but would also take razors, sun cream and hair products. Sports stores were good for T-shirts and other clothing, and as he reached his teenage years, sex toys from Ann Summers also sold well. He and his friends would find stores with poor security and proceed to 'pick the store empty' or until security measures improved. They would work out the best method – entering the store individually, in pairs, or as one big, intimidating group. Over time the group's skills developed:

> We used to go out dippin' down the town, get proper organised, three or four of us like. We used to be all about taking the tags off, go in the changing rooms, or lining the bags and walking out. But that's all shite really, makes no sense. It's just basic.

Here Billy is talking about removing security tags from items of clothing. His *modus operandi* appears to have involved taking a number of items into a changing room, as if to try on the clothes, then surreptitiously removing the security tags, hiding the clothes in a bag or underneath his own clothes, and walking out of the store. This task is not as straightforward as it may seem. Store workers may attempt to ascertain how many items are being taken into the changing room, and make sure the correct number of items is returned when the customer leaves. Importantly, trying to remove tags can result in an alarm sounding and the rapid arrival of a security guard. Furthermore, if the tag isn't removed properly it can damage the item that is about to be stolen, cutting down its eventual sale price. 'Lining the bags' is a standard shoplifting method of lining a large shopping bag with an insulating shield that prevents the security system picking up tagged items being removed from the store without payment. Using this method, the thief calmly walks around the store and drops the items to be stolen into a large shopping bag. Usually the security system detects tagged items passing through entrances and exits, sounding a loud alarm. Billy and his friends line the shopping bag with a covering, usually baking foil, which prevents the alarm system responding to the security tags as the items are removed. This method is far from foolproof, and can often result in an alarm sounding and a subsequent chase through the shopping crowds that clutter the city centre's major thoroughfares. Billy, however, is keen to draw our eye away from these seemingly innovative criminal technologies and emphasise the more traditional method:

> Just walk in, clock the bloke, keep moving, keep your bottle together, fucking grab it, up your top, out.

For Billy, shoplifting is best understood as a very basic form of theft. It's about bottle, showing nerve, grabbing what you can, hoping not to be observed, and getting out quickly. Billy's shoplifting career is chequered, to say the least:

It's fucking stupid. I got caught loads of times. Chasing round the town and that. It's a laugh. You can make a canny knot out of it, though.

The 'knot' he refers to is money, a knot, a wedge of cash. In the overall glossary of acquisitive criminal acts, shoplifting is relatively easy and requires little forethought, but it is, nevertheless, accompanied by some quite pronounced risks. However, to cast doubt on the criminological theory that the excitement generated by risk and transgression is the main motivation (see Katz 1988), Billy is suggesting here that he is drawn not so much to the adrenalin 'buzz' created by the transgression of law and the threat of capture, but to the financial gain that lies in store for those who have a successful day 'doing the shops'. This criminal endeavour, in which Billy is willing to acknowledge but not talk up his involvement, doesn't seem to hold any great attraction for him, and he is keen to marginalise his interest in it as he seeks to portray himself as a wily criminal entrepreneur, a drug-dealer worthy of respect rather than your run-of-the-mill street criminal. Items that he doesn't keep for himself are easily passed on to momentarily quench the estate's voracious appetite for cheap consumer items. As Billy says:

Take the stuff in *The Wolf* [local pub on the estate], sell it straight away, or if it's something big, like we were getting sat navs, you want a hundred, hundred and fifty quid, just sell them to the dealers, the fucking gangsters. Anyone with money will take it straight away.

On an estate like this, the distinction between criminal and non-criminal is not always clear; buying stolen goods appears to provoke little moral discomfort for the majority of the inhabitants. In most cases this process of selling on stolen goods is not done in a furtive, clandestine manner, but in an 'open market' where the highest bidder usually takes the prize. As Billy implies, those with the money to buy valuable items are often criminals themselves.

Billy views these minor league criminal acts as relatively unimportant, a risk he occasionally takes for purely instrumental ends. If he needs the money, or he sees an easy opportunity, then a crime occurs. He may then profit from the endeavour or he might be caught and punished. He appears to be in no way morally reflective about these criminal acts, and while he acknowledges they are indeed criminal, his involvement in them elicits no great introspection or discomfort. He does not ruminate too much about the stark realities of his life and pays little attention to the consequences of these petty crimes, for himself or his victims, or the reasons why he commits them. His life is akin to a leaf being swept along on a strong wind: he believes himself to have little or no control over his unfolding biography, and his various personal and criminal failures are understood simply as bad luck rather than bad judgement. Billy does, however, have some ethical rules about shoplifting:

Our lass used to go out [shoplifting] with the bairn and I used to blow up, man. With the fucking kid though?! She's been nipped a couple of times ... She does well, though [financially]. Takes her time and that. Makes some money.

Here the irritation Billy feels about the involvement of the mother of his child in shoplifting, accompanied by his astonishment that she would actually commit these crimes while looking after his child, is partially mitigated by the fact that she often does quite well financially from these shopping excursions. It seems that he isn't really deeply offended by this, and if he is actually attempting to access a staple discourse related to traditional masculinity and the differentiation of gender roles in bread-winning and parenting, he is not taking its 'authority' too seriously. He wants to create the impression that he is appalled by these events, but ultimately he is happy to bestow an element of admiration upon her criminal ability, and because she 'makes some money' by committing these crimes, everything can be forgiven. As Engdahl (2008) argues, for those whose lives revolve around money and economic crimes, there is a constant tendency for convenience, expedience and egotism to overrule ethical values and traditional social norms.

Billy is keen to consign shoplifting to the past, despite the fact that he admits to having been recently arrested for this crime. Once again he is quick to portray his contemporary reality in evolutionary terms; these basic crimes are now, it would seem, giving way to more sophisticated and profitable enterprises, crimes that earn respect. But despite all this, Billy is a criminal who finds it hard to turn down criminal opportunities, even those he sees as beneath his current, and notional, criminal stratum. He explains, 'It's your duty to steal stuff if the fuckers aren't looking after it proper.' There are some crimes, it seems, from which Billy cannot walk away if the opportunity arises. He sees his childhood involvement in shoplifting as 'not real crime', not even youthful high jinks, just standard playfulness, a means of solidifying his place within his friendship group and acquiring things he wanted. Billy appears to assume that all young men, or at least all the young men that he can immediately bring to mind, get up to this kind of thing, and while he admits to receiving a fleeting 'buzz' from these crimes, even as a child the real motivation was always financial or acquisitive.

Possessing consumer items, actually holding them in your hands, having them as yours, even if they have been attained illegitimately, is hugely compelling for young men such as Billy. Even on those occasions when he sold on the goods he had stolen, a further acquisitive motive was clearly apparent; the money he received would be used to buy other symbol-rich consumer items, or to buy beer and dope. Looking back at it, it was a laugh, a way of having fun with the lads, something deeply engaging to do while truanting from school. Stealing from stores also allowed him to possess items which, at the time, he couldn't afford to purchase legitimately. Billy says the first things he stole were chocolate bars, things like that, things to eat, things he knew he wanted but could not afford to buy. He then progressed on to other consumer items he desired, small toys and so on, and then on to things he could sell, and then on to anything.

Billy offers little justification for his childhood actions other than to suggest that it 'serves the stores right, making money off people'. And it's their own fault for not defending their stores well enough. We should note here that there is no anti-capitalist moral position; Billy was upset that it was the stores that were making money from people, not that making money itself is wrong, and as such they should be prepared to defend their position of advantage in the trading relationship from those who will naturally seek to gain their own advantage in the situation as it presented itself. They were asking for it, and why should you have to pay if people weren't watching and didn't care? However, it must also be said that Billy shows no real commitment to any of these explanations or moral justifications; if things were entirely different, perhaps more just and equal, our researchers were left wondering how much he would care. He hasn't given a great deal of thought to his criminal motivations and instead appears to access some of the standard justifications he has heard elsewhere, which sometimes appear more like Matza's techniques of neutralisation while at the same time seeming to be disarmingly guileless expressions of a pervasive social Darwinist morality that lies just under the surface of Western liberalism. However, he is keen to ignore all that and tell the story as a series of amusing anecdotes and make a few very basic attempts to accentuate his criminal acumen without addressing the meaning or cause of his actions.

Billy also admits to breaking into and stealing from cars, although he says he was never particularly interested in actually stealing the cars themselves. He explains:

When I was a bairn everyone was into it round here, it was fucking mental. Robbing cars was the fucking thing to do, just for a laugh, right, chased off the coppers ... It's all right for a laugh and that, but I wasn't that bothered. We'd go all over the places just scoping out cars. I mean like five year ago, you could get a canny knot just off [car] stereos, the CD players. But people are fucking daft man.

Leave fucking stuff on the back seat, it's only glass, just, bop, and it's off, I'm away. You can't get caught really. Takes couple of seconds: smash and you're off.

Over the years this seems to have been a standard criminal enterprise for Billy, one from which he claims to have made quite a bit of money. There is no sense that he finds it exciting; in fact very often it's almost too easy, a routine fall-back. He appears to keep coming back to this particular crime because he's aware of how very unlikely it is that he will be caught. Once again, if a criminal opportunity presents itself he finds it hard to pass over it:

Mostly it's bags, like, a sports bag, maybe a handbag. But you get daft stuff, tools, fucking shopping bags with brand new gear, fucking gin, we got this car with six bottles of fucking gin in carriers [bags].

We used to try and find vans, like store vans or work vans. Tools are good coz people always want them, and you can use the gear for getting in [meaning breaking in] to things. We did this chemist's van, right. [They'd] left the fucking gear right in the back ... [we got] trays of deodorant and that, toothpaste, and some smelly stuff, women's perfume. Nice touch [meaning a good criminal score].

Billy also burgled some houses when he was younger, an issue upon which he refuses to elaborate. He appears to maintain some connection to the old criminal maxim that house burglary is dishonourable, and seems keen to distance himself from the more recent association between house burglary and drug addiction. Billy is keen to disassociate himself from this lowly class of deviant, and he clearly wants to bolster his credibility as a serious, professional criminal, despite rather stark indications to the contrary. He is happy to discuss one or two shop burglaries and the time he broke into a local pub. These are crimes, Billy admits, but it's not like he is 'raping people or killing kids'; he is 'not blowing people up on trains and stuff', is he?

He talks at length about the pub burglary, about the emotions that accompany the crime, about the Alsatian the pub manager kept as a guard dog ... and leaves that tale hanging in the air, possibly because the encounter with the dog suggests an unsuccessful mission. He describes how he had personally broken into an armed bandit and got away with nearly £200 in change. He and his compatriots also managed to liberate some cash and cigarettes from a vending machine, and struggled out of the pub with the additional burden of some bottles of booze. He suggests they had planned to kidnap the manager and get him to open the safe; why this plan rapidly dematerialised once on the property isn't clear. 'It just didn't come off, it just didn't come off,' he says.

Billy has to be pressed to consider other crimes. There's violence, of course, but that's not like a crime, is it? It's just fighting. He makes a brief initial attempt to portray himself as a bit of hard man, but quickly abandons it. On the estate where he lives, Billy has yet to make it into the big league. He is not a hard man or a criminal of any significant repute. That said, nobody around here appears to doubt that he could be dangerous. The old hierarchies of violence and criminal competency continue to exist, but even the big-time criminals accept that there are now many dangerous men in the lower echelons even on this relatively small estate. Billy and the intimidating group of young men standing outside are unpredictable, and in these places unpredictability can induce a deep-seated sense of trepidation and fear. For Billy violence appears to be simply a behaviour that may ultimately be deployed to produce a specific instrumental end. He does it when he needs to and that's it. Unlike some other people we have interviewed, Billy does not see violence as particularly thrilling and it appears to produce no deeply emotive reaction when it makes its brief entries into his life. Importantly, he tells our interviewer people are always violent, it's just the way people are. He has seen it since he was a tiny little kid.

He has robbed a few people, he says. Billy and some mates used to knock about in one of the city's major thoroughfares and try to rob drunks or students who were walking home late at night. Again, this is a 'funny' interlude in the discussion, not 'real crime'. The opportunity to tell a few amusing stories, nothing more.

Billy has been in custody twice. With regard to his first sentence, it's not clear what he was actually charged with, but it seems to be a list of offences involving theft. The second time he was charged with possessing drugs with intent to supply, and for having burglary tools in his possession. He has also been arrested recently. He was caught shoplifting, and there also appears to have been some kind of domestic disturbance that he prefers not to talk about. He says, 'They always come up here. Once they have got your face they pull ya every time they see ya.' He was complaining that the police now know him as a criminal and target him, stopping him every time they see him on the street. This causes him a great deal of inconvenience, not so much as an infringement on his civil liberties – something he has never heard of – but because it precludes him carrying large amounts of drugs available for immediate sale.

Billy's main income now comes from drug sales, he says. He sells pills and speed, the old powdered kind, when he can get it. But his main business is dope. He pulls out a big bag of grass, and insists that our interviewer smells it. Like all committed salesmen, he is quick to expand upon the merits of his product, and resolutely portrays this dope as the 'best in the city'. Mostly the stuff is sold in half-ounce bags, but he also claims to sell much larger amounts. He is growing dope in a house rented by the sister of the mother of his child. Billy and Mandy are no longer together, but they appear to remain closely tied, and this marijuana-growing operation has resulted in him spending a lot of time in the house. He is new to this production side of things, although he tells our researcher that he is currently making leaps and bounds because he is being taught the techniques by a local expert. He spends ten minutes discussing the cultivation process, the rigging of the gas meter and the stealing or buying of high-power sodium lamps. There's not much of an attempt to hide what is going on in this house. Fumes are wafting out of the front door. Billy tells our researcher that he doesn't live here, so he is 'not bothered'. He suggests that nobody is going to call the police. Nobody ever phones the police around here.

Billy starts to make a joint. He says he likes to be doing something with his hands; it helps him to think. He is happy to talk about the dope business, and wants to discuss the cultivation process in detail. After making a half-hearted attempt to talk up his criminal competency in front of our interviewer by hinting that he is running the whole dope growing and selling venture, it gradually emerges that the dope plants aren't really his, although he appears to be ultimately responsible for the security and production of the weed. As our interview progresses, a young woman knocks at the door and shouts into the house for Mandy, Billy's ex-partner. She wants a bag of dope and the negotiating goes on in front of our interviewer. Billy interrupts and starts shouting. He wants Mandy to deal with it but he can't stay out of the proceedings. He runs upstairs and returns with what looks like a small ziplock bag of weed. He tells the woman not to come back to the house, but to ring ahead and Mandy will come and meet her. The young woman leaves, Mandy returns to the kitchen and Billy starts to complain about people who only want to buy small amounts of grass and the 'pain in the arse of bagging it up and sorting everything out'. I ask Billy about the number of people who come to the door, and he says he prefers to keep them away from the house, but you can't tell people; it's Mandy's fault, it's her mates who come to the door.

Billy's description of his dope business is vague at best, but he appears to have agreed to accommodate the growing operation upstairs in return for a fee. He also earns money from direct sales, some of which he conducts from the house, but the majority of which he conducts elsewhere on the estate. Billy says Mandy's sister, whose house it is, doesn't mind what goes on and he gives her a bit of cash and a free smoke. He says he keeps most of his stuff hidden away, not because he fears a police raid, but because he fears armed robbery. He makes sure someone is in the house at all times.

Despite these nagging feelings of vulnerability and uncertainty, Billy wants the dope business to grow. He wants to set up more production operations in other houses around the estate. He tells me whatever he can produce he can sell very quickly, despite the fact that he is by no means the only dope-dealer in the neighbourhood. It eventually transpires that he buys his ecstasy tablets from his cousin, although Billy goes through the established protocol of appearing to be secretive despite the fact that it is his cousin who set up our initial interview. While Billy's cousins apparently organise the production of the dope, his ecstasy business appears to be his own, but very much a sideline to the dope-dealing. In all likelihood it is Billy's cousins who are making the real money from the dope-growing operation and others like it elsewhere in the city. The sale of ecstasy tablets is also unlikely to be particularly profitable. As prices have fallen, dealers such as Billy are forced to take smaller profits for the same risks. As these are Class A drugs, even a relatively small number found in one's possession can result in a significant prison sentence. On average, we would estimate that Billy receives £2 or £3 in profit from each tablet. Customers who buy in bulk demand lower prices, but most of his customers buy for personal use and consequently pay £5 for each one. Buying more than twenty reduces the charge to around £4 per tablet, and buying over a hundred might reduce the fee to less than £3, but that's a matter for vigorous negotiation, the result of which is dependent to a large extent on Billy's vague estimates of his cash flow. This, coupled with the money he makes from the dope-growing operation and the direct sale of the weed, does not provide him with a significant weekly income, and even an active criminal such as Billy is still at least partially dependent on welfare.

Billy is keen to move away from here, but the details that might realise this aspiration are notably vague. He has no destination in mind, and has yet to think through the processes that might aid this transition. However, it seems that anywhere will do, anywhere away from here. During this particular interview, Billy appears to have appraised the broad spectrum of his life and arrived at the conclusion that all his current trials and tribulations would immediately dissipate were he to actually move away from this place. However, at the same time it remains perfectly clear to both Billy and our researcher that this estate is Billy's natural habitat, a place where he fits in, knows people and can instantly invoke practical responses to the perils of everyday life without ever having to think too much. His whole life, or at least the periods during which he hasn't been institutionalised, has been lived on these streets and his attitudes and ingrained dispositions are an immediate reflection of this rather painful fact. He appears to know little about the geography and nature of the rest of the city, never mind the wide world beyond. In these rare moments of self-analysis, Billy appears keen to apportion 'blame' upon his immediate environment and, rather naively, he envisages his eventual destination as a freeform material nirvana where the mass of practical and legal impediments he faces on a daily basis vanish without trace, where he can have what he wants and do what he wants. He imagines this new world to be ordered, predictable even, in such a way that enables him to indulge his every whim. Despite its powerful appeal, his image of this mythical destination is only roughly adumbrated as he appears to have little practical hope of moving away from his estate and little knowledge of what lies beyond its boundaries, but the fact that he has come to recognise his current environment as unstable and perilous is telling. His view of the estate and the people who live on it is bleak but prescient:

> Look around here. It's fucking shit, there's fucking nowt, is there? No one cares. Fucking depressing . . . People around here know I'm not one of the fucking pussies, the fucking scumbags. I've got more money in my pocket now than all them out there put together. I've got the gear, got the best fucking weed. Fucking bit of bottle is all it takes.

And this view carries over into his assessment of his criminal life on the estate:

> When you're selling gear you've got to have your head screwed on or you'll get done over left, right and centre. People round here just try to rob you, beat you out of a fucking quid, man. You've got to have your eyes open 24 hours a day . . . people trying to break in, steal your fucking shit. Mates and all. It's just the way it is, man.

Billy's ingrained expectation that everyone is a potential enemy reflects how aggressively competitive these impoverished estates and their associated criminal markets actually are. Billy acknowledges that his friends may actually be willing to commit crimes against him and are unequivocally instrumental in their attitudes towards social life. They look at his friendship, and then they look at the potential score, and then, by whatever criteria, they decide:

> Q: *Your friends would rob you?*

> Why aye, man. If they thought they could have me over. That's just the way it is . . . I've had bother like that in the past . . . look, it's just, they know I'd carve them up if I ever found out.

Here Billy is again acknowledging the expectation of instrumentality in all friends or acquaintances who may unpredictably and abruptly curtail friendship and pose a threat to his interests. He doesn't see this as a particularly upsetting aspect of life on the estate, but rather an indisputable fact about the nature of human relations. His suggestion that he would have to 'carve them up' relates to a quite deliberately constructed threatening image which he hopes will dissuade potential foes or friends-turned-foes from deciding to steal from him or harm his interests in some way. This has become so ingrained in the overall culture of the estate that all friendships, relationships or passing alliances are approached in a rather tentative manner and can collapse or be suspended at any time. Sometimes, during periods where relationships are stable and undisturbed by events or structural problems, a shallow form of conspicuous attention is given towards the practical and emotional needs of the other, an almost desperate attempt at spectacular 'matiness' to convince the other that they can be relied upon and trusted. Built upon the inherently unstable cultures of self-interest that dominate interpersonal relationships in this locale, these gestures are often seen as indicative of weakness or interpreted as a camouflage, masking more sinister aims. All who move in the estate's criminal culture seem to accept that everyday social life necessarily involves a constant Darwinian battle for criminal success and social significance via the display of consumer symbolism. For Billy, friendship has always been understood in relation to these hazardous pitfalls, and it can be conceived of in no other way. In the same way that he is remorselessly self-interested in his own social, cultural and criminal life, he cannot conceive of others behaving any differently.

In a related discussion, Billy again reinforces his earlier suggestion that his crimes are almost purely financially motivated. He does what he does for the extra money. The money 'off the welfare' is a 'fucking joke', you can't get anything with it, it's not even enough to pay for drink and fags, he tells us:

[Why should I] live like that? It's daft, man, just never having any money, never having nowt, never going out, never having no gear. What's the point, people round here, just waiting on the dole?

Billy is fully immersed in the hypnotic symbolism of the consumer economy, and the desperate desire to own the ornamental trinkets that bestow existential significance and social distinction upon him propels him towards crime. For him, this is the only way to explain his day-to-day crimes. A life without the indulgent hedonism that has become routine in consumer society is a life wasted, a missed opportunity that induces exasperation, guilt and regret, a fact which he believes too many others on the estate have clearly failed to grasp. Billy plans to get a plasma TV sometime in the near future, despite the fact that burglary is a fact of life on the estate and he is rarely in one home long enough to make the most of such a purchase. He wants a car, a fast one. He has no great allegiance to a particular brand, but he does express the desire to have a top of the range stereo system installed. He wants to go abroad on holiday, and at the moment is particularly taken with the prospect of a jaunt to Ibiza next summer with some of the lads, although he has yet to book it. There's also the prospect of a weekend away in Amsterdam coming up.

These consumer dreams are, however, merely a sideline to his most seductive consumer fantasy, the heart of his dream: more clothes and gadgets. He has a particular liking for trainers, and he tells our interviewer that he has an impressive collection. He wants some of the new Nike trainers that have just come out, and he is very particular about the style and colour. He wants some 'proper' gold: big chains, watches and rings. He wants a new leather jacket and some designer polo shirts that he has seen in a store in town. He wants his teeth 'blinged' with gold and diamonds. He would like one of those new Xbox 360 games consoles. His list peters out as quickly as it began; in fact the list is quite short because his actual desire for objects themselves is weak. It's clear that although there are a few particular consumer items he can identify as those he would like to own, what he actually wants is the ability to indulge his consumer desires whenever the mood takes him and to be seen doing so. This ability, wherever it can be known to others, is at the heart of the culture and social value of consumerism in his neighbourhood. It is not specific consumer items that he desires, but rather the constant ability to go to town and acquire something new. When pressed further, he suggests that he would like to get his daughter loads of presents. He also wants to have enough money to be able to walk into the local pub and pull out a big wedge of cash. He wants the champagne, the cars, all the rest of it. He wants a big house and a swimming pool, just like anyone else, and should it happen he wants everyone to know about it.

However, he doesn't appear to have a great deal of faith in his ability to actually make these dreams come true. Unlike some other criminals on this estate, he doesn't appear to delude himself that this promised land of perpetual conspicuous consumer indulgence is just around the corner. He tells our interviewer that he is 'rubbish' with money and just 'blows it'. He buys coke and spends a lot on drink. He isn't talking about having big nights out in the city's thriving night-time economy; he is talking about going to the local pubs on and close to his estate. He isn't talking about sniffing coke in expensive nightclubs; he is talking about sniffing it off the toilet cistern in the local working men's club, or in the kitchen, or round at his mate's house. He gives some cash to Mandy and her sister, some to his girlfriend, but mostly any money that comes his way is used to provide quick-fix highs: drink, drugs, shopping. He seems mildly annoyed at himself for not being able to build up enough money to enter the drugs economy in a bigger way, but resignation quickly returns. Things are just how they are. 'No one cares,' he says. While his perpetual financial predicament is exacerbated by his attachment to sniffing coke and smoking dope, he is not unaware that these tendencies are preventing his ascent into the more profitable criminal markets that some of his peers have already managed to access. He explains:

> You can't save, how can you save? I've tried man, you've got, just everything is costing you money innit? . . . [If I could save] I'd be able to make more money coz I could be buying loads of coke in, selling more pills, it's just common sense. I've tried . . . cutting down on [my own] smoke, stuff like that, but it's torture, man, that's like, if you can't even have a fucking smoke what's the point?

Billy's business interests are closely tied to those of his cousins, two brothers who have ascended to a higher criminal stratum and no longer live on the estate. It appears that Billy's dope-growing venture is fully or partially owned by his cousins, and Billy suggests they are teaching him the various techniques required to grow and harvest the plants successfully. Billy's ecstasy business also appears to come from this source, and his admiration for the criminal competencies of his cousins is clearly apparent. He is quick to dismiss the inhabitants of his estate as 'scum, just users, trying to rob you', but his cousins are different, and it's their ability to get away with crimes that has enabled them to escape this terrible place. Billy is keen to emulate their success, and the presence of these real, local and believable iconic representatives of the *ego ideal* is the only thing that prevents Billy's underlying fatalism dragging him down to the depths of despair:

> It's not as hard as what people say. Fucking, just, you know, keep earning a bit here and there and don't get locked up. If I can get set up with the draw here, do it proper and learn the full bit, you can be making fucking thousands, man . . . just the best of gear, clothes and that, [stuff] for the house. Get out of here. Go on holiday and that, fucking top-notch bike, a fucking Merc and a jet-ski. Just, look man, just look at this [meaning the house we're in]. Fucking do shit [meaning do things, stuff], just fucking go . . . fucking anywhere. Fucking holiday, fucking Ibiza and that, man . . . Fucking our Kev [his cousin and partial sponsor] is away all the time . . . See the older lads [meaning more successful criminals and/or people who

actually have a job] in the pub giving it the big'un, fucking drinking all day and the coke and that, fuck off leather jackets, fucking covered in gold. All it takes, man, just keep me head screwed on.

Underneath these dreams lies a profound sense of fatalism. Billy might one day make enough money to go on holiday or spend all day Sunday in the pub drinking and sniffing cocaine, but he ultimately appears to accept that this version of the high life will not last. It seems that he accepts his profoundly unsatisfying life of broken relationships and petty crime as a *fait accompli*, a depressing collection of events that might occasionally be interrupted by an explosion of consumer spending and drug-taking after some fleeting criminal success. He can conceive of no realistic means of structurally and permanently altering his present circumstances, and his material aspirations are inextricably linked to criminal activity. Billy's world-view is an example of the ability of the acquisitive goals and symbols of contemporary liberal capitalism to continue to filter through to every social strata and local culture. He may be a committed criminal, forever unable to enter mainstream society, and his bearing and everyday life may be starkly at odds with the pacified cultures of contemporary liberal governance, but just like so many in the economic mainstream he continues to be totally beholden to the allure of consumerism, at least partially embodied by his cousins, and the status it can bring; only immersion in this dream prevents him from his big fall into the abyss of reality, which is why the dream and the regular capture of some of its symbolic objects become ever more seductive, comforting and vitally important as his real situation deteriorates.

Tony

At the age of 41, Tony is the very epitome of an individual totally dedicated to a life of crime. The maturation process has not cleansed him of his youthful commitment to deviancy, and the civilising influences of a committed relationship and a legitimate career have not significantly influenced his attitudes, values or identity. For Tony crime was never really a game or a proto-political act, or even the continuation of the petty childhood attachment to the symbolic parricide that in the West has been sublimated into harmless acts of disobedience or challenging authority for no real political purpose. Nor was it a form of testing the boundaries of acceptable social behaviour or injecting an element of excitement into an otherwise dull lower-class cultural environment. From a very early age Tony understood that committing crimes could produce important tangible benefits. In a neighbourhood blighted by serious poverty, crime could potentially provide the money to buy the standard flotsam and jetsam of youthful consumerism. And as Tony was quick to learn, it could also elicit the respect of his peers, transforming the self into a 'somebody in a neighbourhood of nobodies' (Pileggi 1987). These concerns did not dissipate as he grew into a man, and his everyday life now clearly displays a powerful and unrelenting commitment to acquisitive crime. Criminal activity is now deeply ingrained in his *habitus* and self-identity, and it is inexorably linked to his close attachment to 'living the good life' of consumer indulgence as the most reliable means of doing so. His tough upbringing has not shielded him from the rich symbolism of ornamental consumerism and he clearly equates the ability to display wealth – as the product of his personal performance in a notably tough sector of the market – via the symbolism of consumerism with his own self-worth and status among others in the multitude of competitive individuals that has now largely displaced community in many parts of the Anglo-American world. Tony is a diligent and committed criminal who has succeeded in generating a significant reputation across the city of his birth, and his criminal career has had some notable highlights that at one time allowed him to swim deeper into the waters of consumer symbolism. Now, however, Tony is ageing and before he could make the real big-time, criminal markets changed in ways that accommodate the younger and more flexible 'network' criminals. His reputation as a 'top boy' in the local criminal fraternity continues to enable him to make a living by crime, but having climbed within sight of the real heights of criminal success, he deems his current financial situation profoundly unsatisfactory. He desperately wants to earn more money from his criminal endeavours and hold on to his hard-won reputation, and it is these central concerns that dominated our discussions. Tony's dream of accessing the elusive criminal 'big-time' is now probably unobtainable, yet his entrepreneurial zeal continues to drive him towards new markets and new strategies that might one day allow him the life he wants.

Tony didn't have a particularly auspicious start to life. The slum clearances of the post-war period propelled his family into a hastily conceived new council estate that quickly became blighted by the tangle of pathologies usually associated with extreme economic exclusion and concentrated relative poverty. This shiny new estate quickly lost its sheen and was eventually demolished, forcing Tony's family to move again, this time to a nearby council estate of terraced and semi-detached homes. These moves appear to be of little consequence to Tony as during the same period he and his mother and sister were abandoned by his father. Tony explains:

Can't remember me old man being at home, I grew up knowing who he was, I used to see him about and I knew he was my dad and that, but we never spoke to him. He has died now and I can't say I'm bothered. He was a waste of space from what me old lady's told me, just a piss-head really.

Tony's mother struggled with the burden of two young children and both he and his sister were effectively raised by their maternal grandparents. Tony remembers them with great fondness:

They were great, me nana and granda, spoilt us both rotten when we were kids. They were lovely people. We still used to see me mam all the time, it's just we lived with them and I liked it that way. I knew even at the time we were better off with them. It's just one of them things, isn't it? It wasn't really me old lady's fault, fuck knows.

This quite pleasant arrangement continued up until the age of 11 when the increasingly ill health of his grandfather meant Tony and his sister were forced to go back and live with their mother. Tony's mother appears to have provided a far from ideal role model and was rarely available to supervise her children. The burden of work coupled with an active social life made her a fleeting presence in the family home:

That's when it started really, it was little things that kids do, throwing stones, we smashed up a bus stop and that, just daft kid things, the things bored kids do. Then the usual, bits of shoplifting, house burglary at the age of 13, I screwed me school when we were 12, we didn't even really pinch anything, just made a mess and I let the rabbits out of the school garden, we all got caught and got 'scrubs' for it, it was me first charge sheet (laughs). The shoplifting thing was the only way I could get sweets and that, then it developed into clothes and stuff, it was just really to get stuff for meself, to have decent gear coz me mam didn't have the money. Me nana still used to get us stuff but you just want more, don't you? I was a punk at the time and you had to get the clothes, the records, go to concerts and that, that's when we were screwing houses the most.

Tony cites his sixteenth birthday as a pivotal stage in his offending career and the desire to own a motorbike was of particular significance:

A few of me pals had gotten bikes when they turned 16, Honda fizzies and that, there was no way I was going to get one bought for me, not even off me nana and granda. You know when you want something, really want it? I was desperate to have one, this older lad I knew asked me to do a smash and grab with him, he would drive and I'd do the deed. We ended up doing three: two jewellers and a fucking camera shop, just blatant in the middle of the day, brick the fucking window, grab the gear and nash. Proper crazy stuff. I got me bike, though.

According to Tony the desire to possess consumer items was always at the heart of his criminal activities, and he is scornful of accounts of criminality that proffer excitement as a causal explanation:

These fuckers who say people do it for the buzz, for some sort of jolly, what a load of shit. You don't fucking risk your liberty for a buzz. You do it to get things you couldn't get any other way. Fair enough, it is exciting sometimes, I've been on a couple of ram-raids, getting chased and stuff, of course it's a buzz, only if you get away. But that's like an extra, it's not the reason you do it, though. There's fuck all excitement in spending weeks planning something and not getting it, or when you're literally shitting yourself and that before a bit of graft. You do crime to get the prize, end of story.

He continued on his career of 'prize-hunting' and eventually made his way into a professional burglary gang which throughout the 1980s was responsible for stealing millions of pounds worth of cigarettes with a string of raids on cash-and-carry stores, supermarkets and distribution warehouses across the country. It was this highly successful period that cemented his place in local criminal folklore and equipped him with the reputation and advanced criminal status that are so important to him today. Tony also made a few forays into armed robbery, one of which involved a raid on a main post office distribution depot which earned him and his comrades over £30,000 each. Tony's youthful dreams of wealth and consumer significance through crime appeared to have reached their fruition during this period, but these successes also instilled a strong desire to endlessly recreate these accomplishments. He constantly desired more money, and he now knew a way of getting it. He was within touching distance of the big-time:

How the fuck can you go and work your arse off for a couple of hundred quid a week when you've experienced that? You can't buy what you want when you work, you can't fucking live the way you want to live, you have to watch the pennies, save up. Fuck that. Where's the fun in that?

As the 1980s drew to a close, Tony's succession of remunerative criminal highs was rudely interrupted by a catastrophic low. An unsuccessful burglary on the cash machines of a TSB bank ended in his capture, and that of his long-time criminal partner, Kenny. They both received six-year sentences. As Tony reviews these events, what bothers him most is not the distress caused by his arrest and eventual imprisonment, but the fact that this inconvenient hiccup in the continuity of his criminal career prevented him from accessing a developing criminal market that would have transformed his fortunes:

> It was just when the drugs were really taking off. Es, the rave thing was going through the roof, people wanted loads of speed, the whole fucking thing was going mental and I was stuck in the fucking factory. Not that jail bothers me, it's fuck all especially when you've got a few quid behind you, it's the poor divvies with fuck all that jail hurts. I had everything in the jail, loads of phone cards, nice food, radio, little telly, it was sound that way but every cunt on the out was raking in the money. It used to fucking eat ez up thinking about it.

When Tony was released four years later he found himself in a whole new ball game, a game in which his former associates had a distinct advantage. His past ways of earning money, particularly burglary and robbery, were no longer viable options, as increasing technological advances and the ever-rising numbers of private security firms (see Matthews 2002) made it 'too much of a fuck on for too little reward'.

Despite the numerous offers by his peers to 'sort him something out', Tony realised very quickly that those who had overtaken him during his time in prison were not simply going to haul him up to their level and share their success. Tony feels no great animosity towards his former comrades, but radiates a pronounced sense of dissatisfaction at the perceived injustices that have enabled the careers of others to thrive while his atrophied during his time in prison. A powerful current of instrumentalism runs underneath the criminal milieu in which Tony operates, and he views the various forms of self-interest displayed by his former peers as mildly disappointing but entirely normal and predictable:

> I came out and these fuckers, some of them anyway, were fucking minted. I remember one lad I know, he had made it proper, cunt's a millionaire now. He invited me over to Tenerife as a treat for being out, he had a villa over there and was supplying half the island with coke and ecstasy. He was living in a different fucking world. When I was there some spic came in to the house with fucking nine kilos of proper pure cocaine, I mean proper as well, froze the fucking face off ya. Nine fucking keys, man! That was normal for him as well. It's obvious when people are making that much they're not just going to let you in on it.

Since then, despite some relative success in his own right, he has had to make do with 'working' for those who used to be his equals. He still has his reputation and he is still a well-known criminal face in the city. He drives a flash BMW and he is seen out and about in all the right places, he eats in nice restaurants and he is always immaculately and expensively dressed. However, he admits that most of this appearance is 'pure front' and that in real terms he owns very little by way of either property or liquid assets. He doesn't own a house, his car is 'on bail' from Wally, a friend and a very successful dealer, and he spends whatever money he earns from 'running around' for Kenny, Wally and others on keeping up this faux-glamorous lifestyle:

> Even a night out with people like that costs a fucking fortune. I was with Wally last Saturday afternoon and he lost a grand at the bookies on the fucking roulette machine, a grand on a Saturday afternoon, it didn't even bother him losing it. There's loads of examples like that, money means fuck all to them unless it's tens of thousands. One kid I know spent three grand on fireworks on New Year's Eve, just to piss his neighbours off coz they all work and don't like the idea of him being better off than them. I should have that kind of money.

The envy and resentment in Tony is almost tangible and serves to highlight both the variability and the importance of demonstrable success in the area's criminal milieu. Whereas for some of those in our study, success is a new pair of trainers and an ounce of coke and is, therefore, relatively obtainable, for Tony, having had tantalising glimpses of the Promised Land, relative success is measured against considerably more than that. His former peers constantly remind him of what always appears to lie just beyond his reach, thus condemning him to a state of perpetual dissatisfaction with his circumstances and instilling in him an unquenchable desire to emulate their wealth:

> I just keep thinking, I used to earn more than any of them fuckers, I'm not being a big-head but I'm much fucking smarter than most of them, I've got the balls, why can't I fucking just get a lucky break? Thing is they have got it all sewn up.

Tony's ongoing addiction to accruing the outward signs of real wealth, and his associated status anxiety, continues to propel him back to the market in search of the 'opportunities' that might enable him to reach the big-time of ostentatious wealth and hard-earned respect. His life has become a desperate scramble for criminal success, and this focus comes at the expense of other areas of his life. He sees emotional connections as a sign of weakness, and he is not willing to take on the burden of a committed relationship. His believes his entire life needs to be dedicated to the pursuit of his criminal goals, and to this end he is currently attempting to organise a drug importation scam with some 'old pals [he] was in jail with'. He now hopes pre-packed and vacuum-sealed packages of skunk imported from Amsterdam will be his ticket to the high life that comes with the position of being a rich, independent entrepreneur:

> If I can get them to bail me a biggish amount, twenty–thirty kilos, I can get going, fuck these jokers off and work on me own, be me own man again. It's just getting a start again really.

However, to date nothing has come of this latest venture and Tony appears to admit that it is likely to come to nothing:

> You get promised the fucking world but nowt ever comes of it, there's always some excuse at the end, the whole drugs caper, it's one big fuck on, always waiting about for some cunt who never shows up. But what else is someone like me going to do, you tell me?

True believers

What the above case studies show quite clearly is that we cannot simply assume that persistent criminals who inhabit areas of permanent recession have somehow come to understand the nature of their oppression and have subscribed to proto-political criminal cultures as a way of misguidedly 'kicking against the system' (Cohen 1955). Further, these men do not appear to have been inculcated with a distinct value system born of the political and cultural history of the English working class, one that might distinguish them from the core values and ambitions of today's undeniably Thatcherite social mainstream. It is clear that they lead distinctly unlawful lives in which they appreciate crime and what it can bring at a personal, experiential level, and they are oriented towards it at as a potentially effective strategy that gives birth to a rather paradoxical set of norms, but this does not mean that they have been cut adrift from the mainstream social order and its underlying cultural values. Both our ethnographic observation of Billy and Tony and the words we managed to get on tape reveal just how tightly they are bound to the acquisitive and instrumental ethos of consumer capitalism and its symbolic objects as the sole means of constructing an identity that affords them status. What they value fundamentally is not at all distinct from the foundational value system that currently structures social engagement in the western world. They want the security that a measure of financial success can bring, but they also hope to push past this point and access the opulent heights of indulgent hedonism and *haute bourgeois* status whose images are now broadcast incessantly across the globe by the marketing industry and mass media. They want respect and financial, emotional and psychological security. They want success in their chosen field. They want to know that their lives count for something. And above all, they believe in this value system. They do not question the acquisitive and competitive nature of contemporary social life. They do not grasp the vacuity of consumerism, or the oppressive social system and exploitative economic system that has cast them and their ancestors to the bottom of the pile and watches intently to gauge how many will try to climb back up as an indication of the strength of its hegemony. Rather, the constant waves of consumer symbolism and the partial democratisation of opulence in the consumer/service economy renew their desire to acquire, to go out and be seen to be successfully wrestling significance from a harsh world. They aren't disgusted that they have so few of the material advantages that others might have in abundance. Instead they want a piece of the action and will continue to search for ways to overcome the multitude of impediments that restrict their access to a place of significance in the hyper-real spectacle that services the consumer economy.

Both Billy's and Tony's dispositions have steered them towards illegal methods of achieving cultural and financial success, and these methods have together become one of the standard techniques of 'social mobility' in the deprived neighbourhoods in which both were raised and continue to live. However, utilising criminal techniques does not necessitate a rejection of the values that underlie our current system of liberal capitalism. While it's clear that our respondents continue to be subjected to significant economic hardships, we cannot assume that their marginalised position is a result of their status as 'flawed consumers' (Bauman 2001a, 2004). Rather, our respondents are deeply committed and competitive consumers, and as such they are the kind of consumers the market prefers; it is our contention after years of observing life in these areas that those with a genuine potential of escaping total immersion in consumer symbolism and embracing genuine politico-cultural forms of rebellion tend to be law-abiding and politicised in the traditional manner (Hall and Winlow 2007). Even Billy, whose whole life has been experienced in a position of material disadvantage, low status and very loose normative strategies – which until quite recently would have placed him in an ideal position for the possibility of traditional radicalisation – begins each new day as an active and competitive market performer and consumer ready to take risks to acquire the rich symbolism that structures subjectivity and status in the current economic order. His acquisitive techniques in no way threaten this order and his powerful desire to acquire is not a passing aberration. Billy's involvement in theft is in fact his own tiny contribution to the economic well-being of the burgeoning security and insurance industries. His day-to-day crimes make people want to move away from 'his kind' to more salubrious areas of the city, pushing property prices up for those affluent enough to care, and reducing the prices in those areas where people don't vote. Even if he is caught and convicted of a crime, his resulting incarceration can easily be commodified; the neo-liberal rhetoric about reducing tax and state interference differs significantly from its real tendency towards expensive authoritarian rule. Spending on the criminal justice systems in Britain and the USA continues to be very high indeed as the neo-liberal state is forced to sweep up the inevitable problems created by the various and sometimes quite desperate means by which human beings and their organisations try to maintain their vital performances in the market. The fact of the matter is that in the 1970s the guiding lights of neo-liberal thought envisaged the growth of the pronounced economic marginalisation and the social problems that have, since the 1980s, become such prominent features of contemporary social life (see, for instance, Wilson 1975), but clearly regarded this as a price worth paying for what they hoped would be a vibrant, efficient and prosperous market economy. To buttress their economised version of a liberal society, a broad range of reworked hegemonic processes have reshaped concepts of freedom and equality, breaking down collective sentiments and authentic forms of solidarity and fostering individualised and instrumental cultural forms that have served to reaffirm and re-naturalise – after a century of powerful and damaging social critique (Badiou 2007; Boltanski and Chiapello 2007) – the socio-economic status and preferred cultural practices of what Harvey (2007) terms the 'global elite'. The criminal acts of our respondents and their virtually total immersion in consumer culture's symbolism, and in the mainstream values of competitive individualism and independent entrepreneurship, are so tightly woven into the fabric of late modern society that to identify these men as either 'socially excluded' or 'rebellious' – or even on the other hand 'co-opted' and 'incorporated' – simplifies, as we shall see in the following chapters, the far more complex nature of their position.

Chapter 5

Consumerism and the counterculture

The previous chapters have examined ways in which various criminals pursue their consumer desires. Before we can unpack these desires and locate them in broader sociological contexts we need to know a little more about consumption itself. There is no space in this book for a thorough résumé of consumer development in the Anglo-American West (see Galbraith 1991), but suffice it to say that the outward spread – from the aristocracy and gentry through the middle classes to the multitude – of the desire and ability to consume at a level far above basic needs has been a feature of these societies since the eighteenth century (see McKendrick *et al.* 1983; Veblen 1994). Consumerism was not suddenly 'invented' in the 1950s; humanity has always to some extent 'consumed' and attached social significance to specific objects of consumption, and consumerism has been the essential complement to the development of capitalism's productive forces throughout its history. It was not until the immediate post-war period, however, that the desire and ability to consume ever further into the realms of luxury and technological gadgetry became part of everyday reality for most citizens, and consumerism could be described as a truly 'mass' phenomenon (Galbraith 1999).

What is consumption? Within rational and ecological limits there is nothing wrong with producing and consuming better products that allow a better quality of life for everyday people; even a bit of luxury is a good thing, as long as we recognise that 'luxury' items will quickly lose their allure if they become too commonplace. A critique of today's advanced form of consumerism is not, of course, a critique of actual consumption itself. A serious analysis of consumption will focus not on the ability to consume and the initial asocial ethical questions that it might beg, but on consumerism as a set of cultural practices replete with meanings connected to social power relations; the question is not what we consume and who should benefit from the development of our ability to do so – the answer is, of course, everyone – but how we consume as a complex set of social practices. For Karl Marx, whose thinking is usually associated with production and society's productive relations, consumption was no less than the realisation of species-being, the end-product of labour and production at a specific point in a society's historical development. For him the problem was that capitalism ruptured the relationship between labour and consumption, and the workers' compulsion to sell labour power for the purpose of mass-manufacturing commodities for sale in the market meant that they no longer created products that truly reflected their immediate needs, desires, creative urges and identities (Marx 1999). As the labour-process became rationalised, specialised and professionalised, mental and manual labour became rigidly separated, and the emergence of marketing and the co-option of art into the exclusive design professions emptied, for the majority, the whole process of production and consumption of any creativity or meaning (*ibid.*). Workers consumed the products of the labour of others and produced for the consumption of others, all for the ultimate purposes of circulating commodities in the marketplace and making profits for owners and investors. In the same way that individuals as workers become alienated from the products of their labour, as consumers they become alienated from the social meaning of the products they acquire. We live in a world of phenomenal forms, separated from our essence.

In Emile Durkheim's rather dour Aristotelian/Hobbesian vision, consumption is a compelling and seductive activity that must be restricted lest it feeds into the 'malady of infinite aspirations' and drives the individual beyond the restraints provided by the collective's moral boundaries to the realm of *anomie*, a condition of normlessness that threatens the integrity of these restraints, which are vitally necessary for holding society together (Durkheim 1992, 1984). However, for us these centripetal forces of moral and normative restraint exist in tension with the centrifugal thymotic forces of 'distinction', recognised by Max Weber in his theories of culture and status but explored in more detail by Thorstein Veblen (1994) in his theory of the 'leisure class'. For Veblen, the purpose of conspicuous displays of consumption was to indicate a high status that separates the individual from the practical dimension of social necessity; but it's not the ownership of the goods that counts, or indeed any benefits they might provide, it's the knowledge that they have been obtained by means other than manual work, which, of course, implies that at some point in the process of acquisition everyday moral boundaries might well have been transgressed. This ties in with

Bourdieu's (1986) notion of 'elegance', the effortless acquisition and display of wealth and power, and the ability to bequeath it all to children, which is a 'natural' consequence of the qualities of high caste; an entitlement to take, display and hand down what is rightfully theirs. Veblen posits this as the vestige of an ancient barbarian tendency that has survived throughout modernity (see also Mestrovic 1993). In contrast, the lower orders are fit only for mundane work and service.

It seems that the association of some individuals with the social alienation and anomic tendency posited by Marx and Durkheim as pathological conditions has been regarded – at least when ordered in a hierarchal form – by our ancestors as a source of distinction and status, which is one of a number of reasons why Marx regarded our previous social systems as examples of our barbaric 'pre-history'. If we combine these three insights, what the democratisation and the outward spread of luxury consumption, its drives and its social symbolism seems to have done is to release the potential for the formation and reproduction of an essentially alienating, unethical, anti-social form of social distinction from the custody of the privileged power-elite and diffuse it throughout the social body. As a result, the surplus, the 'accursed share' (see Hubert and Mauss 1981; Bataille 1992; Baudrillard 2001), is now exempt from its ritual destruction, free to endure, roam and cause trouble wherever attempts to monopolise it might be made. Older divisions such as class, religion, ethnicity and gender have been constantly intersected by the division between those who were happy to identify themselves as communitarian producers and the restless malcontents who, as self-alienated and atomised consumers, sought identities of distinction in order to stand out from the crowd (Hall 2000); Maoism contained within itself a failed attempt to surgically remove this tendency from Chinese society, but in the West it was systematically cultivated. As Gary Cross (2000) argues persuasively in his studies of consumerism in the USA, by the 1930s the values, meanings and desires of this latter group had already begun to filter down and, encouraged by the dominance of bourgeois hegemony, grow within the working class, who as a consequence began to assume the 'prejudices of consumption'. This, of course, was during an economic depression when political radicalism was rife among the American and British working classes (see Rose 2002). Nevertheless, increasing numbers began to display the willingness to forgo material necessities in order to obtain and display luxury consumer items that would enhance their social status, hiding themselves away during times of extreme poverty, eschewing all forms of political resistance and re-emerging only when the recovery of personal affluence allowed them to symbolically rejoin the public as successful market performers and distinguished consumers. The virus was alive, and for so many this preference for luxury over necessity is today an ingrained cultural trait throughout everyday Anglo-American culture, as suggested by recent consumer research on the selection of gifts and prizes in promotions and competitions:

> A substantial segment of consumers choose hedonic luxury rewards over cash of equal or greater value; consumers typically explain such choices based on the need to precommit to indulgence, to make sure that the award does not end up in the pool of money used for necessities. (Kivetz and Simonson 2002: 199)

However, between the depression and the so-called 'cultural revolution' of the 1960s the consumerist virus had not penetrated the core of the British working class. Richard Hoggart (1957) recognised the proud isolation of some cultures in the pre-TV age, which was their sole protection from the mass consumer culture that was developing in the USA and filtering across the Atlantic, encouraged, of course, by Keynesian demand management and the post-war boom in production and employment. By the 1960s, however, de-skilling, affluence and rehousing joined the mass-media and marketing industries to penetrate and corrode these politically volatile working-class cultures. As the hard-line politics that Thompson (1991) had seen as the basis of working-class culture began to soften somewhat, the working class's internal processes of self-identification and cultural reproduction within their diverse traditional collectives began to break down. Hoggart (1957) and Williams (1971, 2005) noted that by the late 1950s all but the most isolated and militant working-class communities in the heavy industrial heartlands began to evaluate the world in economic and individual rather than cultural, moral and political terms.

This increasingly 'enrolled' individual became a major sociological concern, especially as it became a predominant form of identity among 'embourgeoisfied' affluent workers in the 1960s (see Goldthorpe *et al.* 1968), but this discourse was flawed because it failed to recognise that working-class individuals were becoming affluent and indulging in consumption on their own terms rather than 'converting' to middle-class mores. During this period the study of class, politics and identity in British cultural studies moved in fruitful directions as the work of Barthes, Lacan, Althusser and others was utilised to investigate the western individual who, despite palpable social injustice, strength in numbers and a rich political tradition, refused to revolt against the capitalist system. Althusser's claim that this individual was the interpellated subject of ideology – beckoned and ensnared by dominant ideological apparatuses – achieved temporary popularity, while Gramsci's more enduring concept of hegemony, which allowed for more relative autonomy in the individual, found a comfortable niche in critical cultural studies despite its brutal conversion into popular usage. However, the rather deterministic linguistic structuralism upon which all this work was based tended to ignore the dull compulsions of everyday life, the active embodied agent and the emotive seductions of consumerism, and, for an Anglo-American palate weaned on orthodox liberalism, it failed to place the autonomous individual on its rightful pedestal. In the 1970s the notion of individuals as passive recipients of ideological manipulation was replaced by the British idea – borrowed from American sub-cultural theory and located in the context of class – that each new generation of young people uses consumer products to construct surrogate communal identities, subverting and resisting the norms and values of the dominant system (Hall and Jefferson 2006; Hebdige 1979). Even though the new generation of cultural analysts accepted that working-class political and communal traditions were eroding, in these sub-cultural reincarnations they still lived on as cultural politics. This idea grew in strength in the early 1980s as the economic base and traditional socialist politics of the working class were being systematically dismantled by the brutal and very thorough Thatcherite regime.

It is our contention that both Leftist factions were quite possibly wrong: the tragic fact unfolding in these decades was that a politically significant majority of the working class had on their own terms strengthened their allegiance to capitalism and cared little even about its social democratic reform, much less its revolutionary transformation. Somehow, consumerism was supplying working people with what they wanted; not simply material goods but a new and very appealing means of constructing a flexible identity that would, allegedly, never suffer humiliation and rejection, and never fail to achieve social distinction in the minds of its subjects and their significant others. There is little doubt that mass consumerism developed first in the USA, but it was not simply imposed on Europe. Rather, the success of the US model, based on its huge and expanding domestic market, allowed it to suggest the rules and procedures required for success (de Grazia 2005; Sassoon 2005) as the European nations began to integrate as a common economic unit. The influence started earlier, in the 1920s, with the gradual importation of Fordist production, Rotary clubs, chain stores, brand identifications, corporate advertising, cinemas and the Hollywood star system. Paramount among these influences was the provision of workers with a 'decent standard of living' to expand the commodity market by increasing consumer power, which gave the working classes access to the cash and the fashion items needed to mount a cultural assault on the hated European 'upper classes' and their system of privilege. Class struggle was very cleverly deflected from the relations of production to the relations of distinction via the spread of a counterfeit gentrification. Where politics had failed, culture would succeed, with no need for a revolution or even stringent social democratic reform. After World War Two, the principle of increased consumption also fitted neatly with the Keynesian strategy of managing the inherently unstable market by adjusting the money supply and manipulating demand, so it received universal support from both sides of the establishment. The art of popular politics became inextricably bound up with the promise of widening and increasing access to consumer goods, which was the magic bullet for the oppressed workers seeking social parity and the business classes who wanted to prevent another economic crisis of the magnitude of the Wall Street Crash in 1929 and the ensuing Great Depression (see Hobsbawm 1995). Voices against consumerism were all too easy to discredit and caricature as romantic cries from misplaced Feudalists who wanted the workers back in their place and the entrepreneurs' wings clipped, or from naive Romantics, miserable Puritans or 'evil commies' who wanted to ruin the whole show for the sake of an unrealisable dream that would inevitably end up as a totalitarian disaster.

Nor were cultural forms and identities simply dreamt up by American designers, mass marketed and imposed on populations. So effective was the American technique of taking in cultural forms – first from Europe and Latin America and then from around the world – and turning them into commodities with global appeal that it is inappropriate to posit America as the generative source of global consumer culture. It was more like the clearing house and distributor selling various cultures' ideas – including its own – back to themselves (de Grazia 2005). Consumer products, made up of bits from all over the world, could subtly combine exotica with homeliness and street relevance to increase their universal appeal. It is thus extremely difficult to resist these consumer goods with a turn back into localism, or to cultures outside capitalism, or with the conceit of autonomous sub-cultural creativity, because everything, including the elements necessary for those symbolic moves and more, is already contained within them. Consumer products are thus tiles in the Lacanian mirror in which the subject identifies itself; they have no symbolic existence in themselves and their symbolism cannot be 'created', as we discuss in more detail in the following chapters.

Six decades of this totalising form of consumer culture has made the world a different place, especially the USA, and for our purposes, Britain. Research recently carried out by the National Consumer Council (undated) led them to declare the existence of a 'new shopping generation', and the marketing industry continues to invent ever more ingenious methods of inculcating messages about consumer products into the psyches and cultural lives of young children (see Barber 2007). By the age of ten 78 per cent of children list shopping as one of their favourite activities and they have been inducted to the world of brands and labels; the average child of this age displays extreme familiarity with 300 to 400 brands. Seventy per cent of three-year-olds recognise the McDonald's symbol before they recognise their own surnames. The children's market in Britain is now worth £30 billion, and the marketing industry is a major influence – if not *the* major influence – on children's identities, desires and values. For many transatlantic marketing executives children are not children but evolving consumers (see Bakan 2005) who can be encouraged to 'nag' their parents into making the purchases they want. The marketing industry sponsors school activities so it can plaster schools with adverts, creating 'brand enclosures'. Ofcom (2007) figures show that 86.1 per cent of homes now have multichannel television, and the majority of channels are plastered with marketing messages. The average British or American child views between 20,000 and 40,000 TV ads per year. Ninety-eight per cent of children and young people have used the internet at school and at home, and the marketing industry has also swamped popular sites with adverts: between January and March of 2005 over 12.2 million children visited commercial websites promoting food and drinks. Peter Thiel, the libertarian venture capitalist, self-styled 'futurist philosopher', co-founder of the virtual banking system *PAYPAL*, founder of the hard right-wing journal *The Stanford Review* and initial fundraiser for Mark Zuckerberg's immensely popular teen site *Facebook*, quite unashamedly boasts of the site's ability to take advantage of the 'sheep-like' tendency of young people to copy and follow one another around without a great deal of reflection – an application of his mentor René Girard's (2005) concept of 'mimetic desire' – to herd them onto his site and expose them to numerous adverts (see Hodgkinson 2008). The 'mimetic desire' of young people was no doubt a major selling point in the process of raising investment capital for the site, but later, in our discussion of Lacan (see Chapter 9), we will see quite clearly that Girard's concept is a crude naturalistic notion that belies the complexity of a phenomenon that requires cultivation in the midst of numerous sociocultural prerequisites. In corner shops and newsagents, magazines targeting children as young as four are saturated with advertising. Public services are increasingly being used as advertising spaces, and the marketing industry has also tapped into children's enjoyment of collecting things, which encourages purchases and repeat purchases of products such as cereal, fast food and washing powder. The marketing industry is now forging ahead with the aid of neurosciences in the 'neuroeconomics' and 'neuromarketing' fields, where brain scans can show marketers how to stimulate the parts of the brain that seem to deal with envy and emotional and cognitive awareness of relationships with co-consumers (Lewis and Brigder 2005). The whole package creates a surrogate world in which active identification processes are ensnared.

If marketing agencies and their products sell one cultural image above all others to young people it is 'cool'. Nancy Shalek, president of the highly successful Shalek Agency, quite unashamedly revealed that advertising at its best can implant in the psyche the idea that without a certain product an individual will be seen by others as a 'loser', and performing such operations of mass psychology on children is easy because they are so emotionally vulnerable (see Palmer 2006). Using pop, movie and sports stars as cultural icons is the most common strategy for establishing 'cool' and associating this sociocultural position with products (Rojek 2001; Cashmore 2002). The role of the brand as a primary 'mirror of identification' (see Lacan 2006) does not necessarily diminish as the child matures, but, in a weakened symbolic order whose ability to prohibit narcissism and encourage an alternative political relationship between the subject and reality has been diminished (Žižek 2006b), it becomes more potent and influential at important points in the construction of individual and group identities:

> Our findings identify the period from middle childhood (ages 7–8) to early adolescence (ages 12–13) as key to understanding how children view brands in relationship to their self-images. Not only do we see increases in the number of self-brand connections during this period, but also changes in the nature of the self-brand connections being made. Our findings also suggest that older children have deeper self-brand connections because they think about brands in a very specific way – as having personalities and symbolising group membership – that provides a natural link to their self-concepts. (Chaplin and John 2005: 127)

National Consumer Council research (undated) concluded that 'brand-aware' children were more likely to display symptoms of unhappiness and mental ill-health. As the 'adultification' and sexualisation of children's clothes increases, the possibility of experiencing a meaningful childhood with space for learning and establishing an organic identity begins to evaporate. Marketing guru Martin Lindstrom once suggested that brands and their surrounding iconography are replacing religion (Palmer 2006). The whole consumer edifice is based on two hedonistic commands: enjoy yourself by pursuing your base desires to their limits, and exercise your inalienable right to enjoy yourself in this way as much as those who seem to enjoy life the most, both of which are inextricably connected to the young person's relationship to brands. The marketing industry's iconographic production apparatus is well developed in its capacity to supply young people with an endless procession of hedonistic icons, people who have it all and know how to flaunt it, the latter-day saints of consumption. Consumer objects, needed as portable mirrors and displays of fragile identities that are constantly under scrutiny, become extensions of the self, leaving many young people susceptible to profound feelings of lack and humiliation:

> The onset of adolescence is a time when the self-concept is especially fragile ... and heavily influenced by the reflected appraisals of others. When adolescents ridicule peers about possessions, and by extension themselves ... they threaten their fragile self-concepts and perpetuate a pattern of seeking material solutions for identity problems. Concerns about name brands and jokes about poverty were especially prevalent among informants from working-class neighborhoods. This observation is consistent with symbolic self-completion theory, which predicts increased self-symbolizing behavior among individuals who face barriers to achieving self defining goals. The notion that expensive goods are pursued most aggressively by consumers who are not necessarily among the most able to afford them has important implications for public policy. (Wooten 2006: 196)

However, the iconography is connecting to forces more complex than envy and gentrified 'conspicuous consumption', and it plays on the ubiquitous notion of achieving social positions by means of distinction (Bourdieu 1986; Frank 1997; Heath and Potter 2007), distinguishing the self as a 'cool individual' from others cast as the hapless, moribund 'herd'. It is no longer necessary – although it still remains optional for those who have difficulty in mastering 'cool' – to become spectacularly rich and ostentatious to be a dedicated consumer with high social status. Liberal cultural studies' enthusiastic misrecognition of the media-marketing apparatus as the supplier of malleable symbolic material to an autonomous, creative plurality external to itself – a theoretical development that occurred at the same time as the countercultural icon of the 'cool individualist' was replacing the responsible collectivist – is quite striking. Decades of gleaning information about local tastes has allowed the marketing industry to be not merely responsive or productive in the supply of tractable polysemic symbols, but formative in the sense of being an active and perhaps dominant partner in taste-formation:

> The process of translating consumer meanings into promotional texts and product designs suitable for larger consumer segments removes them from their local contexts. This process of abstraction inevitably transforms their distinctive character. What starts out as a concrete, local, and contextualized fashion, something that may be perceived as not yet commercial and therefore authentic, is drained of its original sign value as it is marketed and mainstreamed. If one's

customization of the code appears authentic, it has value, which is exactly what marketing research communities are after. When the consumer's appropriation of countervailing meanings is done in the context of distinction, then commercialization of the style creates a staged authenticity, and the consumer may move on to something new. This makes the construction of a distinctive style a continuous struggle involving a tug-of-war between life worlds and social systems. This interpretation is consistent with contemporary ana-lyses of marketing and consumer culture suggesting that the interpretive positions of consumers become important information for market researchers . . . (Murray 2002: 439)

The aspect of the media that makes them 'mass' is that, apart from public broadcasting institutions, they are all driven by advertising, and the visual and audio culture of their popular programmes and adverts diffuses the images of the consumer dreamscape into every street, house, commercial building and vehicle in the western world. All diverse values and opinions are simply lures to attract a purportedly plural audience that becomes 'mass' as soon as it connects with the images that represent lifestyle dreams and directs consumers towards the general audio-visual style of the commodities that promise to realise them. All diverse cultures from the life-world, ranging from the mainstream to the alleged counterculture, are drawn into a bazaar that can cater for their differences yet simultaneously homogenise them around the common factor of the commodity. Regarding this issue, Stuart Hall, in a statement that typifies cultural studies thinking in the 1980s and 1990s, was ambivalent:

> Consumer capitalism works by working the markets: but it cannot entirely determine what alternative uses people are able to make of the diversity of choices and the real advances in mass production which it also always brings. If 'people's capitalism' did not liberate the people, it nevertheless 'loosed' many individuals into a life somewhat less constrained, less puritanically regulated, less strictly imposed than it had been three or four decades before . . . Thus, the Left has never understood the capacity of the market to become identified in the minds of the mass of ordinary people, not as fair and decent and socially responsible (that it never was), but as an expansive popular system. (Hall 1988: 215)

This concept of 'loosening', however, is flawed. There is nothing more constraining and relentlessly demanding than the fetish, the fixation, and Hall is missing the Lacanian distinction between the *aim* and the *object* of desire, which is what lies underneath the more anodyne term 'identified' that he selected. Of course, consumer items are diverse and therefore can allow choice as a part of the object of desire, but the fetishistic aim of desire that is cultivated by consumerism – to circulate eternally around these objects – remains the same. For those with little enthusiasm for alternative sets of symbols this allows no choice whatsoever, a subject we explore in more detail in Chapter 9. The valuable concept of abstention as the principal form of resistance, a refusal (see Žižek 2008) that can be encouraged by the prohibitions present in a traditional form of symbolic order, had by this time virtually disappeared from the debate; although, writing in the same year, Judith Williamson (1988: 20) was perhaps a little less ambivalent in her assessment of the liberal *canard* of autonomous choice:

> The great irony is that it is precisely the illusion of autonomy which makes consumerism such an effective diversion in people's lives. At a time when such power in the economic and political spheres seems very distant, the realm of the 'superstructure' is, for consumers and Marxists alike, a much more fun place to be. Certainly it offers more fun than trying to deal with the frustrations channelled into it but created, predominantly, by the economic realities which are still the major constrictions on most people's lives. And also more fun than trying to envisage new ways in which some of the needs and desires appropriated by consumer goods can be met.

However, by foregrounding the 'fun' aspect of consumption Williamson failed to recognise the compulsive drive, the powerful combination of narcissism, fetishism and super-ego injunction that propels the consumer subject into the realm of enjoyment and, for some, beyond the boundaries into the painful realm of *jouissance*, where life is not much 'fun' at all (Stratton 2001; Žižek 2002, 2006, 2007). Some consumer researchers now argue that this core problematic should be revisited (see Murray 2002). Thomas Frank's (1997) strident answer to this problem was to argue that Anglo-American cultural studies, in its haste to portray the consumer as actively autonomous and argue that young people could 'resist' at the point of consumption, neglected the immense formative power of the marketing industry, the manufacturer of consumer culture's symbols, a profound strategic blunder:

> Today corporate ideologues routinely declare that business has supplanted the state, the church, and all independent culture in our national life. Curiously enough, at the same time many scholars have decided it is folly to study business. For all of cultural studies' subtle readings and forceful advocacy, its practitioners often tend to limit their inquiries so rigorously to the consumption of culture-

products that the equally important process of cultural production is virtually ignored. (Frank 1997: 18–19)

Frank's powerful and perceptive analysis, eschewing the incestuous intertextuality and theoretical convolution of cultural studies, cut into the heart of the marketing industry, showing us that not only resistance but even our distaste of the artificiality of consumerism itself had for a long time been incorporated into marketing strategies. By the 1990s we saw 'the consolidation of a new species of hip consumerism, a cultural perpetual motion machine in which disgust with the falseness, shoddiness, and everyday oppressions of consumer society could be enlisted to drive the ever-accelerating wheel of consumption' (Frank 1997: 31). In other words, the marketing industry had learnt to generate its own internal dynamic by containing the cultural explosions caused by the friction between 'uncool' and 'cool', which can now be recycled endlessly as the waste produced in the process is brought back into fashion as 'retro-chic' (see Baudrillard 1993). Even the ostensibly subversive activities of the culture jammers (see Lasn 2001) calling for the 'uncooling of America' were hijacked by the ever-alert 'funky business' machine of the marketing industry (McGuigan 2006; Ridderstrale and Nordstrom 2002). Now, because everything is eminently commodifiable in the image, even seemingly 'organic' critiques of consumption are part of the marketing strategy:

> As the voluntary simplicity lifestyle becomes appropriated by experts, packaged, and sold, it loses its distinctive character. When this happens, even a lifestyle based on anticonsumption becomes defined in terms of commodities, possessions, sign value, and commercial success . . . What started out as an 'emancipated space' ended up just another packaged, historical identity. (Murray 2002: 439)

Anti-consumption's core drive was essentially a product of the consumer's self-disgust at seeing his own enthusiasm for such transparent artificiality reflected back at him; a means of selling self-protection for the persistently embarrassed fashion-victim, allowing her to ward off the feelings of humiliation that might cause withdrawal and collapse the whole game:

> But rather than a revolutionary vanguard, such consumers are more accurately theorised as participants in a countercultural movement that, working in concert with innovative firms, pursued market-based solutions to the contradictions of modern consumer culture. Consumers are revolutionary only insofar as they assist entrepre-

neurial firms to tear down the old branding paradigm and create opportunities for companies that understand emerging new principles. Revolutionary consumers helped to create the market for Volkswagen and Nike and accelerated the demise of Sears and Oldsmobile. They never threatened the market itself. What has been termed 'consumer resistance' is actually a form of market-sanctioned cultural experimentation through which the market rejuvenates itself. (Holt 2002: 89)

This sort of 'disgust' now appears to be merely a middle-class variation of the humiliation that has always operated as a powerful motivator among the post-war consumer mass. Humiliation has been adopted and developed into a sophisticated and symbolically violent cultural practice in young consumer groups. This involves a complex inversion where activity becomes passive and passivity becomes active:

Recent efforts to understand how aggressive marketers . . . materialistic parents, and influential peers . . . affect children's consumption patterns have advanced knowledge of the social forces and experiences that contribute to consumer socialisation. The present study contributes to these efforts by exploring a powerful mechanism through which influential socialisation agents provide feedback about consumption missteps. Although teaching is seldom the motive of teasers, learning is often a by-product of teasing. (Wooten 2006: 196)

The assumption that consumer culture is a site of creativity, fun and freedom must be questioned. Frank (1997) and others (see, for example, Heath and Potter 2007) have recently demolished the voluntarism at the heart of cultural studies by showing that the 'cool', rebellious identities reflected in the consumer mirror were essential marketing tools for the attraction of younger generations and the maintenance of the system's dynamic movement. The 'cool' identity manufactured and promoted by consumer marketing as today's structural *ego ideal* cannot be assumed to be either progressive or benign. In fact the Anglo-American 'rugged individualist' image on which the 'cool dude' appears to be based – the 'man who forges his own path' – dovetails with Veblen's barbarian mentality (see also Mestrovic 1993; Slotkin 1998) in which individual distinction is achieved and secured by violent, predatory and anti-social means. This is not the product of creative freedom but a reworked tradition that foments narcissism, envy and both the character and the mimetic emulation that Thiel and Girard seem to think are universal and natural. Everyone wants to distinguish the self from the herd, but everyone wants to emulate those who are seen as capable of doing so, and therefore the herd itself is reproduced and energised. The achievement of 'cool' seems to be driven by a cultural dynamic in which pleasure/pain, determinism/voluntarism and emulation/differentiation all appear to create dynamic oppositional dyads in a multifaceted system, which is more restrictive and compulsive than 'free'.

If 'cool' is not a product of autonomous creativity, what is its real source and how and why did it become such an essential aspect of consumer culture? The answer may lie in what is commonly referred to as the Anglo-American 'counterculture', which emerged in the late 1950s and spread quite voraciously thereafter. This counterculture focused exclusively and rather one-dimensionally on pleasure, distinction and voluntarism and systematically ignored any development that might contradict its claims to be the historical agent of freedom set to lead us away from advanced capitalism's dull compulsions. We can see the legacy of this movement at the heart of cultural studies and in some aspects of contemporary cultural criminology. Many liberal theorists in Anglo-American cultural studies and contemporary cultural criminology have rather hastily conflated and politicised the search for pleasure as the quest for freedom and, through that, social justice. Heath and Potter have been quite strident in their critique of this assumption and its countercultural roots:

> According to the countercultural theory, 'the system' achieves order only through the repression of the individual. Pleasure is inherently anarchic, unruly, wild. To keep the workers under control, the system must instil manufactured needs and mass-produced desires, which in turn can be satisfied within the framework of the technocratic order. Order is achieved, but at the expense of promoting widespread unhappiness, alienation and neurosis. The solution must therefore lie in reclaiming our capacity for spontaneous pleasure – through polymorphous perversity, or performance art, or modern primitivism, or mind-expanding drugs, or whatever else turns your crank. In the countercultural analysis, simply having fun comes to be seen as the ultimate subversive act. Hedonism is transformed into a revolutionary doctrine ... Is it any wonder then that this sort of countercultural rebellion has invigorated capitalism? It's time for a reality check. Having fun is not subversive, and it doesn't undermine any system. In fact, widespread hedonism makes it more difficult to organise social movements, and more difficult to persuade anyone to make a sacrifice in the name of social justice. In our view, what the progressive left needs to do is disentangle the concern over questions of social justice from the countercultural critique – and to jettison the latter, while continuing to pursue the former. (Heath and Potter 2007: 10–11)

To us, it appears that the countercultural left of the post-war period confused conformity with obedience, and, perhaps more to the point for this study, nonconformity with disobedience. To resist conformity one simply had to be conspicuously disobedient. In pursuing this line, the countercultural left have omitted the crucial fact that the culture industries of advanced capitalism have systematically transformed 'disobedience' into the accepted way to conform.

Casting a critical eye across the consumerised expanse of Anglo-American postwar culture begs the question: was the 'counterculture' really a force for progressive social transformation? In the arid desert of liberal-conservative Western culture, its 'newness', its posturing and its supposed challenges to the prevailing orthodoxy appeared to suggest that it had taken over the baton of leftist radicalism from an exhausted traditional socialism with tremendous vigour and would push onwards towards an ultimate victory, heralding a new era of civilised social justice. With its wellsprings in the libertine worlds of music, art and radical individualist philosophy, by the 1960s the counterculture had made revolutionary and reformist variants of socialism seem outdated and rather staid. Further, the presumption that socialism necessitated a form of state authoritarianism jarred with the evolving post-war cultures of libertinism and openness. After the Nazis had used broadcast media technology to mobilise the masses, and the Soviets and the Maoists had created geopolitically dangerous collectivist states, for many liberal thinkers in the West the very concepts of 'state' and 'mass' became the epitome of 'absolute evil' (Badiou 2002, 2007). Theodore Roszak (1969), for instance, vulgarising the rather more subtle analyses of critics such as Mills (1959), argued that the political state and the corporate technocracy had merged; the military-industrial complex whose mission was to enslave humanity had, no matter what its political hue, become a totality to be resisted at all costs. Social democratic reform was useless while socialist revolution led to the Gulag and the corrupt totalitarian state; only rejection of the whole 'system', as the first move in a quest for the absolute freedom of the individual, would suffice as a political strategy. However, in their fervour these new cultural revolutionaries entirely ignored the evidence that the only two institutions capable of combining to effectively oppose – or at least regulate – consumer capitalism and its military-industrial system were themselves highly collectivist: the traditional working class and the democratic socialist state (Reiner 2007).

However, whereas Marxists and socialists simply sought complete or partial common ownership and control of the means of production to abolish exploitation and prevent the plutocratic monopolisation of wealth and power, the counterculture wanted to abolish everything. The ambitions of Marxism appear rather modest in relation to this kind of hubris, yet, ironically, it was those modest ambitions that profoundly changed the world in the twentieth century while the wild, unrestricted countercultural ambition of total change eroded the political and replaced it with 'an increasingly narcissistic preoccupation with personal spiritual growth and well-being' (Hall and Winlow 2003: 59). Marxism became totalitarian due to its perverse enactment, while the counterculture was totalitarian in its conception, in its abolition of the collective. In political terms, of course, its grand design to abolish everything was totally unachievable, and consequently it makes sense to see the post-war counterculture as momentarily captivating but ultimately toothless in its quest for progressive social change. It relied on post-scarcity conditions to allow the space for free play and fun, but because capitalism was the system that had proven by far the most effective for economic and technological growth, it seemed to be fundamentally reliant on the machine that it wished to destroy. Psychology and culture came to the fore as changes to individual consciousness and inter-subjective meaning were deemed to have political consequences more profound than direct political change itself. Our evidence suggests that cultural and individual meanings are heavily influenced by life in the conditions created by economic processes and managed by politics, but this was rejected as old-fashioned.

If politics is based on culture, the counterculture told us, then 'all social injustice is based on repressive conformity' (ibid.: 63). However, what the agents of the countercultural movement could not see is that without some sort of system of symbolic prohibitions the subject fails to mature and lives on as an infantile narcissist, reproducing whatever specific form of organised narcissistic identification happens to characterise the times. The movement creates a void in place of the symbolic order by dismantling old 'repressive' prohibitions and failing to construct replacements to regulate the anti-social subjectivities and activities that capitalism's competitive individualist culture encourages. Many of social democracy's regulations were instituted for the protection, assistance and endorsement of vulnerable individuals who were losing out in the unforgiving social competition exacerbated by the growing complexity of market ideology. Removing many of the prohibitions about sexual relations did not increase sexual freedom for women, as countercultural feminists had argued in the 1960s and 1970s – concealed pre-marital sex and other illicit relations had been going on for centuries – but it certainly opened the doors for the pornography industry's commercial exploitation of female sexuality, as later feminists noted with grave concern. It seems that the wave of right-wing libertarianism that closely followed the hippy counterculture was inevitable, because both are cut from the same theoretical cloth: an enchanting dream of individual freedom exercised to its outer limits, beyond desire and into the realm of *jouissance*. The naive Manichean world-view of the New England transcendentalists – Emerson, Thoreau and their acolytes – had taken up faith in the essential goodness of human nature, beyond even the tempered suspicions of Rousseau, to the absolute, and it was this that underpinned the ethical dimension of the counterculture's belief-system; people should be set free because they are essentially good, and it is the imposition of restrictions that frustrates their nature and turns them to 'evil'. This swing of the Manichean pendulum away from the traditional Christian-conservative view of humanity as essentially wicked and in need of the teachings of Christ and the discipline of the institutionalised church ignored all the caveats and conditions that one must take into account in order to plot a feasible course out of excessive repression into optimised freedom. The vital caveat is, of course, that if extant cultural practices, social relations and material conditions create and reproduce the sort of hostile and acquisitive subjectivities which make life difficult and unpleasant, and if this mode of being is naturalised by ideology, morally justified by culture and systematised by economics and mainstream social life, then real freedom in a civilised form for the majority is impossible. By dismantling many of the formal and informal regulatory codes that softened the system's inherent brutality and its tendency to accentuate the worst aspects of human nature that it draws upon for energy, the counterculture assisted in the creation of the unfreedom in which the majority now exist and the surfeit of barbaric freedom enjoyed by the new elite.

The counterculture's significant contribution to the destruction of politics and the transition to neo-liberalism's preferred age of para-politics was the conflation of deviance and dissent (Heath and Potter 2007: 83; see also Frank 1997; Žižek 2000). Resisting domination and tyranny is not the same as doing exactly what one desires. The counterculture's blurring of this vital distinction fuelled the consumer economy, legitimising narcissistic hedonism by ascribing to it the highest affirmation available in the western modernist ethical order; it was part of the fight against tyranny and the journey out of slavery. The Hegelian lesson was forgotten: consumer culture was the ultimate modernised form of the Western liberal-bourgeois conception of freedom, which was not a fight against or a journey out of anything, but a competition with the feudal Master and a fight for his social status position, marked by the achievement of individual distinction, should he be deposed. Thus freedom was associated with the mimetic desire for barbarian aristos – and yet again we can see Girard's and his rather unthinking acolytes' false naturalisation of a historically specific cultural form – the essence of the source of tyranny as *amour-propre*, the id-driven ego seeking freedom won at the expense of others, and the countercultural reproduction of this desire prolonged the subject's immersion in a specific form of narcissistic identification throughout the life-course. As we've seen in previous chapters, many of our interviewees were convinced that freedom could be attained by means of narcissistic identification with the post-production gentry, the new entrepreneurial aristocrats of the marketplace.

The current phase of hyper-modernity is characterised by a decline in interpersonal trust (Sennett 1998, 2006; Bauman 1995, 2001b), which Hobbes (2005, 2007) saw as the root of human insecurity and anxiety in the state of nature where the prohibitions of the Freudian symbolic order are absent. Preoccupation with the self and its quest for personal freedom in a competitive system characterised by horizontal divisions of wealth and status reproduces this lack of trust, which pollutes the relations of recognition and mutual pledges that are vital to the processes of identification and social interaction. The subjects of the counterculture, living with the constant expectation that the unreliable other might choose to prioritise the self's search for pleasure and social promotion and break some fragile obligation, lived, like eighteenth century rakes, on their wits in a climate of heightened anxiety. In this condition of chronic insecurity, people are prone to attacking one another, normally in sublimated, symbolic ways but occasionally with real violence (Winlow and Hall 2006). The symbolic order of a functioning civilisation will insist upon prohibition and repression when necessary, but that is not how capitalist culture functions; it functions by systematically organising conditions of social insecurity, lauding individual hubris, stimulating aggressive competition and applying immense effort to the construction and maintenance of channels of sublimation in which diverted psychic energy can be harnessed to the economy, dealing with the inevitable spillage with means of repressive control. The counterculture's puerile rejection of all social traditions and norms threatens the existence of essential institutional regulations (Heath and Potter 2007), but because in a liberal-capitalist system these regulations are specifically designed not to penetrate and interfere with capitalism's fundamental method of institutionalising insecurity and stimulating anxiety – turning as many aspects of life as possible to the vagaries of the unforgiving market mechanism – the regulations as they stand, and in the current direction they are headed, are specifically designed to repress drives *after* they have been vigorously stimulated. If these drives are focused on consumer products, the subject becomes an autopoeitic resistor of any institutional rules that prohibit the quest to circulate permanently around these products (the basis of the 'fetish', which we discuss in Chapter 8).

Individuals are allowed to take their quests for personal pleasure and infantile thrills right to the edge of morality's toxic core because the counterculture, now established in some university departments as well as corporate offices, has glamorised the violation of norms as a blow struck against the system that represses us all. Thus transgression is good simply because it is transgression, which is what each and every good libertine is compelled to do, or cease to feel 'free'. This is rather odd, because the system itself has been taking exactly the same thing to its extremes since the 1950s, when business realised just how lucrative it was to sell young people images of harmless, depoliticised transgression against what were then quite restrictive social norms; signposts on the beautiful journey out of repression, on which the *ideal ego* of narcissistic identification could magically merge with the *ego ideal* of mimetic admiration to create the most seductive talking mirror in which a lifelong process of identification could take place. Of course, obsolescence could be built in so that specific images would function only for a very short time, and the customer need not wait for something to wear out like a refrigerator or a power drill, so product innovation was absolutely necessary not in the technical but only in the stylistic sense.

The counterculture's colonisation of the political has been disastrous. It played an active part as cheerleader and contributor to the libertarian armoury in the dismantling of social democracy's regulatory project in Britain and the USA during the Thatcher and Reagan era. In the 1980s, so many of the public countercultural intellectuals from the 1960s became Thatcherite entrepreneurs (see, for example, Hoffman and Simon 1996; Hoffman 2000; also Dennis 2006; Branson 2006). Oddly, the punk entrepreneurs accused the hippies of selling out while they were transparently working their way towards doing precisely the same thing, rejecting concrete political reforms in favour of 'deeper' attempts to transgress the totality of capitalist culture, without realising that they were feeding precisely the same sort of transgression that fuels consumer capitalism's dynamic as it flies its elliptical orbit around the boundaries of pleasure. 'Destroying' consumerism in a flurry of cultural subversion, like the 'culture-jammers' (Lasn 2001), would be just another one of the impossible promises that constitute the fabric of today's spin-sodden para-politics (Žižek 2002, 2007), which is an indication of how the counterculture functions to support corporate capitalism by glamorising transgression and discrediting regulation. Today, it joins the chorus of right-wing libertarians and corporate mouthpieces, decrying any serious effort to impose institutional regulations on consumerism – banning marketing campaigns aimed at very young children, placing quotas on the importation of the junk element of American media production, placing quality controls on satellite TV, censoring gratuitous violence and the extremes of the pornography industry and so on – as the actions of the 'nanny state', the slippery road to the 'Absolute Evil' of totalitarianism.

It's perhaps worth reiterating that what cultural criminology defines as the 'crime-culture nexus' is inextricably bound to the consumerisation

of the 'means of identity'. What cultural criminology needs to understand is that the essential force driving consumerism since the 1960s has
been a systematically depoliticised critique of 'mass society' that favours
individual freedom over collective politics. At the sociogenetic and
psychogenetic roots of this force is the deliberate stimulation of anxiety:
to put it simply, people were made to feel unhappy about being
ordinary, about being too much like everyone else, about appearing
'unfree', about failing to look distinctive and stand out from the crowd.
Simultaneously, people are made to feel anxious about displaying forms
of difference that lie outside of the hazy parameters of consumerised
popular culture. Youthful consumers tend to struggle with this complex
double-bind most acutely, and research clearly indicates that wanting to
fit in and stick out has a profound impact upon youthful identities (see
Miles *et al.* 1998).

In the long-term historical view we can see that the initial bourgeois-
individualist rebellion led by ambitious entrepreneurs against the forces
of feudalism has been gradually democratised and spread outwards
throughout the social body as a fake reproduction. The failure of
twentieth-century socialism means that this culture now has no real
enemy and no real resistance, apart from reactionary nationalism and
religion, as it continues to colonise the sociocultural landscape after
already totally colonising the economy. The counterculture is not a
reaction against the tyranny of the system that rules us, a spontaneous
rebellion drawing upon some suppositious natural urge to transgress, it
is the ultimate populist element of the bourgeois-derived system itself.
Its *avant garde* acts as a scout to detect the latest 'cool' street style that is
itself a variation of the bourgeois individualist cultural code that has
already been diffused into the streets. Young people are quite right to
feel proud that they have created the style, but they played no part in
the creation of the principle, the basic cultural code itself, although they
play the crucial active role in its reproduction. It is the ultimate form of
participatory assimilation, a vast 'hothouse' market research exercise that
has perfected the art of pre-empting changes in fashion just before they
actually catch on in a wider market.

Consumer culture has become like an arms race in that most
consumption is defensive, an effort to avoid humiliation and the possible
destruction of the self's fragile place in the vicious social process of
identification. Art, as 'commercialised beauty', has come to be defined
by costliness and the ability to buy. To those with aspirations of joining
the new urban gentry, an object is beautiful and desirable because
someone like Charles Saatchi has bought it and put it in a collection. To
those whose aspirations remain enclosed within old class boundaries
because of inherited disrespect for the urban bourgeoisie – a disrespect
that now reproduces itself in the absence of its historical origins and

political language – an object is beautiful and desirable because it has been bought and proudly displayed by some successful local 'name' or some celebrity carefully manufactured as an icon of the working class. The common factor is, of course, money and the ability to pay, so the need for money is no longer driven by the insecurity of the potential lack of basic needs but by the need to acquire 'positional goods' (Hirsch 1976) as marks of social distinction (Veblen 1994; Bourdieu 1986) in the symbolic order of competitive consumption. The counterculture was a product of the marketing industry's realisation that the most potent and valuable mark of distinction in a society saturated with bourgeois values is simply the individualistic achievement of distinction itself, the Slave's mimetic revenge on the Master (Hegel 1979, 2005a, 2005b; Žižek 2006a). Thus it could short-circuit the whole process of social distinction, which is otherwise quite capable of creating positions of authentic distinction that could stir up heroic opposition to consumer capitalism. It is not the desire for comfortable conformity to 'mass culture' that drives competitive consumption but the desire to be seen by the self and others as an individual who has successfully completed a rebellious quest for distinction.

The argument that the cultural products of youth rebellion are created in a flurry of autonomous creativity and then simply co-opted by the system does not wash. Manufactured and mass-marketed rebellion must be passed off as 'co-optation' in order that the perpetual cycles of competition and obsolescence in which the subject feels trapped can be blamed on the oppressive 'system', rather than the true source in the underlying code of bourgeois individualism manifested in the competitive consumption of positional goods that signify individuality (Frank 1997; Heath and Potter 2007). The 'system' is an amorphous but ultimately oppressive 'thing' that dares to impose rules and regulations on the rebellious individual, and thus 'the counterculture has always had a tendency to romanticise criminality' (Heath and Potter 2007: 141). Those who indulge in harmful anti-social practices to benefit themselves in the quest for conformist marks of distinction – whether in the streets or in the suites – can thus hide behind the interpretation that the powerful forces of the counterculture have been busily institutionalising in political and cultural discourses since their heyday in the 1960s.

The 'Peacock Revolution' of the 1960s encouraged men who tended to own very few clothes to expand their wardrobes and become dedicated followers of fashion, each change a symbol of their rebellion against mass conformity. Yet, the 'mass conformity' of the traditional male-dominated working class – combined with a hefty dash of politically charged contempt for the fashion-driven culture of the urban dandy – seemed to act as a powerful protective shield against the marketing industry's invasive strategies. Oddly, this contempt for the fake rebellion and its cultural elevation of superficial novelty was shared by the old warhorses of High Tory culture (see Eagleton 1994, 2000), who were portrayed by the marketing industry as the working class's timeless mortal enemies, even though the industrial project that had laid down relations of crass exploitation in the economic base and hooked working people into the consumer treadmill was not their doing; in fact, they were often its harshest critics (Clayre 1977). The rebels have always insisted that the system co-opts styles that originate on the street. However, in the absence of this working-class 'mass conformity' that, often inspired by middle-class intellectual critique (Rose 2002), once produced political opposition to the primacy of private enterprise and sought to regulate its toxic excesses, the entrepreneurial spirit pervades the street, and this has throughout western history been manifested in criminal forms (Hobbs 1989). In other words, most style-based 'sub-cultural' forms are born already co-opted, like pre-faded blue jeans. As entrepreneurially realised individualist rebellion is inscribed at the heart of Anglo-American culture as the most potent mark of social distinction, it poses no danger to the system and neither does it need to be constantly co-opted by the system: it *is* the system (Frank 1997).

Competitive consumption is now drilling down to the core of Anglo-American society, seeking to colonise social relations and desire at the youngest age among the broadest social demographic. Our own previous research has revealed the saturation of the lives of young people since the 1990s with the paradoxical novelty of 'cheap luxury' goods and the intensified competitive consumption that that encourages among individuals whose traditional sources of identification in work, class and community have all but evaporated (see Winlow and Hall 2006, and 2008, forthcoming). As Heath and Potter argue (2007) we should now stop daring to be different and dare to be the same in a rejuvenated political sphere separated, as it should be, from culture. This is not a simple matter, because consumer culture also covers sameness as well as difference in the sense that competition cannot work with real difference and it is always a struggle over a shared value. Consumption has become autopoeitic (see Luhmann 1986) because the core value is competition itself, and the binary code that configures and drives it is, of course, win/lose.

Frank (1997) quite rightly alerts us to the real source of cultural change in the USA and Britain, the two pioneers of the counterculture, which was, of course, consumer marketing rather than millennial visions of a cultural revolution against the 'uniformity' of the mainstream. Seeking to manipulate culture and generate a powerful dynamic force in the economy, the marketing industry seized on the one politically safe and economically functional form of revolutionary consciousness that had emerged during modernity as a democratised legacy from the barbarian past: the rebellious quest for a self-image that distinguished the individual from the 'herd'. The post-war consumer revolution allowed its subjects to buy marks of social distinction with which they could imagine themselves as the *Übermenschen* in transcendence of the suffocating norm, while actually being press-ganged more effectively into the ranks of the *Last Men*. We could call Anglo-American consumerism the era of perverted Nietzschean economics.

Frank (1997) charts the emergence of a huge number of management and marketing texts that appeared in the early 1960s for one common purpose: to release the creative power of individuals chained together as designer, marketer and consumer in a way that would energise the economy and increase profitability and growth. Consumer capitalism was not about to 'co-opt' the rebellious spirit of the day but rather to rediscover its revolutionary individualist roots – which are now 'conservative' in the sense that they are themselves vital and need to be conserved and reproduced if the organism is to survive – with a view to taking over the means of inspiring rebellion in the form that most suited it. The business writers of the day, as Frank's diligent and illuminating study demonstrates, were quite candid about their quest to create a new form of consumer subjectivity. Rather than catering for segmented markets that already existed within a framework of traditional social categories, the marketing industry's plan was to create new segments, focusing mainly on upcoming generations at first and then later moving into adult territory as adults themselves became convinced that the retention of youthful characteristics was a way of discovering a 'wholeness' of self that had been denied by repressive tradition.

Business invented the counterculture. Ironically, the Old Right saw it as a serious attempt at a left-libertarian revolution driven by utopian visions of freedom, which was about to inflict untold damage on the precious traditional values and institutions that held conservative society together. Because it occurred directly alongside a number of serious civil rights movements in the 1960s that furthered the causes of blacks, gays and women, and in the midst of an unpopular war in Vietnam, many among the liberal-left also regarded it as an authentic cultural current driven by a collective wish to change the world for the better by freeing individuals from the oppressive yoke of traditional institutions. In fact it had nothing to do with these movements except that they provided useful cover, and neither group could see it as a product of marketing campaigns grounded in the underlying logical 'needs' of the consumer capitalist economy, the success of which they and every other political party were beginning to rely upon for popular support. The system was creating its own preferred electorate of 'consumers', and this meant the unravelling of not only traditional conservative culture but of all culture, and the concomitant domestication of all political institutions and ideologies to turn politics into a market management machine (see Frank 1997).

What at first glance seems like a rather odd elective affinity between traditional conservatism and socialism becomes quite understandable when we see the collectivist values on which both ideologies were based – the former strictly hierarchal and the latter egalitarian – in direct conflict with the acquisitive, competitive individualism whose energy can be harnessed by a social system that is fluid yet loosely structured by symbolic marks of distinction, and which is an absolute requirement for the growth of liberal-capitalism's market economy. The failure of the conservative critique is the tendency of their vitriolic one-dimensional commentators on both sides of the Atlantic – Bloom, Gingrich, Burgess, Peter Hitchens and a host of others – to place the blame for social atomisation and the degeneration of civilised interpersonal relations squarely on the Left's welfare system and its 'permissive' values and institutional practices of the 1960s. Canada's and Western Europe's welfarist social democracies maintained very low crime rates alongside low imprisonment rates despite being the pioneers of sexual permissiveness in that era, which suggests that Anglo-American societies were promoting permissions that ran far deeper and ranged far broader than sex. What distinguished the USA, and later Britain, from the other nations of the industrialised West is the extent to which the former adopted consumerism and encouraged acquisitive competitive individualism as the sociocultural drivers for economic growth and adopted neo-liberal politics as the means of managing this process, and the inevitable social destabilisation and cultural corrosion that would follow.

The ultimate purpose is to promote continuous taxable economic growth in a capitalist economic system prone to the overproduction of goods yet reliant on a tightly controlled money supply, a system in which individuals must work hard to create commodities and buy hard to consume them. There is no sign that this remorseless growth above a reasonable level of comfort has promoted human happiness and social stability; in fact many research studies show notable decreases in both (Frank 1997: 102; see also James 2007), brought about not only by endless consumer dissatisfaction and debt but also by the increasing pressure exerted on workers as they are placed under authoritarian regimes in downsizing companies (Ames 2007), in order to produce cheap goods under increasing competition and earn the money to pay their debts. It is a zero-sum game because there is no end to it; each winner produces losers, and the irony is that as soon as the mass acquires symbolic goods that are valuable as marks of social distinction the goods lose that value, and the mass once again becomes a bunch of losers. This sense of loss is compounded by guilt, which, as we shall see later (see Chapter 8), has profoundly reoriented the western super-ego. As well as the mounting problem of consumer debt, it appears that competitive consumption – which amounts to a brutal struggle over means of identification and marks of distinction driven by the new super-ego injunction to take every opportunity to enjoy some dubious pleasure that one imagines that others might have experienced – has intensified and altered the whole shape of guilt in the Anglo-American West. There is no evidence that this unhappiness is a product of some overbearing feeling of enforced conformity to any authority other than that which compels the consumer to adopt and display the latest image and demonstrably experience the latest 'sensation' and live the latest lifestyle of the 'cool individual'. The whole thing could be deemed a waste of effort and resources except for the economic fact that the accelerated circulation of commodities increases profits and maintains 'economic growth'.

What appeared as cultural hostility towards the 'system' was in fact the sound of the deliberately ignited and cleverly contained explosions in the psycho-cultural cylinders that were connected to capitalism's economic engine. The important added bonus of selling this late modern version of the archaic delusion of ultimate personal freedom and social distinction to the public is that compared to this great transcendental romance, which places the self at the apex of the world, real politics seem distinctly uncool and unrewarding. Even real revolution, which is over in a quick burst of violent insurrection, leaving an enduring social administration headache that would dispirit even the most earnest bureaucrat, looks comparatively tedious; a bit of a flash-in-the-pan, really. On the other hand, the solipsistic fantasy revolt is a narrative in which the autobiographical self is a temporarily admired winner each time he manages to sidestep a convention with an exhibition of spectacular elegance, the mark of 'cool'. The transience of the admiration is both a burden and a bonus, multiplying the opportunities for admiration if the individual has the creative energy and resolve required to keep on rebelling into style. No blood, no sweat, no sacrifice, no diligent planning, no risky execution, no comrades, no traitors, no shouts of joy or tears of bitter defeat are required; only regular visits to the shopping mall.

The organised conformity of mass society was in fact an impediment to economic growth much more than it was a dead weight bearing down on individualism. The critique of writers such as Mailer (1968) and Reisman (1953) was little more than a lament for a past characterised by the mythological free spirit of the rugged 'inner-directed' individual, but they had conveniently forgotten that this individualism was the foundation stone for the historical-economic process that had inevitably led to the specific form of mass society, with its plutocratic ruling elite, that they thought they despised. It was a thoughtless, nostalgic yearning for a return to the beginnings of a system that lacked the ability to go anywhere other than where it is right now. The beginnings of capitalism in Britain and America were romantically recast as bohemian and libertarian, rather than a disruptive and exploitative phase of brutal primitive accumulation, chaotic social upheaval and organised violence (Hall and Winlow 2007).

However, the argument favoured by today's liberal commentators, working under the compulsion to be balanced and subtle even when what they are commentating on looks decidedly imbalanced and crude, is that mass-manufactured culture is simultaneously the site of oppression and rebellion. Frank (1997: 17–18) sums up this standard argument:

> Even as it is calculated to exploit consumers, it unintentionally provides various groups with the implements of empowerment ... the 'power-bloc' intends that the public be conformist, complacent consumers while the 'people' rebel through a million ineluctable, unfinalisable, individualistic devices ... by its nature, capitalism requires rigid conformity and patriarchy in order to function. The transgressive practices of the hipster are innately modes of resistance, and mass culture only makes concessions to them from necessity.

However, he has already exposed this 'resistance' as a fake, and for us these 'rigid modes of conformity', comprised of many elements that intersect politics and culture, constitute the Smithian regulatory insulation that the wiser and more cautious among capitalism's agents constructed to prevent the economic dynamic overheating and diffusing its toxic radiation into politics, society and culture. We have two choices: revolutionise the economic system or reconstruct the insulation. In the meantime, the initial ideological steps along this road are, first, to transgress the liberal taboo placed on criticising consumers that is upheld by the judgement that doing so is mere snobbery and tantamount to labelling individuals as 'consumer dupes'; and secondly, to discard the assumption that consumption is the site of potential resistance. To argue that consumption is not a site of resistance, and to point out that transgression and resistance are two entirely different practices, is not to suggest for one moment that human beings are incapable of resistance to that which dominates them. The practices of the marketing industry itself have changed dramatically since the 1950s, and it can no longer be seen as the purveyor of mass conformity or even as that which co-opts authentic resistance and turns it against us. To us it is the generator of fake resistance in a rolling wheel driven forward in cycles of aimless transgression. It displaces the potential for real resistance, which requires critical thought, a new radical subjectivity and real politics. We are convinced that if cultural criminology is to progress it needs to incorporate this key point into its general framework and address the various ways in which the fetishised 'hip consumerist' version of the cult of competitive individualism is practised in various circumstances. The more difficult the circumstances, the more ruthless will be the methods that some employ to achieve their marks of social distinction, avoid humiliation and survive the relentless challenges of others.

Chapter 6

Critical reflections on the intellectual roots of post-war criminological theory

What we might call 'liberal-pluralist' criminology emerged as the dominant critical form during the 1960s. The Mertonian integrationist orthodoxy that had dominated critical criminology in the USA, serving as the main opposition to classical/correctional criminology throughout most of the New Deal project, was challenged by an insistent voice that posited society as essentially and ineluctably plural. The ideas that the monolithic system of values and goals that constituted the American Dream could assimilate individuals along with traditional and emergent cultural groups as active agents, and the corollary that diverse, mutating ways of life were simply methods of coping with that assimilation, were firmly rejected. Despite the social successes of the state-centred New Deal project, which maintained some of the lowest crime and murder rates in recorded American history (Reiner 2007; Hall and McLean 2008, forthcoming), this new paradigm of American criminology was firmly anti-interventionist. If British criminology resisted developments in American social theory and clung on to its rather staid administrative pragmatism, it was to a significant extent because British social democracy's post-war economic management and welfare programmes were proving more successful than their diluted American counterparts in the tasks of reducing economic instability, social polarisation, crime and violence (Hall and Winlow 2003). The British had at their disposal the political will and the means – such as an expanding public education system, a public healthcare system, nationalised industries, public works and full employment policies – to redistribute wealth, guarantee some degree of socio-economic security, improve underlying conditions and nurture the cultural values that hold most criminological problems in check.

Despite the New Deal and the brief interlude of revived intervention-ism in the 'Great Society' project of the 1960s, the USA retained and intensified its underlying culture of competitive individualism and minimal state intervention. Becoming the victim of stigmatisation and discrimination in the less protected sectors of the labour market could have devastating repercussions for the individual. This situation was further intensified in the Reagan era when huge pressure was placed on workers in downsizing industries that were facing ever more fierce competition, creating the conditions for a rash of workplace revenge shootings in the 1980s, 1990s and early 2000s from disgruntled em-ployees who had been pressured, humiliated or fired (Ames 2007). When American liberals recoiled in horror at stigmatisation and discrimination, it was mainly because, compared to Western Europe, in a 'flexible' hire-and-fire business culture the underlying socio-economic conditions were extremely insecure and the apparatus for helping the disadvan-taged was significantly less well-developed. In the full-employment economy and the more stable society of Britain, less skilled or intellec-tually able people could be hurtfully ridiculed and discriminated against in the class-ridden socio-economic hierarchy, but at least most could still obtain some sort of secure tenured job, or benefit from increasingly open access to state education, and a reasonable level of welfare support if all else failed. In the USA it was all too easy for the stigmatised to slide rapidly down into the ranks of the 'casual poor', a realm of chronically insecure livelihoods and minimal welfare protection from which it was often extremely difficult to escape (Sennett 1998; Ehrenreich 2002, 2006); hurtful words were accompanied by a barrage of heavy sticks and stones.

The commonly held belief that transatlantic criminology and the politics of liberation made their greatest gains during the 1960s and 1970s appears somewhat misguided if we consider the socio-economic turmoil, intellectual inertia and political failure that descended upon the Western world in the latter stages of this period. If this belief were true, why has violent crime risen so much since the 1960s (Reiner 2007; Young 1999)? Why are young people in such an anxious state (Currie 2005), and why do we wake up every morning to the glorious sights of an expanding prison population, increasing surveillance and the joys of para-political 'risk-management' – a far more cynical, dismal and reactionary form of social management than anything we encountered during the social democratic era – and why does criminology in particular and our intellectual culture in general seem bereft of ideas that might instigate progressive moves out of this situation (see de Haan and Loader 2002)? Compared to the USA, not only was British sociology at the time much more amenable to Marxist and socialist ideas (Sumner 1994), but also, in line with much of mainland Western Europe, Britain's economic management and political welfare apparatus was more developed (Hutton 1996, 2003), its working class communities more secure and its labour politics more militant and collectivist. Put simply, Americans had been compelled to use integrationist sociology as a means to lobby for what Britain to a large extent already had. By the 1960s America's long history of *laissez-faire* liberalism was already beginning to replace the country's brief flirtation with progressive social democracy, and the increased strength of liberal-pluralism in intellectual and politico-cultural life appeared to cast further doubt upon the basic principle of social democratic interventionism.

In the dying days of the New Deal project, what had seemed like radical American sociology was actually rather pragmatic and acquiescent in its quest for a political compromise with corporate capitalism, far more so than the social democratic intellectuals and politicians who had been influential in Western Europe since the end of World War Two. To secure this compromise with the 'conservative' power-bloc that dominated American political life – which, although named 'conservative', was in its politico-economic thinking founded on the utilitarian philosophy of classical liberalism – American sociologists were compelled to couch their radicalism in terms of the economic liberalism that was enshrined in American culture, and which stamped its authority across the whole political spectrum. Thus the social democratic underpinnings of Cloward and Ohlin (1960) were able to mutate quite easily into the more overtly liberal-pluralist discourses propagated by the likes of Lemert (1967) and Becker (1967). From that point American criminology's measured and apologetic pleas for the socio-economic management that was necessary to prevent unstable locales and regions collapsing at their weakest points into brutal and punitive social disasters were once again compelled to sail under the colours of individual liberty.

In the USA of the 1960s, urban deprivation was described in terms not dissimilar to those of Engels (1987) or Mayhew (1985) in nineteenth century Britain (see Rainwater 2005), but the structural relationships between the state, labour politics and the economy were always bypassed in favour of analyses of cultural and phenomenological dynamics (see Sumner 1994), a tendency still predominant in culturally reductionist American sociology and criminology (Wacquant 2002). The deeply 'conservative' American power-elite – remembering the social interventionist calls of the 'Progressive Movement' at the turn of the century and its friendly links with the then very active American Communist Party and Eugene Debs's ominously successful Socialist Party of America – just did not want to know about democratic socialism and serious supra-Keynesian economic intervention, which to them was the road to 'communism'. Those who worked in its mainly privatised university system and therefore depended upon trust-funding and private fees are likely to have been mindful that this was a boundary over which one could not step. Apart from Landesco (1979), Thrasher (1963) and a few other accounts, American sociological criminology since the Chicago School had been firmly focused on minor delinquency, and there was a tendency to leave serious crime and violence to the psychologists and psychiatrists to classify as the product of individual pathology rather than the serious socio-economic tensions that Merton had roughly adumbrated two decades earlier. Despite the lobbying of Shaw, McKay, Sutherland and some of the other more politically aware Chicago sociologists, who supported interventionist measures such as public housing and education, the political focus was on the amelioration of cultural dissonance, the buttressing of latent currents of organic sociability that supposedly existed in 'disorganised' communities and the equalisation of opportunity for competing individuals in the dog-eat-dog world of commerce. This tradition still continues (see Wacquant 2002). There was no real call for deep socio-economic intervention over and above the equalisation of opportunity and a very diluted and tentative form of Keynesian demand-management in the market. Even Sutherland's (1985) seemingly revolutionary focus on the crimes of the powerful did not throw up any challenge to the fundamentally individualistic belief system that underpinned American capitalism and its minimal-state political philosophy.

If indeed the maximisation of the individual's existential and economic freedoms is the unquestionable cultural shibboleth in the USA, then the 'orthodox' Mertonian mainstream, with its inherent orientation to social integrationism, ethico-cultural censorship and political intervention was far more radical in its opposition to this core value than the compromised liberal-pluralist positions that emerged during the 1960s. The left-liberals' focus on the more punitive wing of the social democratic state's control apparatus as the generator of secondary deviance, combined with the theoretical elevation of secondary deviance above primary deviance and its deeper socio-economic causes, harmonised sweetly with liberal-capitalism's anti-statism and its claim to be the guardian of individual rights against totalitarianism in all its forms. The inescapable fact is that all forms of extreme liberal-pluralism depict the collectivist state, whether secular or theological, as the potential embodiment of Absolute Evil (Badiou 2002) and as such they can be hijacked with consummate ease by the libertarian Right in the project of deregulating and destabilising political economy and culture for the purpose of exploitation. Although many moderate liberals share with democratic socialists an acknowledgement of a positive role for the democratic state, this theoretical movement in criminology tacitly contributed to a general culturo-political current that emerged in the 1960s, irreparably split the Left and unconsciously aided neo-liberalism in its concerted effort to discredit and weaken the social democratic opposition that was finally swept aside in the Thatcherite and Reaganite revolutions.

Each development in liberal criminology can be seen as a move to prevent the emergence of a sustained focus on deep structural and ethical problems, and together they constituted an *a fortiori* intellectual process that engineered systematic moves away from the radical socialist and social democratic implications present in the claims of Marx, Freud, Durkheim and other classic theorists. The American people's foremost aspiration to exponentially increase material wealth and consumption by competing as individuals in the market was not open to debate. For instance, when Cloward and Ohlin's 'Mobilisation for Youth' project got up and running as part of Kennedy's 'Great Society' programme in the early 1960s, it ran into trouble as soon as it encouraged young people to protest against their structured socio-economic position rather than their lack of individual opportunities, to make political demands for the structural elevation of their collective position and to challenge fundamental business practices, such as setting private rent levels in tune with free-market principles. Cloward and Ohlin had achieved government approval and been appointed to government posts by diluting Merton's formulations with pluralistic sub-cultural ideas, and Merton in turn had been allowed to formulate and publish his ideas by diluting Durkheim's much more potent ideas, which were considered mildly conservative by European socialist radicals. Despite this, they were still labelled 'commies' by the deeply conservative elements that dominated American culture and politics. We must understand how deeply and aridly conservative American society actually is, and how its liberal opposition has been consistently forced to dilute its politics simply to survive. Almost twenty years before the Great Society programme, Britain had nationalised many of its major industries and services, invested in public health and education and erected a welfare safety net, aiding the retention of lower crime rates, a lower imprisonment rate and a murder rate that was in the 1950s one-tenth of that of the USA. Why did British sociologists need diluted pseudo-radical ideas that had emerged in the severely compromised politics of the impossible American quest for the things Britain already had? Nevertheless, as with rock'n'roll and Hollywood movies, in contrast to British post-war austerity they looked exciting and new, so British liberals grabbed them anyway.

The American integrationist orthodoxy was replaced by a liberal-pluralist and culturalist orthodoxy that sat uneasily alongside European democratic socialism and tended to dilute it to a consistency that was far less intellectually nourishing and politically effective. Culturalists such as Albert Cohen (1955) preferred to see the 'middle class' as the source of status and values, and although he saw competition as inter-class he avoided linking classes to the means of production, the relations of production or the structure of political power, preferring instead the cultural definition of class. The orthodox Marxist flaw was to ignore the quest for status and distinction (Weber 1991; Bourdieu 1986) and explain class cultures purely in terms of the relations of production, as effects of occupying positions in an economically based social structure. In our own past work (see Hall 1997; Winlow 2001) we have been partly guilty of explaining working-class cultural traits and *habitus* as products of functions and lived experience in the social and geographical locations constituted by the relations of production in the classical capitalist era, and downplaying traditional oppositional values that were culturally transmitted across time (see Thompson 1991). However, unlike Merton, genuine cultural-pluralists disconnected almost entirely the source of value and meaning from history, economic function and social structure, relocating this capacity in the free negotiations of autonomous inter-subjective groups, some with malleable historical traditions and some newly created, which is what even Cohen (1955), in his efforts to retain the basics of strain theory, was reluctant to do. However, none of these discourses could explain why the traditional politics, identities and value system of the working class – outlined by Lasch (1991) in America and Hoggart (1957) and Williams (1971, 2005) in Britain – which had for a long time been substantively different from those of the middle class were beginning to lose their influence over the members of the working class in the post-war era, or indeed why the middle-class way of life came to be regarded as so attractive and worth competing for, rather than against.

One very important and neglected aspect of the answer to this question, as we saw in the previous chapter, was the marketing industry's increasingly sophisticated ability – aided by the bogus radicalism of the counterculture – to loosen and manipulate the Anglo-American world's structures of social distinction by diffusing the seductive image of 'cool individualism' throughout a set of cultures that were in the process of being deracinated from their historical, structural and cultural roots and would finally become totally dissolved. Through-out its classical industrial period, the logic of capital regarded the labour power of the working class as more important than its values, dreams and desires. Among the traditional working class, levels of consumer desire that were adequate for the task of keeping production rolling and profits accruing could be maintained in the realm where technological product innovation serviced basic material needs. As long as product supply and market demand were in rough equilibrium and the money supply was managed efficiently, the role of the working class was secure. As far as its members were concerned, capital did not require, as Foucault (1991) claimed, the 'soul' of the individual worker, who outside of work in the classical capitalist era was far freer and 'indisciplined' in the cultural and intellectual sense than today, and prone to extremely radical forms of political activism and organic intellectualism (Rose 2002). Early classical and neo-classical economists were, of course, mistaken in their belief that the free market has a natural tendency to equilibrium, and the crash of 1929 and the ensuing depression taught salutary lessons. After these disasters, the post-war era in western politico-economic history was founded upon the absolute necessity, whether by Keynesian or monetarist methods, to expand and maintain consumer demand at a high level, which was compounded by the parallel ideological need to 'out-produce' the Soviet Union. After the 1980s, the tactic shifted, relapsing the socio-structural and economic situation to something akin to the early nineteenth-century free-trade era before full industrialisation, where an insecure domestic economy prioritising service and distribution became the receptacle for cheap goods manufactured in low-wage economies abroad. Maintenance of consumer demand was paramount. If capitalism did not really need to 'seek the soul' of the individual in its classical industrial period, then it did now. The full employment economy required by post-war reconstruction was capable of paying higher wages to facilitate this new demand, and the newly affluent sections of the Anglo-American working class passed through a uniquely reconstructive and partially consensual period in which its wages and conditions improved markedly. Gradually, militancy began to decline and the working class became ever more absorbed into a proliferating, mass-mediated consumer dream-world whose creeping commercialisation of everything disrupted old cultural values, to the chagrin of traditionalists from all classes (Eagleton 2000). By the 1960s social values, aspirations and identification processes were no longer being reproduced in cultural groups that inhabited intersecting social structural positions on class, gender and ethnic axes; the capacity to generate and reproduce these vital organising and motivating devices was gradually being wrenched away from its organic sources and confiscated by the marketing industry.

From the 1960s to the present day, apart from a dwindling band of working-class militants and middle-class radicals, most Anglo-American individuals were recruited as enthusiastic workers, performers and above all consumers to service the stringent logical demands of the market economy (Harvey 2007). This means that the source of any shame and humiliation felt as a result of 'failure' can no longer be attributed to internalised middle-class 'attitudes', as Cohen (1955) claimed. Rather, personal failure reflected the inability of the subject to meet the new performative demands of the highly competitive and unstable labour markets that dominated the new, and supposedly meritocratic, social order. In this formulation the middle classes are simply a benchmark of performance on a common scale – those who 'do well' – not a source of unique cultural values. Western society was moving into a phase where the shame that some commentators still see as a potential means of controlling and adjusting behaviour (see, for example, Braithwaite 1989) has a basis not within or between class or cultural forms but in objective, performative self-assessments measured in the spaces between unaltered values and rapidly altering norms and normative strategies. It is our contention that the motivation for most property-oriented crime is produced not in the structural or post-structural power relationships between individuals and sociocultural forms, or between individuals and institutionalised authority, but in the relationship between the individual and the consumer economy's cultural symbolism, with which he/she identifies. The criminals we interviewed were not reacting to the symbolic labelling and criminalisation of powerful groups, but to their own self-assessments of their own performances in the market, which are oriented to the achievement of positions of social distinction above the 'herd' of 'mugs' that must always exist below them. What at first glance looked like 'new' sub-cultures were simply groups of relative winners or losers drawn together by elective affinity at a time when traditional class cultures were being systematically dissolved by consumer culture.

In the mid 1960s crime and public violence rates began to rise in Britain and the USA despite concomitantly rising affluence and what looked like increasing personal freedoms, which threw criminology into an aetiological crisis (Young 1987, 2002). Post-war capitalist culture had been founded upon the political principle that increasing prosperity and individual liberty would bring lasting peace, security and civility. The lightly managed free market was thought to be the best way to fulfil this aim, raising the bar of overall prosperity and bringing individuals, classes and nations together as skilful, property-owning, free-trading partners. The very idea that rising crime and violence might have something to do with this affluence and emancipation was unthinkable, even among many on the Left. Despite the 'War on Poverty', 'Operation Head Start' and other programmes aimed at equalising individual opportunities, crime continued to rise in the USA, and it also began to rise slightly but ominously in Britain despite full employment and a mature welfare state. The possibility that these American programmes, designed to increase individuals' 'fitness for competition' and tackle social inequality by stimulating personal struggles for self-elevation, might in this nascent context have fed into the toxic dynamic of social distinction and contributed to a cultural current that was actually intensifying the pressure for demonstrable success and the humiliation instigated by failure, was rarely discussed in criminological theory. The one possibility that few American liberal-left intellectuals – apart from some notable but largely ignored exceptions such as Galbraith and Packard – could contemplate was that the human energy that drove capitalism forward was generated by the interminable struggle of individuals for completely unattainable equality at a socially and ecologically destructive level of affluence. If the ambition for equality on which their nation was founded could ever be realised, the problem of contentment might arise, and too much contentment in the dimensions of wealth and status is the dysfunctional nemesis of the capitalist method of sustaining economic growth.

For many British criminologists the way out of this aetiological crisis revolved around Runciman's (1966) concept of 'relative deprivation'. Much of what has been written on this topic appears to rely on the Kantian assumption that human beings possess an innate sense of social justice on which normative being and its constructivist projects rest. This can be expressed readily in terms of consumerism's status-system; being in a position below others rather than in relation to absolute poverty is felt to be unjust and thus causes a reaction, political or otherwise. This, of course, led many to see that some crimes might be misguided proto-political acts (see, for example, Presdee 2000). However, as we have seen, our respondents were energised by a sense of personal performance rather than by a desire for social justice, and this appears to be a product of the narcissistic form of identification with socially undefined 'others' rather than identification with the symbolic order, without which individuals cannot develop a sense of the place that they and other individuals occupy in the social order. In the market-based culture of narcissism all individuals see themselves in positions of reflective clarity that exclude and demote others, and rather than feeling deprived they cannot understand why that imaginary position does not square with a reality in which they seem to be buried in the nether regions of the herd that they so despise. Therefore, for us, the individual's tendency to criminality is driven by personal assessments of the preferred degree of alienation from others, by a narcissistic fantasy, rather than direct comparisons of wealth and status made from a position of perceived deprivation. Those who felt aggrieved by their positions of relative deprivation were seen as 'whiners' and 'losers' by our intrepid narcissists, who say good luck to those who succeed and regard them as the elite alongside whom they might one day become fellow travellers on the road to alienated distinction. More fruitful aetiological explorations can be carried out in the realms of anxiety, narcissistic identification, social distinction and the cult of cool individualism, the mechanics of which are discussed in more detail later (see Chapter 9).

However, the fundamental pluralist principle that human societies are constituted by a broad diversity of radically different beliefs, values, goals and ambitions is even less useful than relative deprivation insofar as it denies the theory that human energy can be generated among the whole population by the American Dream's promises of affluence, freedom and distinction. After the perceived failures of Kennedy and Johnson's Great Society project, moves were made in American criminological theory to explain delinquency as the product of the precise opposite of the failure of specific groups and individuals to achieve goals; liberal-pluralism and its concept of cultural diversity as the bedrock of all societies thus took centre stage in critical criminology, a position that we now briefly explore.

Edwin Lemert (1967) was one of the liberal-pluralist pioneers in criminological theory. His interpretation of anomie as a 'modal tendency', rather than what Durkheim and Merton claimed it to be – the destructive psychosocial effect of the cultural stimulation of a latent emotional desire in a context of social disruption or structural inequality – was a transparent straw man, and his misunderstanding of anomic values, as reproduced simply by normative control without the accompanying enforcement of the concrete, everyday desires, practices, relations and market imperatives of which Durkheim originally spoke, could, to the cynic, seem quite deliberate. When so many of the putatively exotic and diverse sub-cultural creatures that proliferated in the 1960s, such as former 'Yippie' Abbie Hoffman, became capitalist entrepreneurs when the party was over – although one could argue that they were precisely that when the party was in full swing – the fact that Lemert, Becker and others continued to present cultural-pluralism as indisputably superior to strain theory suggests the existence of dogma. Lemert (1967), for instance, insisted that we see the potentially 'free agent' adapting to the mainstream 'value order' while coping with the countervailing pressures exerted on him by 'various groups to which he has given allegiance', by which, according to Downes and Rock (2003: 135), he probably meant family, occupation, religion, ethnic groups and political ties. Here, there is no mention of the mass-media, the marketing industry, the unforgiving economic logic that enforces practice at work and in business, the tendency of religions to accept and support mainstream economic values and normative controls, the assault on politics and the slow assimilation of ethnic groups into consumer culture. The criminological focus was wrenched away from these immensely powerful macro-cultural forces that were connected firmly to the shifting needs of the capitalist economy and switched to the practices of meaning-generation in youth peer groups that convene temporarily around fashion-fetishes, which pluralists liked to call 'sub-cultures'. This was the beginning of a post-war intellectual paradigm in which capitalism itself, the economic system we all inhabit, was simply no longer mentioned (Boltanski and Chiapello 2007). If today's more penetrative theorists are, with the benefit of both hindsight and harder thinking, correct to posit these sub-cultures as variations of the identity of cool individualism promoted by the counterculture (which, as we saw in the last chapter, is itself a construct of the mainstream marketing industry), then Lemert's claim that the power of the 'mainstream' can be 'mediated' and 'reduced' by sub-cultures appears slightly absurd; in effect, the mainstream would be mediating and reducing itself. If we give this very persuasive new critique a Freudian/Lacanian twist, sub-cultures can be seen quite clearly as little more than temporary staging posts that appear along the sublimatory channels that allow the narcissist's aggressive-acquisitive energy – generated by the anxious need to obtain the means of constructing ephemeral identities that promise social distinction – to be safely released and productively oriented to the objects that circulate in the consumer economy.

Lemert went on to criticise Merton's theory for neglecting the state bureaucracy's power to 'shape' deviant behaviour by confronting it with opposing norms, which in our formulation is not a critique at all but a misrecognition – based on the conflation of regulatory norms and underlying values/practices – of the dynamic relationship between generative values and restrictive norms. The idea that state reaction produces secondary deviation from primary deviation needs to be questioned. The primary action is not a real 'deviation' at all; in fact it is a practice carried out in full compliance with underlying core values and economic logic in a way that contravenes the system's regulatory norms. The bourgeois state labels this as a full deviation and punishes the offender for a number of reasons, but mainly in an act of public denial, in order to relabel the unlawfully performed act of compliance as fully deviant. There is no real deviance at all, no disturbance of the game's values or goals, only an uncontrolled eruption of foul play and a penalty, which maintains the public image that the game itself is fundamentally fair, noble and reasonably well managed by bureaucratic agents willing and able to punish infringements made by a few dirty players. Thus only a minority will suspect that, underneath this relentless public relations exercise, free market capitalism is an inherently dirty and violent game prone to breeding many dirty and violent players. Lemert (1967) claims that the original causes of the act are pushed into the background by the state's spectacle of disapproval and reaction. However, it must be said that it was also Lemert and his symbolic interactionist followers who pushed them into the background and did little to bring them back into the foreground for honest analysis. In fact the liberal-capitalist state and its attendant mass-media do everything they can to maintain crime in the foreground so that in the usual lurid fiend-fest the 'evil act' can be ritually renamed as deviant (against values) rather than merely unlawful (against regulatory norms), which conceals the system's core values under the normative order's shroud of ritual purging. This is not merely an epiphenomenon, but the primary purpose of the exercise. Capitalism is secretly ashamed of itself, and it must punish those who enact their narcissism and acquisitive individualism illegally lest whatever mark of social distinction they obtain might be discredited first by the public, which may raise suspicions about the whole system – whose social order is little more than a huge historical edifice of such marks of distinction obtained as outcomes of competition and exploitation – and the ethical credibility of the cultural way of life that exists within it. Yes, scapegoating and labelling are taking place, not primarily in the name of repressive 'othering' and the reproduction of relations of domination – which if too rigid are deleterious to a system that after all requires enthusiastic assimilation and the constant efforts of the dominated to achieve alienated parity with the dominant – but rather as a vital part of a strategy designed to protect a fragile image from the suspicions of a population that, no matter how assimilated, can always find cause for protest and the weakening of allegiance.

The consequence of the confusion between deep values and regulatory norms, and the assumption of homology rather than dynamic tension in their relationship, was the absence in criminological theory of really penetrative explorations by the Mertonians, the early sub-culturalists or the liberal-pluralists of the specific source and nature of the underlying values and desires that permeate mainstream society and its criminal and delinquent 'margins'. In other words, although these theorists appeared to be arguing about the question of whether deep values and goals were monolithic or plural, the argument was actually restricted to the question of whether norms and practices were monolithic or plural. The genuine liberal-pluralists who mounted a challenge to the Mertonian orthodoxy and its sub-cultural variants argued that plural belief and value systems were the natural constitution of society – the foundation that is not really a foundation (see Rorty 1989) – and thus the source of natural differences and resolute resistance to any attempt to impose a monolithic way of life on a whole population. However, although the general liberal-pluralist critique of the strain theorists' assumption that working-class youth had bought into middle-class values could have been useful had that assumption been true, it was simply another wrong turning. The liberal-pluralist counter-assumption that diverse values existed ready-made in cultural groups, or that they could be creatively reconstructed in inter-subjective groups, under-predicted the background static of harmful crime and delinquency that had – in different forms and largely unreported and unrecorded – for a long time permeated American society from the ghetto to the boardroom. Both camps suffered from the same problem: the deep values of personal freedom won in competitive struggles between individuals, expanding economic opportunities, exponential economic growth and increasing consumption had faded into the background and become customary. Most Americans from all positions across the political spectrum who were brought up in a culture that prized this sort of individualised economic freedom, and in many ways portrayed itself as freedom's 'exceptionalist' historical zenith, simply refused to believe that the consumer economy and the marketing industry were not only dictating the lives and shaping the desires of the mainstream but had also, in a colossal effort to displace potentially dangerous political opposition, systematically constructed a bogus counterculture into which radicalism itself had been assimilated and desires were being manipulated in more seductive and effective ways than the old conservative regime could ever muster. In the shadow of this refusal to reverse the durable suspension of disbelief grew a debate about different strategies of coping with capitalist life, a debate in which the different norms that were established and reproduced in the everyday practice of these strategies appeared as different values. Thus the normative strategies of law-abiding consumers differed from those of criminals and appeared as distinct values and practices, whereas in actuality deep, economically functional values with their accompanying desires and goals remained precisely the same. The big mistake is to assume that there is a different, constitutive deep value and desire underneath each different set of norms: in this formulation the American Dream itself was an intensifier and organiser rather than a generator of deep capitalist values, desires and goals, which ultimately belong to consumer capitalism and the historical cults of possessive individualism, narcissism and social distinction: in other words, what had been in our past, under a far less stringent normative regime, *barbarism*.

The confusion that reigned in American criminological theory was imported into Britain during the post-war period. J. B. Mays (1954) was the first to transport the 'conflictual sub-culture' notion over the Atlantic, failing again to see the difference between deep values and behavioural norms and remaining entirely innocent of the counterculture's origin as a marketing exercise. He studied young people in inner-city locations where, as Hobbs (1989) argued, they were more exposed to proto-entrepreneurial market values than in the working-class communities of the industrial heartlands. Carter and Jephcott (1954) and Morris (1957) observed the separation, by elective affinity and the market aided by housing policy, of industrial working-class areas into larger 'respectable' and smaller 'rough sections', which, after a long period of attempted integration, started to occur again in the 1990s. This was a transitional phase of partial differentiation of values and norms, wherein the values generated by the principle of social distinction by means of competitive individualism were revived indigenously as classical liberal culture slowly re-emerged in the dying embers of traditional working-class cultures and the artificial national communitarianism engendered by the war effort, and also began to filter across the Atlantic on the back of American cultural products. These values were taken up first by a pro-entrepreneurial minority among the working class who continued to reproduce them across their own history as the disorganised 'casual poor', whose precarious condition was more conducive to egotism and demoralisation than political solidarity (Stedman-Jones 1976; Bonger 1916). Yet, among many working-class cultures, especially those in the industrial heartlands, traditional non-utilitarian values were still quite strongly reproduced. Consumerism's move was to depoliticise and individualise these values and encourage them to mutate into regulatory value/norm hybrids that would sublimate the competitive individualist ethos that was to be re-established in the country by consumer capitalism and its attendant neo-liberal political project. When this occurred during the 1980s, large numbers of the 'rough' section quite rapidly became heavily involved in shadow-enterprise, much of it semi-legal or criminal, while the regulatory norms of the 'respectable' section held, creaking and groaning, to ward off predatory behaviour and supply the service industry with workers and the expanding higher education sector with students (Winlow and Hall 2006). It was during this period that the reinforcement of the normative insulation by means of the restoration of traditional family socialisation techniques became perceived by conservative forces as more vital than ever in the prevention of the drift of even larger numbers of young working-class people into predatory crime; in many cases, of course, this afterthought came far too late in communities already devastated by capital retraction and the cult of narcissism.

The great liberal-pluralist denial was the refusal to accept that, from the very beginning of the capitalist project, hedonism and narcissism had been cultivated and harnessed as economic drivers and spread outwards as the general population was incorporated as seekers of social distinction by means of conspicuous consumption. Smith, Ricardo, Marx, Keynes, Polanyi, Galbraith and many economically literate thinkers recognised this. Over the course of the project these basic and highly functional proclivities became core cultural values and psychological drives, and they had to be opposed and controlled by behavioural norms that could regulate the powerful psychic tension caused as they were stimulated, internalised, socially configured and economically harnessed. However, these regulatory behavioural norms could not be allowed to mutate into oppositional values and affects that themselves could be psychologically internalised over generations and thus become capable of attenuating and eventually transforming the human motivations behind the whole project. As we shall see in Chapter 9, these pseudo-pacifying norms could not be allowed to mutate into values that might underpin truly social and affective human civilisation, lest the economic drive be attenuated below the level of intensification required for the optimisation of consumer demand to meet the production system's developing ability to supply cheap goods, exploit labour and ensure capital accumulation.

Separating out culture, values and status from the economy was a bad move, certainly not one made by Max Weber (1991), who is often cited as a major influence on liberal cultural theory (see, for example, Geertz 1973). During the historical waves of the long-term consumer-capitalist revolution status was defined more and more by economic success, which was in turn defined more and more by the 'cool' entrepreneurial individual's adroit performance in the market, eventually unleashed into previously unexplored regions of human desire and identification by the cultural entrepreneurs of the counterculture. In this way individual market performance became established as the principal strategy of distinction that in mainstream culture overrode the tradition of contributing modestly to the collective good, which began to fall into disrepair and obsolescence. People who succeed in the marketplace, such as Bill Gates, Madonna or Paris Hilton, become admired and influential; Gates, it was often said by cultural commentators at the time of his rapid ascent to riches and fame, did more than anyone else to make the nerd 'sexy'. He did, however, furnish the world with a technical invention (although some dispute this), but his real success was achieved by ruthlessly marketing the product and marginalising the competition. Pop celebrities such as Madonna or Paris Hilton achieved wealth and fame by cleverly constructing and marketing their 'rebellious' images in an equally ruthless way; methods of making it as the cool individual are diverse, yet the core value and identification process remain the same. The problem liberal-pluralists had with strain theory is that it assumes that most people conform to 'mainstream' values and goals, but what they did not recognise is that the counterculture had operated on behalf of the marketing industry to expand and diversify the mainstream's normative order to the absolute limits of social acceptability; the mainstream and the periphery were merged in a relationship of dynamic tension, and diverse opportunities proliferated for the cool entrepreneurial individual to 'succeed' in the sense of constructing a temporary identity of distinction. The identities themselves can shift substantively around the solid central pivot of mimetic admiration educed by the achievement of distinction, which is, of course, the ideal 'pitch of axis' for the marketplace, and iconic winners can thus become leading influences in the normative shifts and expansions that are required as consumer capitalism develops through its phases. The key process is a diversifying and proliferating normative order energetically pitching and tumbling around a rigid axis defined by the core value of entrepreneurial individualism.

What we are dealing with here is a loosening and expanding set of norms that can masquerade as values because the actual core value upon which they rest has become so customary that it is invisible and taken for granted. For instance, the 1960s 'permissive society' can be presented as a major causative influence on the genuinely progressive break-throughs in the struggle against the conservative core values that hampered the formal 'civil rights' of women, gays and blacks, whereas it was actually a shift in normative standards around core values that continue to be generated, reproduced and enforced as practices by the everyday experience of living with the market economy's compulsions; women, gays and blacks were 'set free' not to forge a completely new way of life but to explore avenues of competitive individualism and distinction within the mainstream, and thus they were liberated only in a tight orbit in the system's gravitational field. At this point we must suspect that many alternative values have, over the course of the capitalist project, been transformed as they were assimilated into normative strategies that evolved to continually reconstitute human desires and goals as functional economic drivers. The criminological corollary is that when the economy demands it, in order to sustain core values and the compulsory practices that reproduce them, normative standards will shift in either authoritarian or libertine directions, or complex combinations of both, whether people like it or not, and, more importantly, whether they can cope with it or not.

Strain theorists and early sub-culturalists tended to argue that anomie is the product of a lack of moral regulation. In our formulation, as we shall see later (see Chapter 9), it is actually the product of a surfeit of tension generated by moral stimulation in an unstable insulation of normative restrictions that has become ever more diaphanous and fragile as it has diversified. Public perceptions of this fragility have accelerated the revival of the strict moral codes of nationalism and religion; norms have not been corroded by pressure from the natural 'malady of infinite aspirations' but rather they have been systematically relaxed to allow the proclivity of narcissistic desire to be artificially stimulated and harnessed by the economy. Sykes and Matza (1957), in their concept of 'techniques of neutralisation', stumbled upon an important aspect of this tension, but tended to conflate moral values with the rules governing normative strategies. The belated and perhaps guilty invocation of normative rules, after breaking them as a means of enacting deep desires, shows a life-world permanently suspended in what might appear as a plural order, but whose forms are entirely unable to engage creatively and politically with the deep ethical and economically functional core around which they orbit (see Žižek 2000, 2008). This is just a utilitarian normative game, and Sykes and Matza misnamed these rules as 'non-delinquent values'. In fact they were, and continue to be, anti-delinquent norms that have been cultivated to prevent the deep values, desires and enforced practices that generate the human energy that drives forward capitalism from following through with their predatory, hostile and anti-social tendencies and spilling out to poison the social organism. Forty years ago the British criminologist David Downes (1966) put this succinctly: 'Far from standing as an alien in the body of society, the delinquent may represent instead a dangerous reflection or carica-ture,' and the only minor correction we would offer is that it is not the 'social body' being represented in an unruly manner but the underlying suite of moral, psycho-emotional and practical forces that drive forward the capitalist economy. The stronger these drives become, and the more compulsory their enaction becomes in the effort to avoid humiliation, the stronger the normative order must bear down upon individuals by means of legal and cultural restraint; the punitive turn and the recent increase in incarceration (Garland 2001a, 2001b; Zimring and Hawkins 1995) is a product of this increase in the pressure, not from an incorrigibly punitive elite, but as an expression of the sensual detection of overheating in the core energy source and its drive mechanisms and the possible corollary of eruptions of disorder. The upshot is, however, that whether liberal-pluralists are looking at crime, violence, political protests, countercultural imagery, extreme expressions of sexuality or outbreaks of charity, they are looking at outbursts of unruliness, in the sense of normative strategies moving into an eccentric orbit, splitting and creating gaps, but not substantive differences in values, desires or goals.

In a doctrinal effort to escape reruns of the previous Statist repression of what had been labelled pathological, liberal-pluralism's counter-labelling of crime and delinquency as diverse forms of creative ethico-cultural diversity and proto-political resistance made a small but potent contribution to the political complacency and naivety that flourished in the 1960s and 1970s, weakening the spirit of the democratic socialist projects that had already superseded repression with far more progress-ive and effective political programmes, and accelerating its hefty defeat by the neo-liberal Right in the 'Restoration' of the 1980s (Badiou 2002; Harvey 2007). The revolutionary call for socialist diversity (Taylor *et al.* 1973), for instance, was politically useful to the regrouping neo-liberal Right because it was completely impossible, rather like Young's (1999) current call for a just meritocracy among plural forms to prevent antagonism developing in the chaotic reward system. How can we contemplate a 'socialist diversity' when some political elements of the diversity will be virulently and perhaps violently anti-socialist, which would once again force socialism into a repressive mode? And how can we have a consensual meritocracy as the organising mechanism among a diversity of normative strategies and narcissistic identity projects when conceptions of merit will be based on myriad conflicting normative means of achieving the same basic goals; will constant losers simply accept without any reaction that their particular difference is just not the sort of difference that is likely to be the basis of success? Each signifier of the impossible adds to a vast constellation of impossibilities that, by outshining and displacing the honest and at least partially effective reforms of the social democratic era (see Žižek 2000, 2007; Reiner 2007) and permanently curtailing the Big Impossible that would transcend the banality of current cultural differences with a new phase of human development (see Badiou 2002), ensures that nothing ever really happens.

The attempt to mix the liberal-pluralist shibboleth of diversity with Marxism and socialism was less than successful. The latter were unashamed attempts to extinguish bourgeois utilitarian values and, by political force, temporarily replace them with what until very recently was a rich and deep seam of working-class non-utilitarian values, until such time as a new, stateless and altruistic world would appear. There was nothing remotely pluralist about it, yet, compared to the counterculture's wish to abolish everything so that the individual could be set free to ensnare herself in webs of social distinction, its ambitions, as we have already said, were quite modest, especially in its reformist social democratic form (see also Heath and Potter 2007). To insert the ethic of diversity into the socialist project, one had to assume that 'plural forms' were all benign (see Badiou 2002; Žižek 2000; Eagleton 2000). In fact some cultures, for a number of reasons well known to orthodox criminologists, were unsuccessful in their attempts to socialise young people into these core functional norms. In fact Bonger (1916) was entirely correct when he observed these values eating into the potentially more collective, non-utilitarian values that continued to survive among the working class, understanding very well the demoralisation that would ensue from living in such intolerably insecure conditions while simultaneously being swept up by the ethos of competitive individualism: 'Look after number one, coz nobody else will, and don't let nobody trample over you' has been the advice from the lips of countless parents trying to bring up children in these extremely difficult conditions. A self-confident, secure, non-utilitarian working class would not care about the wealthier class's constant ostentation in their struggle to maintain their marks of social distinction, a moral contempt that might well constitute the emotional drive for some sort of political opposition, but, unfortunately, this tends to be restricted to the 'new puritans' (see Schor 1998, 2000) of the middle-class Left and older generations of the traditional working class. The positive values of traditional cultures – especially those concerned with friendship, altruism and mutual obligations beyond kinship – had been metamorphosed into the negative form of normative restrictions, which complemented the formal legal restrictions in the normative order in the way that Smith had recommended. These former values, once ends in themselves in some cultural groups but now relegated to the role of a general means of control, were no longer ordering society and driving it forward but policing its potent yet dangerously toxic economic drives. What appeared as a set of plural values and sub-cultures was in advanced capitalism's functional reality a rainbow of co-opted and metamorphosed values functioning as normative configurations that, with varying degrees of success, prepared individuals to practise competitive individualism and seek status through performance, acquisition and conspicuous consumption in legal yet minimally sociable ways. When the Blairites informed us that we were 'all middle class now', they did so without recognising the immense power and toxicity of the energy released when the competition for social distinction became open to all and the opportunities available for competitors began to leak past the boundaries that mark the limits of social order.

The liberal-conservative slugging match that has bogged down and stalled criminological theory is a Manichean battle between two constant 'moral panics', which are in turn fuelled by two quintessential fears, two 'Absolute Evils' (see Badiou 2002): the fear of the totalitarian state and the fear of the pathologically unruly individual. Myths are, of course, created not out of thin air but from *synecdoches*, specially selected and exaggerated bits of reality that claim to represent the whole and more complex picture (see Barthes 1972; Eagleton 2000; Fiske 1989). Dangerous pathological individuals do exist, and so do totalitarian states, but not every criminal is Ian Brady and not every state is the Third Reich. Liberal and conservative criminologists are always keen to point out the crude synecdochal myth-making at the heart of the other's discourses but far less keen to reveal their own, tending to mystify their metaphysical hearts with a wall of caveats and concessions, which give the impression of sophistication and balance. However, the literature abounds with give-away moral judgements that put hearts on sleeves. The advantage shared by the democratic socialist and the milder, more centrist social democratic movements is a more flexible yet more realistic conception of the individual, the state, the relationship between the two and the progressive possibilities that this relationship holds. Left realists outlined these relations in a reasonably sophisticated way, but they simply dismissed the potential role of the state – if it could be wrenched out of the hands of the plutocrats who continue to have disproportionate influence over its policies – as a democratic instrument of deep economic and cultural regulation. Although Cohen (1986) was right to point out that the shift to orthodox legal conceptions of crime, criminalisation and punishment was a regressive move on the part of the Left Realists, it's difficult to give credence to his claim that the main gains in criminological theory occurred 'twenty years ago' in the 1960s and 1970s, the time during which liberal-pluralism disoriented, diluted, romanticised and idealised radical criminology while traducing the political gains that social democracy had made and constantly casting doubt on the socialist attempt to further democratise the state and its municipal authorities. The post-war Western European social democracies, which used the state far more effectively as a means to control the inherently unstable capitalist market and to some extent attenuate absorption into consumer narcissism, were far more successful than Britain and the USA in maintaining low rates of crime alongside low imprisonment rates (Reiner 2007), a feat that was achieved, miraculously, without much help from American cultural studies. To us, the main post-classical, post-bio-determinist gains in criminological theory occurred before that period, from Bonger to Merton, and further gains will be made when we shake off the 1960s and 1970s and their subsequent postmodernist variants a little more. Left Realism did a valuable job of beginning that process, but it became tied up in administrative pragmatism and legal definitions of crime, retained oversimplified structural concepts such as relative deprivation, failed to explore consumerism and consumer culture in detail, and has thus now lost momentum.

Postmodern liberalism, the cooler Continental version of Anglo-American liberalism that dispensed with the Cartesian subject in an effort to arrange discursive closure and renewal without the aid of politics, is more faithful than any of its predecessors to the basic liberal principle of not risking any Evil in the act of being seen to be seeking the Good. All that can be celebrated are depoliticised dissident minorities ripe for incorporation; they are classified as dissident simply because they are classified as cultures. This shares a common root with the Burkeian conservative discourse, which saw culture as a basic metaphor for society, thus shielding actual society and the tainted project of its 'civilisation', along with its underlying political economy, from criticism and politically inspired change. Romantic liberals and conservatives deliberately seek to revive culture as an alternative to politics. Art, fashion and pop culture are the favoured modes because of their ultimate political disinterest and pointlessness, fantasy worlds where cool dudes can fly the flag of the revolution that they believe has just happened inside their wardrobes and CD collections. We are now at the high point of the process of altering and diluting meaning where it is uncultivated and 'uncool' to be committed to anything real; only culture, the great antidote to politics and the great saviour from absolute Evil, can help us to keep up with the times and register our unrelenting dissent against anything that existed the day before yesterday.

Classical theories were rejected because their macro-concepts such as alienation, anomie and consumer fetishism are incompatible with liberal postmodernist para-politics, simply because they expose major flaws in the deep underlying values, structures and processes of economy and culture, which demand serious intervention. Schur's (1973) 'radical non-intervention' became the motif for liberalism's general political cop-out, an excuse for doing as little as possible and giving deep values, structures and processes a wide berth. Andrew Scull (1984) rightly criticised the inevitable fiscal corollary of radical non-intervention – the abandonment of public services – as a sham, an excuse to hand over responsibility of care and control to private agencies, diminish the authority of the state and save taxpayers money. However, as we have already outlined, it is much more than that; it is also a complex defensive strategy to protect the core value of competitive individualism. According to Slavoj Žižek (2002), anyone who supports liberal-pluralism is either stupid or a corrupt cynic; it is now anti-democratic, because its basic aim is depoliticisation of the practical world, at least of the important elements, while the cultural froth, as a surrogate, can pretend to be as 'political' as it wants. It is in the thick of this ontological ruse that we can locate the liberal-pluralist criminology that emerged in the 1960s, part of the attempt to 'suspend the destabilising potential of the political' (Žižek 2000: 190) that had grown to a crescendo in the mid twentieth century, the period which Badiou (2007), in his Lacanian schema of modernist history, saw as the point when we had progressed through the Imaginary and the Symbolic to the Real, and our 'passion for the real' was demanding the implementation of the yearning for social justice that built up throughout modernity. Despite the terrible failures of our attempts to implement that yearning, argues Badiou, the passion still burns with great intensity but it has no voice, only an 'impotent rage'. Para-politics are pragmatic politics, the 'art of the possible' fragmented into a series of innumerable minor impossibilities – meritocracy, diversity, risk management, responsibilitisation and so on – whose tediously slow conception, half-hearted implementation and ambiguous evaluation delay for generations the realisation of their overall impossibility. Authentic politics is the art of the impossible, but not simply making serial impossible demands on capitalism, which is the liberal method of feigning politics, but rather the means by which we can move from what is to what is not. Liberalism secretly tolerates fascism, because fascism is the art of what occasionally has to be done, a relapse into barbarism to make sure nothing really important will ever change, an ambition it shares with liberalism. Fascism revives and reveals the original prejudices and violence that established the gentrified liberal order in Europe, but it cannot tolerate meta-political or ultra-political fascism (Badiou 2007), so it gives fascism the normal treatment: depoliticise, atomise, neutralise. Micro-fascism – the predatory criminal in the cabinet meeting, the boardroom or the sink estate – is therefore a pragmatic liberal preference: by no means an ideal, but something that it is willing to tolerate in place of politics. In its supposed re-classification of the public according to risk, liberalism is actually seeking to declassify publicly its nineteenth-century categories of criminals and victims, and the results of this liberation of the people from modernity's classificatory discourses is that prisons are again becoming generic warehouses for everyone from mental health sufferers and drug addicts to serious predatory criminals. At its best, liberalism is conservatism with a conscience, but at its worst it is penny-pinching classical liberalism, negligent romanticism and solipsistic libertinism with no conscience at all.

At one point in the 1970s, radical criminology risked becoming as absurd as its counterpart conservative criminology, by simply inverting the latter's traditional moral order wherein deviance was Evil and conformity Good. Both camps eventually wilted under the myriad caveats that inevitably appear around such ethically naive and rigid positions, although it must be said that despite this their respective Manichean myths remain strong to this day. The most important political result was that the sight of radical criminology committing suicide in public after it tried to import liberal principles, and the concomitant sight of conservative criminology remaining obdurately wrong at the aeti-ological level while occasionally being right at the level of banal observation, was grist for the mill of liberal-pluralists and postmodern-ists, who were delighted to confirm once again that the world is too diverse and contingent for much to be done about anything. The liberal-pluralists' principal political ambition is to make sure that we refrain from approaching major social problems with too much collective gusto, moral disapprobation and political design, which might result in a demand for forceful intervention in the deep core of the capitalist economy and its peculiar culture of social distinction.

So, where do we locate the intellectual roots of liberal-pluralist criminology at the deepest level? Alain Badiou (2002) confronts liberal philosophy squarely – Rawls, Habermas, Benhabib, Ricoeur, Rorty, Irigaray and others – and American pluralist cultural studies, which had a substantial impact on British cultural studies and constitutes the platform on which stands today's cultural criminology. For Badiou, the root of the problem is that ethics should not concern the 'Other' simply as a victim of misrecognition or violence. As history moves forward from what is – the mundane ontological reality of everyday life as a multitude of differences – by seeking the Same, the legitimate truth and knowledge that is indifferent to differences gathers strength and acts as a unifying tendency with the potential to bring disparate cultures together on a higher ethical plane. Whether criminology likes it or not, it is this project that consumer capitalism has hijacked; while productive capitalism was more indifferent to cultural differences, like an economic Pax Romana interested only in labour power and taxes, culturally driven consumer capitalism is entirely dependent upon culture and seeks to dominate the worlds of emotion, meaning and desire, both in the way we work (Hochschild 1983; Williams 2001) and, more importantly, in the way we seek to acquire and display cultural symbols as marks of social distinction (Bourdieu 1986). Consumer capitalism has thus entered the territory of the Truth-Project, and thus approaches a condition of totality in which it entirely dominates the movement to create homogeneity in ethics through its central icon of the cool distinguished individual, an image that it now exports across the globe.

Despite this move towards totality, the current liberal orthodoxy hangs on to a bogus reverence for the Other, as we can see clearly in the work of liberal philosophers such as Levinas, Derrida, Irigaray and Spivak. Spivak's notion of the 'subaltern' identifies the hyper-exploited and marginalised, which are supposedly – and conveniently, some cynics night suggest – beyond the help of traditional political intervention and can only be reached by becoming 'at one' with them in the sense of an almost spiritual union, an 'ethical singularity'. Liberalism wants the state to legislate on behalf of mystified symbolic communities, ancient or recently constructed, to protect or 'liberate' them within the present system, rather than the freeing of humanity from the manipulations of plutocratic states in the service of advanced capitalism. Thus anything that liberalism seeks to protect will be ascribed an existence as a symbolic community trying to express a political message of protest, including groups of young delinquents, criminals and others trying to scramble to positions of distinction rather than taking part in the politics of opposition. We can see quite clearly that liberal cultural studies and both cultural and managerial criminology are saturated with this core ethical notion as the basis of their shared ontology. Liberalism promotes the 'rights' of individuals as simply the general abstract right to what Badiou (2002) calls 'non-Evil', good seen purely as the negative of Evil, the avoidance of mistreatment, and thus it has nothing positive to say about laying down the conditions for the Good, the conditions in which so many of these groups could abandon their abject positions and return to politics and the building of fraternity. This is an ethical position that systematically avoids engagement with reality on the pretext that it might result in a 'Big Evil'. The claim that it can impose itself globally, even in the negative sense of protecting individuals' rights, is false; it allows the continuation of the reality of the 'unrestrained pursuit of self-interest, the disappearance of or extreme fragility of emancipatory politics, the multiplication of "ethnic" conflicts, and the universality of unbridled competition' (Badiou 2002: 10) which, of course, are the fundamental generative conditions for the worst types of social fragmentation and predatory crime.

In fact, 'cultural difference' is an irrelevant banality of everyday life, simply what *is* and what *has been* for a very long time. Our fascination with this difference is a legacy of vulgar forms of liberal sociology and anthropology, based upon the fascination with 'savages' and all things wild, the ethos that kept the 'zookeepers' of American liberal sociology and criminology (see Gouldner 1971; Sumner 1994) hard at it seeking out fascinating and mildly menacing examples of the internal 'alterity' that in the West were actually products of capitalism's unforgiving homogenising and ranking system (Eagleton 2000). 'Difference' is something that children get used to quite easily, finding it unremarkable if mildly entertaining, and only when it is forced by adults who should know better to mean something in the political culture does it become traumatic (Badiou 2002; Žižek 2000). However, because these different modes of expressing humanity are forced to struggle over positions in a highly competitive capitalist economy that has no value other than money or narcissistic distinction, and whose culture induces political apathy, the population is reduced to a state of 'belligerent impotence' (Badiou 2002), which for over forty years now cultural studies and cultural criminology have mistaken for examples of subversion, resistance and proto-politics. Earlier Mertonian theorists, along with those who seek to revive strain theory (see Messner and Rosenfeld 1997), correctly adumbrated the basic shape of things in Anglo-American societies in their formulation of so-called 'sub-cultural' groups as modes of adaptation to central values and insatiable desires, even though the source and nature of these values and desires were under-theorised and the reformulated concept of anomie over-predicted crime and posited a state of 'normlessness' where there was actually a surfeit of differentiated normative strategies growing in the spaces created by the gradual abandonment of oppositional values and politics.

Post-war liberal-pluralist sociology is not a paradigm within which intellectuals attempted to construct informative explanations of life, criminal or otherwise, in advanced capitalism; rather, it appears to have been founded upon a negative reaction to the collectivist politics of the past that ended up in violent and totalitarian failure. It is little more than a grandly narrated anti-statist cautionary tale whose ethical core renders it unable to see the political failures of the past as products of unique events and conjunctures at specific points in history. In its ranking of Evil, the ultimate is, of course, the Holocaust, and the runners-up are the Gulag, the Cultural Revolution and the killing fields of Cambodia, but we must not lose sight of the fact that the state itself is not necessarily predisposed to oppressive or brutal regimes. For many liberal-pluralists, the cruel innocence of the Little Evils that seep out through capitalist culture's layers of normative insulation is preferred to the possibility of the Absolute Evil State, and thus in liberal-pluralism's criminological variants the causes of crime are either persistently avoided as the focus of study, or alternatively explained away as reactions to the legal rules constructed by the state and imposed upon the innocent cultural groups that 'peacefully' inhabit civil society. This is the grand narrative where left and right liberalism converge, a fairly open secret, and the principal reason why neither branch ever fully supported the idea of even the mildly interventionist social democratic state – or the working-class communities or political collectives that with greater genuine democracy in the political system could have been fairly represented by this state – without serious reservations (see Young 1999). Now, in the advanced stages of the triumphant liberal-pluralist orthodoxy we have entered a metaphysical realm where nothing can really be denoted as a serious crime unless it can be compared to the Absolute Evil, and unless the politics required to reduce that type of crime can be measured against their potential contribution to the return of Absolute Evil.

We are thus intellectually and politically marooned (Hall and Winlow 2007); the whole liberal-pluralist discourse is little more than a subtle method of ideologically hamstringing the political collective just in case history might repeat itself and the collective mutates into the totalitarian state. In that case, there are crimes across the social order that will continue to be committed as the undemocratic neo-liberal state fails to legislate against business crime, and crimes committed by its own employees, as it fails to censor the marketing industry and its ability to promote the culture of insatiable desire, and as it fails to improve the abject conditions of insecurity and nihilism at the very bottom of society that breed predatory intra-class crime. To wrench ourselves out of the political torpor established and maintained by the joint effort of neo-liberalism and liberal-pluralism it is now essential that we develop discourses in a concerted attempt 'to abandon the theme of radical Evil, of the measure without measure . . . [t]his theme . . . belongs to religion' (Badiou 2002: 63). Nazism and Stalinism were singularities, and must be located as irreducible events in history, and therefore we must look again at the project of convening the democratic collective and constructing the political infrastructure with which the collective can control its own destiny and stop suffering social problems like the ludicrous income gap, narcissism, nihilism, violence and crime as if they were unavoidable pestilences wrought upon us by the caprice of angry gods, and rectifiable only by ritualised adjustments of language and meaning combined with the interminable calculations, classifications and machinations of the dismal risk-management bureaucracy.

Chapter 7

Myths of exclusion and resistance: a critique of some current thinking on crime and culture

The Anglo-American Right has always seen criminality as a product of the moral and rational failure of the individual and/or society's disciplinary mechanisms, a position that has been heavily criticised by all schools of radical criminology. Whereas earlier forms of Marxist, socialist and social democratic criminology saw criminality as an expression of the immorality and degeneration that were unavoidable aspects of capitalist social relations and culture (Bonger 1916), Mertonians saw it as a problem caused by society's failure to integrate its population in a just manner. In the mid twentieth century, shifting attention firmly to the state as the representative of the forces of reaction, as we have seen, the liberal-left saw criminality as a reaction – sometimes proto-political – of the innocent to cultural marginalisation, socio-economic exclusion, relative deprivation and negative 'labelling' and 'othering'. Relativists among the postmodernist liberal-left, taking the principle of individual freedom to its libertine outskirts, often argue that criminality is simply a set of 'discursive objects', which, outside of a small number of core harms about which there is consensual agreement, are largely harmless expressions of 'difference' labelled criminal by a dominant order that wishes to impose its rigid moral authority across the whole of society's ineluctably plural and polymorphously perverse landscape. There have been many attempts to integrate these positions, with varying success (see Cullen and Agnew 1999), but a cursory glance at the development of criminological theory should tell us immediately that these prominent explanatory schemas tended to put all their eggs in very small baskets and failed to offer entirely convincing explanations of criminality (see de Haan and Loader 2002). In a recent book on street crime, Hallsworth (2005: 91), following on from Young's (1999) very useful concept of social 'bulimia', makes the following key point in a very clear manner:

> What left-orientated notions of exclusion posed in this manner often fail to see is precisely how far the street robber is also a product of the society whose members they attempt to rob. They are not essentially different ... despite their exclusion ... much of what motivates engagement in street robbery occurs not because street robbers are excluded from society but, on the contrary, from their successful internalisation of its value system. In particular, the need to have and possess desirable material goods.

This short passage, grounded in Hallsworth's own ethnographic work, alerts us to the paradoxical nature of life in the world of contemporary capitalism, a life full of opposites existing in 'double-binds' that put pressure on individuals to deal with contradictory ethical positions and social imperatives (Miles et al. 1998), a shifting configuration of dynamic tensions with which the standard structural, integrationist and pluralist/ postmodernist schemas outlined above have not quite got to grips. Living in the lower echelons of a system whose dynamic forces comprise of contradictory tensions, these young criminals are simultaneously different yet similar, excluded yet included, resistant yet compliant, subversive yet reproductive, deviant yet conformist, and it is quite obvious that if many such tensions abound in capitalist societies then maintaining them all in even a semblance of equilibrium must be immensely difficult. However, for us it seems to be the case that these oppositional poles are no longer primarily the products of social conflict and destabilising tension between genuine 'differences' in ethico-political goals, values or even group interests, as they once might have been in earlier stages of history. As we have already seen, it might well be the case that these everyday tensions and differences are, after a long process of assimilation and harnessing, now vital components of the very sophisticated culturo-economic apparatus that generates the dynamic power required by consumer capitalism. For criminological theory to advance and become relevant to the times, criminality and criminals need to be located more precisely in these dynamic forces and processes, which in turn need to be more fully understood by means of analyses that take place beyond the moral discourses of condemnation or celebration, pessimism or optimism. We have long suspected that the 'excluded' and their specific forms of criminality are part of the way the system works (see Lea 2002), as indeed are 'included' white collar criminals (Tombs and Slapper 1999; Punch 1996) and the everyday part-time malefactors who operate throughout the less than pristine 'moral economy' of market societies (Karstedt and Farrall 2006). However, beyond standard explanations, such as the tendency of the relatively poor to drive down wages and foment anxiety, we are still not sure exactly how they reflect underlying functions that generate dynamic power. Simply pointing out that in consumer culture expectations have surpassed many individuals' ability to satisfy them, or that efficiency, predatory acquisition and the 'malady of infinite aspirations' are aspects of market culture that have leaked from the economy and corroded the ethical regulatory mechanisms of social institutions, as do current Mertonian theorists such as Messner and Rosenfeld (1997) and Karstedt and Farrall (2006), explains neither the sources and nature of these proclivities nor the complex ways in which they function as dynamic forces. As a first step towards this end we need to explore the complexities of the dynamic tensions and dilemmas that pervade the 'new spirit' of global consumer capitalism itself (Boltanski and Chiapello 2007). The main focus of attention in this chapter is the tension between the centrifugal and centripetal forces of exclusion and assimilation, and in the following chapter, rather than simply assuming it to be a timeless aspect of a monolithic 'human nature', we explore the psychosocial wellspring of 'infinite aspirations'.

There is nothing new about our awareness of 'contradictions'. The whole Marxist discourse was founded upon capitalism's inherent contradictions and clashes of interests, and Robert Merton's (1938) original recognition of the various adaptive strategies that were prompted by the tension between mainstream cultural values and socially structured variations in the opportunities to conform to them was the catalyst for a good deal of further discussion. The American anthropologist Walter Miller (1962) argued against Merton's classification of delinquency as a form of rebellious nonconformity precipitated by blocked opportunities, suggesting that it was a product of conformity to the 'focal concerns' of working-class neighbourhoods: excitement, smartness, trouble and so on. This theme was to be taken up by British sociologists such as Young and Willmott (1962), David Downes (1966) and Paul Willis (1977). Downes's study was particularly useful insofar as it questioned and deromanticised Miller's pluralist analysis. He found that young men were conforming to their own peculiar working-class 'values' – a term far less woolly than Miller's 'focal concerns' – yet they felt that their 'values' by no means opposed the prevailing mainstream culture; if there were indeed any clashes of interests these young people seemed to be unaware of them. They sought excitement in leisure to escape the mundane routine and repression of work and traditional culture, an idea that was to be taken up again by cultural criminologists two decades later.

However, radical social science has always tended to focus on conflict as the main product of contradictions. There is little doubt that at specific times and in specific places contradictions and tensions do indeed produce conflict, sometimes even extreme disruption and abrupt change, but there has been far less focus on what we might see as the other main product; dynamism. As we have seen, as the desire for rebellion, existential freedom and excitement grew in popular culture and featured heavily in intellectual discourses it was also being cultivated by consumerism's marketing industry and media machine, which rapidly metamorphosed rebellion into a specific type of conformity. What seems like a partial reversal was occurring in the sense that the dominant culture was now moving outwards and integrating with popular culture rather than attempting to dissolve and incorporate it. This suggests that 'conformist rebellion', always present in consumer culture but never as vital as it is now as a dynamic force in the economy, was being recognised as such, and thus it was in the process of being diffused rapidly throughout the whole society by means of encouragement and cultivation, mainly by the rapidly expanding commercial media (see Gerbner and Gross 1976a, 1976b).

That it would cause problems was also apparent from its early stages in the post-war era, problems that would also eventually diffuse throughout the social body after first manifesting themselves most spectacularly in some distressed working-class locales. Here the strict and vital socialisation techniques required by capitalism's normative order had been weakened in a sequence of disruptions that stretched from industrial migration to slum clearance and the move to satellite estates, yet the intrinsically predatory and amoral nature of capitalism had been experienced more severely and could be perceived more clearly; many of these locales were unstable yet more politically dangerous than most others. From this perspective we can see that as socialist politics came under the corrosive pressure of consumer culture the amorality emphasised by the Mertonians and the existential rebellion emphasised by the cultural criminologists seem to have merged with depoliticisation as complementary aspects of a singular and increasingly nihilistic cultural form. The rapid popular adoption of this cynical yet economically functional hybrid suggests, rather dismally, that by the 1960s many individuals were beginning to lose the traditional knowledge and ethical sentiments necessary either to conform or to rebel in an effective manner; the Anglo-American population was in its first stages of becoming socially atomised and politically ineffectual. It also suggests that this apparent rebellion/conformity hybrid might no longer exist in the realm of values at all; rather, it looked more like a product of an evolving normative strategy, a way of adapting to and coping with far more fundamental values, psychosocial forces and logical requirements that, as we shall see later, lie deeper in the capitalist economy and its cultural history.

Writing in the early stages of the post-war consumer revolution, Sykes and Matza (1957) argued that delinquents conform to much the same 'values' as most others, but because of injustice and marginalisation they have a 'minimal stake' in them. This assumes that the focus of these varying allegiances is indeed a system of values rather than a system of normative strategies that have evolved around an underlying value system, which, after decades of being taken for granted, has become *doxic*, an invisible customary authority informing an everyday 'logic of practice' (see Bourdieu 1990). Most criminological theorists have neglected the extent to which liberal capitalism's consumer culture has reinforced the core economically functional values, desires and goals to which the individual is expected to conform while also diversifying the normative strategies – strategies that converge around the now ubiquitous maxim, 'What's the most I can get away with here?' – required to achieve them by lawful means. Precisely at a time when the nexus of culture and economy was at its most potent as a generator of meaning and motivation, labelling theorists called off the search for the causes of crime within it and shifted attention to the criminalising effect of social control mechanisms, decrying most previous attempts to theorise the sociocultural and economic causes of crime as 'mechanistic'. Many extreme liberal-pluralists and postmodernists argue that there are as many micro-causes of crime as there are individuals committing it, and thus the search for macro-causes is futile. This seems to be a politically expedient way of avoiding issues concerned with deep structures and processes, influenced by liberalism's determination to work within current ethical and social coordinates and its subsequent fear of deep macro-political regulation or disturbance (Badiou 2002; Žižek 2000, 2002) rather than a genuine attempt to improve criminological analysis. There was, for instance, nothing at all mechanistically determinist about Bonger; his position on 'demoralisation' was much more sophisticated than many gave him credit for, and he did not posit it as an automatic class response, but a tendency among the vulnerable:

> [It] is almost superfluous to remark that the egoistic tendency does not by itself make a man criminal ... [it] is possible for the environment to create a great egoist, but this does not imply that the egoist will necessarily become criminal ... [as] a consequence of the present environment, man has become very egoistic and hence more capable of crime, than if the environment had developed the germs of altruism. (Bonger 1916: 402)

Effectively, in 1916 Bonger had reflexively criticised his own discourse and presaged the problem of the tendency of macro-causal explanations to over-predict crime. Drawing upon Engels (1958), he also presaged Hoggart's (1957) and Williams's (1971, 2005) recognition that a strong non-utilitarian culture was immensely valuable to emancipatory politics, if indeed emancipation was to be carried out in a social order whose degree of civility and sociability made emancipation worth the effort, and that it continued to be reproduced among some working-class micro-communities and occupational groups; although certainly not all (see Hobbs 1989). Many among the Rousseauian influenced liberal-left seemed to assume that anti-utilitarian altruism was a natural tendency immanent in all individuals but corrupted by modernist culture, a *sociotropism* that we have criticised elsewhere (Hall 1997), and that it simply needs to be drawn out and cultivated a little more in a non-repressive climate. Since Kant, Rousseau and Marx, the Left have mistaken what is far more likely to be a *sensibility*, a precious and fragile psychocultural quality, as a natural human drive, a mistake that neglected a long history of cultural and political struggle that constituted and reproduced the few fragile non-alienated, altruistic and fraternal cultures that we have seen in the West. Worse, traditional working-class culture itself has often been disparaged by some liberal theorists as a destructive and dehumanising form of self-repression replete with racism, sexism, homophobia and other forms of odium (for useful discussions see Young 1999, 2007; Eagleton 2000). Hostile and repressive it certainly could be – a suite of prohibitions, ensuing discontents and irrational reactions in the classic Freudian sense – but whatever it detested and repressed there were also powerful ethico-political forces bubbling inside it, resisting those tendencies as well as detesting and repressing the bourgeois utilitarian tendencies of exploitation and narcissistic self-aggrandisement that the Left claimed to oppose. We are reluctant in such instances to invoke the old cliché of throwing out the baby with the bathwater, but we must certainly question the motives and wisdom of some members of the self-appointed progressive liberal-left in their many, varied and usually rather furtive attacks on traditional working-class cultures.

Nevertheless, despite the possibility that traditional working-class culture might well have been the sole repository of active rather than formal anti-utilitarian values, many seem quite keen to consign it to the dustbin of history and forge ahead on the wings of a culture that powers itself forward by constantly disconnecting itself from its past. Eric Hobsbawm (1995), arguing in the more romantic vein that throughout his work seems to exist in tension with harder structural analyses, suggested that we are living through a 'gigantic cultural revolution'. Our view is that the chance would be a fine thing, but at the moment we are living through nothing of the sort. Rather, we are witnessing a period of Restoration that includes the dissolution and assimilation of all modernist opposition and the return to modernity's basic bourgeois aims (Badiou 2002; see also Harvey 2007). In the midst of this there can be no 'little revolutions against the routinization of life' (Young 2007: 293) because from the beginning of consumer capitalism this type of micro-revolution itself – which under the faux-ethical surface is merely standard libertinism in its glorious diversity – has been manufactured and routinised; at the moment we are simply witnessing its democratisation and diffusion. The unfortunate outcome of this, which has secular liberal-rationalists and self-appointed progressives fulminating at full volume (see Grayling 2007), is that we now seem powerless to prevent the great ironic twist that characterises the current advanced capitalist phase: the appearance of regressive forms of revolution revived and reconstructed in the political vacuum to oppose the disruptive and non-regenerative cultural effects of routinised modernist micro-revolutions, such as mysticism, religious fundamentalism, nationalism, tribalism or fascism. If people are bored and repressed, it is not just with tradition and mundane work, but with the concept of revolution itself, because it has been hijacked and reduced by consumer capitalism to a carefully cultivated suite of micro-revolutions, which over time have become tedious chores that must be performed to fuel the constant circulation of symbolic commodities.

At the very bottom of the whole process seems to be a tense and irresolvable hybrid rebellion/conformity dynamic that compels human beings to construct various normative strategies to guide them through its confusing, contradictory imperatives. Twentieth-century criminological theorists have been hitherto restricted to the exploration of the various normative strategies constructed by individuals and fluid, shifting interest groups as they attempt to cope with and prosper in the constant domesticated tumult caused by the operation of this dynamic force. At given times some strategies within the general group of *simulacra* might tend towards the presentation of a rebellious appearance, and others appear conformist, while others appear hybridised; these are simply perspectives that reveal themselves to the public as the strategies move through stages of their development. Of course, we must remember that these forms are also infinitely recyclable among younger generations who have no memory of their original entry into the world (see Baudrillard 1993). The major ontological bifurcation in criminological theory and the current attempts to transcend it – integration/plurality and hybridisation – can be clearly detected as ways of conceptualising the main perspectives and stages. Genuine oppositional values are all but gone, along with the productive work functions that accompanied them, and they are thus no longer capable of operating in the dialectic. Now, what passes for 'oppositional values' can be easily dissolved in the diffusion of the elite's dynamic force throughout the social body in the form of an accelerated cultural simulation. The elite's great democratic gift to today's 'emancipated' class, race and gender groups is the unrelenting dynamic that initially compelled its members to apply themselves to the task of constantly seeking and maintaining positions of spectacular social distinction in brutal competition with each other. Perhaps we should reflect a little before we show too much gratitude to the progressive liberals who presented us with this glittering prize.

As rebellious opposition is now asocial and politically impossible, and therefore guaranteed to be safe, the irony is that this guarantee can no longer be applied to extreme manifestations of rebellious conformity. In conditions of severe repression and alienation, taking risks and courting danger can be intoxicating and signify a leap for freedom, and in conditions of elite privilege and social stability conformity can be secure and rewarding. However, now that the rebellion/conformity drive is on its way to being fully diffused throughout consumer culture's increasingly asocial and apolitical body, being compelled to cast oneself again and again into yet another micro-revolution of simulated transgression beyond the boundaries of pleasure into the painful excessive realm of *jouissance*, while never really leaving the conformist core, indicates the completion of the individual's subjugation by a cultural system reaching the height of its totalising powers. What looks like resistance to repression is a product of the new super-ego injunction to enjoy (which we explore in detail in the next chapter), the moral command based on the negation of the negation that once represented true resistance. True resistance in consumer capitalism would be resistance to being forced along the path of simulated rebellion to reach its obscene supplement, the painful excess of *jouissance*, only to discover that one has walked in a circle back to conformity, while the new super-ego with its harsh internal remonstrations heaps guilt on those who miss opportunities to enjoy the trip (Žižek 2002). Criminological theory has not yet quite got to grips with this vital dynamic force. Hayward and Young (2004: 259–60), for instance, seem to have misrecognised the marketing industry's attendant cultural forms by expressing late modernity as a period in cultural history where we find:

[the] extraordinary emphasis on creativity, individualism and generation of lifestyle ... coupled with a mass media which has expanded and proliferated so as to transform human subjectivity. From this perspective, the virtual community becomes as real as the community outside one's door – reference groups, vocabularies of motive, and identities become global in their demesne.

However, as we have argued in previous chapters, it is quite likely that there has been no transformation of human subjectivity, only its further assimilation into the fake revolt. Richard Sennett (1998), much more circumspect in his appraisal of current times, explored the shift to the global free market not just in terms of the changing nature of work and the destabilisation of identities, but in the decline in trust, loyalty and civility in everyday relationships. Sennett sees the general character emerging in this insecure and hostile social environment as what we might call a latent predator, present in more explicit and spectacular forms in the core and the periphery, and in low-intensity forms in the normatively restrained space between them. This is not the 'anomic society', with all the sublimatory channels that Merton (1938) outlined acting as alternative ways of enacting the dream and discharging the pressure, but a society in which the traditional alternatives, especially politicised rebellion, have declined, a society with the greatly increased likelihood of more individuals channelling their consumer-inflated desires for social distinction into privatised, hostile and potentially criminal projects. This is the track on which our creative abilities seem to be stuck, and it leads not to the open spaces in which subjectivity can be transformed but to a terminus of cynical resignation (Sloterdijk 1988) in which various normative strategies must be constructed to prevent the subject sinking down into consumer capitalism's lower echelons.

In a similar vein, Young (1999: 7) argues that the 'rise of individualism heightened demands for fuller and more developed citizenship as well as registering a protest at the lack of equality in the system'. That's what it might look like at first glance, but citizenship in advanced capitalist societies is now based first and foremost on the opening up of opportunities for the narcissistic self's distinction and prosperity (Barber 2007), and for all but the politicised minority the protest is individualised and ultimately centripetal. Talk of equality is entirely negative and solipsistic as it emanates from the self's complaint that its position in the competition has been unfairly allocated. It is essentially an infantilised form of citizenship based on a complaint lodged on behalf of the self rather than a plea on behalf of others (see Hughes 1993; Lasch 1991). The struggle for citizenship in imperialistic market societies has to some extent always been driven by personal interests, by the quest to join the competition and seek elite status as a potentially successful player. This invariably generates hostility, and perhaps Young underestimates the degree of narcissistic instrumentalism that has been created among post-war consumerism's children (Lasch 1991; Sennett 1998, 2006; Barber 2007), and how difficult this will be to dislodge. Liberalism's move to culturalism and personal politics has considerably exacerbated this problem by allowing interest-based personal politics to displace the politics of mutuality and authentic solidarity. Where Young (1999: 8) argues that it is 'chronic relative deprivation among the poor which gives rise to crime', we would suggest instead that, in the absence of traditional sources of identity, ethics and politics, by far the more powerful factor is the perceived absence of opportunities and lack of ability to achieve individual positions of social distinction, to invoke *amour-propre* and lord it over others, making them feel relatively deprived. Our data suggests that rather than striving to be like others, consumer capitalism's subjects want to use consumer symbolism to *not* be like others. Rather than wanting to relieve the sense of deprivation felt by themselves and others in a similar or worse position by organising relations of equality, they want to rise as individuals to positions of social distinction above others, who will subsequently feel relatively deprived of the same opportunities to make others feel relatively deprived; unfairness and inequality are integral aspects of this narcissistic desire and the social dynamic it energises, not simply effects of the structure in which it takes place. In late modernity a specific form of egotism has become normalised, recognised by Rousseau (1990; see also Žižek 2008); from *amour-de-soi*, the healthy form of self-love based on dignity and self-respect that can be felt for others by the empathetic individual, has emerged *amour-propre*, the unhealthy narcissistic form, driven by envy, which seeks pleasure in preventing the enjoyment and seeing the downfall of the other, who is seen as an obstacle to the self's ambitions. If the innate Kantian sense of justice does indeed exist, and it is not merely a sense of personal injustice writ large, it seems to have been firmly repressed. Consumerism's subjects are the product of centuries of competitive individualist culture, which was opposed only temporarily by an opposition whose revolutionary forms discredited themselves and whose social democratic forms were badly beaten in the neo-liberal Restoration. There is no sign of that subjectivity being deposed from its dominant position unless we are inspired to develop a sense of justice and solidarity – and prohibited from adopting a position of extreme destructive self-interest – by a symbolic order that accompanies some sort of ethically rigorous mutualist politics, whose return is essential (Žižek 2000, 2007; Badiou 2002).

However, for us Young (1999: 8) is entirely correct to see late-modern life as a 'race', and our data suggest that all our interviewees believe that, no matter what an honest appraisal of their current conditions of existence, social position, cultural capital and real chances of success might suggest, they are in the race, just one lucky break away from becoming a millionaire. One important finding that pervaded our data in this study was that most of our interviewees constantly indulged in fantasies about being 'on the way' as a cool individual operator to a position of social distinction, 'always in with a chance'. This became crucial to their ability to construct a sense of psychological and social security amid the general culture of insecurity, and most felt driven to realise quickly the positions they imagined themselves to occupy – positions that they tended to present to others in order to impress – or risk the deep descent into permanent fantasy and low repute as impotent 'wannabes'. One important answer to the question of why only some of the young people who occupy similar social positions and circumstances commit crimes while others don't is that no two young people perceive themselves to be in precisely the same position on the same trajectory. This might well depend on cultural variables, but it also depends on how those cultural variables affect the individual's imagined position on a linear trajectory towards a position of social distinction and her attitude towards culturo-legal normative restraints. Our data consistently suggested that those who are sufficiently cynical to reject liberalism's spin about inclusion and meritocracy and have an oscillating, dynamically ambivalent perception of how far they are from success, yet who lack commitment to legally institutionalised norms and thus believe that the achievement of success can be legitimately short-circuited, are the ones who are more likely to engage in crime. Thus, despite the resigned view that there is no justice and 'society' is a cynical and unforgiving competition, there is no conscious knowledge or psycho-emotional feeling of exclusion, no perception of their real plight, because there is nothing solid or stable to be excluded from, and one cannot be excluded from a competition that, in the Heideggerian sense, everyone has been 'thrown into', one can only occupy the position of a (temporary) loser within it. For us, this reflects the damage done by years of liberal mendacity about the existence of equality, rights and freedoms in advanced capitalist societies (Žižek 2002, 2007).

Since the 1960s liberal criminology has presented a premature and wishful conception of lumpen groups as already, without any organisation or education, replete with the signs of political resistance. Here we find the myth of 'organic micro-resistance' operating at full power. The most naturalised and anti-political form of this argument can be found in what is becoming the rapidly outmoded work of Michel Foucault and the gradual collapse of the cult-like intellectual industry that grew around him after his death. Willis (1990) attempted to address this problem when he claimed that consumer capitalism is parasitic on the subversion and resistance that Foucault (1980, 1984) saw resplendent in the petty micro-struggles that permeate liberal societies. Again, however, although this is a useful corrective to some of the less perceptive and critically reflexive Foucaultian analyses that pervaded social science throughout the 1980s and 1990s, it buys into the counterculture's 'co-option' myth. From the eighteenth century, when consumerism presented itself as the ultimate way forward in the expansion of wealth-creating markets, it has learnt how to create a dynamic by actively cultivating the cultural processes that create preferred forms of micro-subversion, which in turn can be harnessed to its dynamic economic drive. It is thus just as appropriate to say that what passes for subversion is parasitic on capitalism, but perhaps much more appropriate to say that they are symbiotic. This game was interrupted partially and temporarily by the threat of organised labour. The intellectual rot set in when cultural commentators such as Raban (1975), de Certeau (1984) and many others overestimated the actor's ability to creatively 'transform' consumer symbolism into autonomous and subversive cultural politics and simultaneously underestimated the system's ability to prefabricate the general symbiotic mode of subversion in which actors performed for the few youthful years before casual labour and the 18–40 debt crisis (or prison) rudely reminded them of their real place in the new order of things. This is indeed nothing like a system in which 'wooden actors passively pursued . . . conventional ends by unconventional means', a position that Young (1999: 11) is right to criticise, but neither is it a system in which creative actors actively seek unconventional ends, a position he does not criticise with sufficient vigour; the conventional/unconventional dichotomy is now meaningless. Real power and real resistance are not 'everywhere' (see Mouzelis 1995), and it was only possible to think that thought in a depoliticised world where real power remained in the hands of a plutocratic minority, and all that remained in civil society was the cultural means of admiring them. What is actually 'everywhere' in the advanced capitalist world is an awful lot of jostling for position and complaining by individuals and custom-built post-sub-cultural groups about their share of the symbolic spoils, Bataille's 'excess', the gargantuan 'accursed share' produced by consumer capitalism's productive engines, constantly paraded in front of the population by the mass media and representative of positions of fake social distinction for those who lack alternative sources of identity. Foucault's (1980, 1984) narrow obsession with the discourses of science and capitalism's state-organised 'disciplinary technologies' as the loci of the constitution and normalisation of the liquid 'subject of discourse' meant that he had virtually nothing to say about mass-media and consumerism, effectively throwing us off the scent of advanced capitalism's most important subjectivising and normalising power.

The existence of so much assimilated subjectivity on the margins supports our argument in the previous chapter that it is not simply the well-socialised individual who is more likely to become a predatory and/or violent criminal, as Young (2002) suggests, or even the badly socialised individual, because socialisation deals with both values and norms and the complex tension that exists between them. It is the vulgar narcissist, the individual who has been well but crudely socialised into capitalist culture's underlying economically functional values and rebellion/conformity dynamic, but poorly socialised into its downsized insulating norms and symbolic prohibitions, who is more likely to be unpleasant, aggressive and self-serving. When social Darwinists speak of the ethical integrity and functional economic benefit of unbridled competition they are, of course, talking about a fight with the gloves on, as Adam Smith (1984) recommended, a fight that takes place within a strictly codified normative framework and which is umpired by the state's legal apparatus. In fact, the individual who is overly socialised into values and poorly socialised into norms, and who subsequently breaks the law in an embarrassingly overt manner, can be seen as letting the side down, a discomfiture, a 'sore loser' in American parlance. As we have already argued, when mainstream culture and its institutions seem to 'other' the predatory criminal with a barrage of negative labelling, it is not because its agents really believe that he is an 'other', but because they secretly know that he is as far as it is possible to be from being an 'other'. In fact they are painfully aware that the criminal is an embarrassingly crude and ill-disciplined caricature of themselves, one who discredits the whole liberal-capitalist enterprise, revealing the perversity and instability of its underlying ethical principles and bringing shame and unwelcome doubts upon everyone who holds them dear. Thus the criminal is not a pariah but a wretched sinner, a fallen insider, a dirty player who could not play the game within the rules, and he sends the group into a painfully repressive bout of silent denial. This is why the mainstream despises the criminal.

In a recent book about crime in cities, Hayward (2004) brings into play Lasch's (1991) well-known Freudian notion that post-war Anglo-American identity has taken shape in a psycho-cultural process of brutally competitive 'consumption-orientated narcissism'. This condition is bound to cause a good deal of social and interpersonal friction, but Hayward perhaps de-emphasises this when he foregrounds a consumer culture that, alongside this struggle of the narcissists, has at least partially transcended what both he and Young (1999) see as the dull productivist and communitarian compulsions of the old industrial capitalist world and now presents opportunities for creative freedom in the construction of identities and lifestyles. As we have seen, liberal commentators such as Hebdige (1979), Featherstone (1995), and Fiske (1989), converted neo-marxists such as Stuart Hall (1988) and many others, have already explored what they see as the positive, creative side of consumerism. The depthless world of expanding and proliferating aesthetic categories could indeed be seen as a playground for individual identity projects, but the withering away of structure is perhaps overstated and thus we tend to be led away from the sociological fact that this atomised struggle for identity still takes place in a hierarchal framework consisting of positions of social distinction (Bourdieu 1986).

The hierarchal structure might be a little more fluid than it has ever been in the sense that its categories shift around here and there and open up a few more opportunities for those with ambitious and entrepreneurial inclinations, but it is still nonetheless a hierarchal structure, and a highly competitive one at that. What looks at first sight like a playful, subversive struggle against the norm in order to explore innovative identities and lifestyles can be seen upon further investigation to be a brutally competitive social struggle against all others, which foments deepening and widening inequality, new class divisions (Bourdieu 1986), the terror of social insignificance and an unprecedented level of interpersonal suspicion and hostility. This has perhaps been downplayed by liberal sociologists whose pragmatic resignation to the notion that the capitalist market is a terminus in economic history guides sociological analysis on a trajectory of enforced optimism, in which too many stones are left unturned and serious social problems are ignored or understated simply to carry on justifying the original position.

Since the late 1990s, however, there are signs that this particular worm is turning and stringent critical analysis of consumer capitalism, fed by tributaries from various left-field positions, is on its way back, if indeed it ever went away (see Jameson 1992; Eagleton 2000; Frank 1997; Heath and Potter 2007; Barber 2007). With a bit of a struggle, it is slowly and rather hesitatingly filtering back into criminology. Hayward (2004), for instance, expresses some reservations about the ability of urban expressions of consumer culture to act as seedbeds for genuine political resistance, but by no means does he fully commit himself to this position. Specifically, he does not acknowledge the possibility that these youth cultures are the sanitised, preferred forms of opposition created by the post-war marketing industry as a means of creating politically safe dynamic tension, despite his acknowledgement of Eugene Gilbert's (1957) classic marketing strategy of stretching adolescence from a brief transitional phase to a whole way of life from 12 to 30 so that disposable income could be tapped more readily over a longer period. However, Hayward's brief yet important correction, that the emotional feelings and desires engendered by consumerism are often destructive and tend to be overlooked by criminological discourses, is an important sign that the critical approach has not been permanently displaced by liberal pragmatism. With a palpable sense that he acknowledges the current cultural situation's gravity and portent, he comments that 'consumer culture and aspirational culture are now locked in a deadly embrace, each begetting the other' (2004: 8).

On the other hand, Hayward is also in some agreement with Katz's (1988) primitivist-essentialist theory of crime and delinquency as expressions of an urge to transgress the repressive norm, driven by the 'existential pursuit of passion and excitement'. This theory rests on rigid, naturalistic conceptions of emotion, desire and their objects – would not many of us, if unaffected by consumerism's constant provocations, desire peace and quiet? – and it lacks a conception of culture as sublimation and maturation and an acknowledgement of psycho-cultural diversity across a history punctuated by changes in human sensibilities and desires (see Elias 2000; Fletcher 1997; Eisner 2001; Hall 2007). However, Hayward (2004: 11) also argues that consumerism 'cultivates tendencies (especially among the young) that can, in certain circumstances, ulti- mately find expression in specific forms of expressive criminal behav- iour', but then, to complicate his position further, he proceeds to argue that 'self-definition' is the demand that late-modernity places upon us. This ignores the very important homology and dynamic tension between the demands of consumerism and the demands of individuality, which has been expressed neatly by Miles *et al.* (1998) as the double-bind command to simultaneously 'fit in and stick out'. Although Hayward's position appears to waver throughout his book, it wavers intelligently and in many sections quite unequivocally acknowledges the power- ful influence of consumer culture and the tension this creates in its relation with allegedly creative, subversive and transgressive identity projects.

As a way out of the impasse created by his wariness of Katz's primitivist conception of agency and the more deterministic structural/ cultural positions alike, Hayward draws upon the Mertonian and Gramscian residues that still exist in the thinking of Young (1999), who, echoing the original British criticisms of early American sub-cultural theory, reminds us that Katz's (1988) analysis ignores the historical and structural contexts, and that desire for transgression can easily be recruited into the insatiable desire for new commodities and commodi- fied experiences. This recruitment promotes the impulsive, short-term desire for instant gratification, which has long been touted by criminol- ogists representing various left-of-centre positions (see Hallsworth 2005; Hall and Winlow 2005; Messner and Rosenfeld 1997) as a principal psycho-cultural cause of crime with an inseparable connection to the consumer economy. Young is to a large extent right about this, but his accompanying idea that the original urge to resist is an organic one that is subsequently assimilated by the system buys, like Willis (1990), perhaps a little too much into standard 'co-option' theory (see Frank 1997; Heath and Potter 2007) and deters us from considering the possibility that the urge to resist is itself being produced and diffused by the marketing industry in the depoliticised, individualised and economi- cally functional form that it prefers. If true, this would mean that what looks like an exhilarating organic triptych of resistance, subversion and transgression is simply the carefully manufactured and politically harmless negative pole in the dynamic tension that is systematically generated to sustain consumer culture's alternating cultural current. Yes, it is perfectly possible that after centuries of evolution this veteran system has indeed become that powerful.

Ultimately, Young's and Hayward's analyses, along with those that predominate in cultural criminology (Katz 1988; Ferrell 2002, 2006; Presdee 2000; Lyng 2006) suffer from a reluctance to confront squarely the bleak reality of advanced capitalist culture and the gravity of the measures and the concentration of effort and sacrifice that would be required if what remains of the Left were once again to become serious about forging some genuinely active and effective opposition. Alas consumerism is only a proliferation of signs, not real diversity, subversion or resistance (Baudrillard 1994, 2005), and these minor eruptions of symbolic mischief – joyriding, pirate radio, graffiti, alternative fashions, culture jamming and so on – are merely *ignii fatui*, not the seeds of effective resistance, because there is no evidence of them ever germinating (Heath and Potter 2007), as politically significant proportions of each new generation of youth sink deeper and deeper into consumerist infantilism (Virilio 2005; Barber 2007) and begin to lose touch with the symbolism and collective memory of political resistance. As for Young's (2007: 203) claim that 'we live in a plural society . . . there is palpably no agreement about desired goals, preferred means, or indeed what is rationality', we have already discussed the general misrecognition of 'goals and values' as normative strategies that preside over deeper values and logical functions that are ineluctably homogenising. Alain Badiou's (2002) reminder that these 'differences' are nothing more or less than timeless apolitical banalities, combined with the enthusiastic adoption of consumerism and competitive individualism among the bulk of the West's population and the lack of electable political resistance to neo-liberalism, suggests that the claim of deep plurality is just plain wrong.

In a recent critique of some of Young's core ideas, Yar and Penna (2004: 534) posited modernity as 'a highly differentiated set of processes in which the "inclusion" of some is dependent upon the "exclusion" of others [and therefore] exclusion and inclusion are part and parcel of highly differentiated and asymmetric historical processes'. Here they have astutely recognised the dynamic and formative tension in the relation between these two positions in the general social field (see also Bourdieu 1990), although they leave this vital point undeveloped. Two problems here however, are, firstly, that they describe social inclusion as an aspect of social policy rather than a product of the economic and cultural functions of specific groups in specific phases of capitalist development; and secondly, they use the term 'exclusion', which supports liberalism's corruption of the genuine position of consumerist loss, which we have already discussed at length. Yar and Penna (2004) are unerringly correct to criticise the crude distinction Bauman (1995, 2001b) and Giddens (1984) make between 'stable' modernity and 'unstable' postmodernity, a conception used perhaps rather too often by Young (1999). As Yar and Penna (2004) suggest, modernity was also ridden with hostile conflicts and instability along with vast inequalities of wealth and power across class, race and gender axes, a point that Young (2004) conceded in a measured rejoinder, but for us this needs unpacking a little further.

What appears to be instability today is an increase in the tension between positions in the tumultuous 'meritocracy' that Young (1999, 2007) suggests might be the mechanism that could release tension and provide an ultimate solution to social injustice and hostility, hopefully effecting a reduction in crime by organising competition into a comprehensible and morally justifiable social order. As we have already argued, it is rather doubtful that, under the pressure exerted by consumerism's inexhaustible and irrational struggle for social distinction, those who exist on either the bottom or the top of any meritocratic hierarchy would accept their positions; how can something that is constantly in motion ever be assessed and how can the amoral and irrational be morally and rationally understood and justified? If we accept that competitive meritocracies do not have to be ethical and very rarely are – Darwinism, of course, is a raw, blind form of meritocracy – then capitalism has to a large extent always been meritocratic. Meritocracy is the polite liberal name for a social world ordered by rule-bound competition, a Hobbesian war hidden behind a thin veil of ethics, the continuation of barbaric social conflict by other means. The problems we face today are products of profound shifts in the economic foundations and normative order in which the competition takes place; the reconfiguration and revaluation of basic functions and norms arranged around ornamental consumption rather than productivism and militarism. The 'vertigo' we feel (Young 2007) has little to do with existential choice and freedom. For us it is a product of the refreshed *amour-propre* and the heady expansion of opportunities for simulated positions of social distinction sensed by us all as we confront the further diffusion of the rebellion/conformity dynamic, and those whose position as losers cannot be accepted and turned into social critique and political opposition are playing a dirty game.

Today's disruptions and anxieties do not signify the simple emergence of instability out of stability, but, rather, a radical alteration in instability's form. Yar and Penna (2004) are correct; modernity was from its inception unstable and unequal – hostile, in fact – in the sense that racist and sexist exclusionary forces were constantly in play, and the institutionalisation of those designated medically or socially inferior was an essential aspect of the administration of this essentially unstable and unequal British society. Today, they continue, the mythical concept of 'citizenship' is just another hierarchal way of organising society, meritocracy is its instrument and 'exclusionary' processes are obscured by the administration of citizenship. We are in broad agreement with most of this, but we would argue that the political framework for socio-economic stability was achieved briefly in the post-war social democratic era, in which radical elements of the British working class were showing signs of transcending defensive tribal hostility and becoming a unified force for political change. Further, we would argue that what is being obscured by today's politics is consumer capitalism's systematically cultivated dynamic tension between centripetal and centrifugal forces – the rebellion/conformity dynamic – rather than 'exclusion', and indeed this important dynamic force is being hidden and protected by the administration's focus on the static categories of inclusion and exclusion. Thus a dynamic force that cannot be managed with liberal democracy's light touch is being replaced in our line of vision by a structural social relation that is more easily depicted as manageable. However, the same dynamic force continues to be generated in a radically recontextualised and reconfigured system of instability and inequality. Although Yar and Penna (2004) are correct to claim that some degree of inclusion – or in our terms a degree of the centripetal force that creates balance and establishes orbital stability – was won by social movements representing different cultural groups that were marginalised by imbalanced centrifugal forces in the old configuration, the effect has been to displace and expose to imbalanced centrifugal forces other groups with a tenuous attachment to the orbital path, along with floundering remnants of the lower-class fractions of the previous structure, in a new round of class division. Some of these groups, such as unskilled lower-class men and women who now entirely lack grounded identity and politico-cultural representation, seek renewed identity and status in archaic, mystic and often ugly forms of nationalism and fundamentalist religion, yet, according to our data, they do not accept their exclusion in the phenomenological sense and remain entranced by the fantasy of quickly regaining a place in an orbit closer to the core. Paradoxically, our data also suggests that neither would many of them ever accept their full and permanent inclusion as part of the reviled 'herd' of 'mugs'.

Genuine resistance, which must carry with it a clear picture of exactly what is being fought for and fought against, was once rife among many proletarian workers whose experience and political discourses kept them painfully aware of their position of exploitation. However, in the West this feeling now exists only among a far smaller group of politicised workers and disparate educated minorities (Hall and Winlow 2007). The better criminological ethnographies of the 1990s, such as those of

Nightingale (1993), Bourgois (1996) and Hobbs (1989 1995), to varying degrees supported the claim of the near total assimilation into the paradoxical dynamic of 'social distinction' of those who lack the political and cultural resources to resist, a position that has been confirmed repeatedly by our own research. According to Nightingale (1993), the 'ghetto', as a metonym for all deprived areas, seems to display a surfeit of mainstream values, and this corrects Albert Cohen's notion that there is something about sub-cultures that tends to create 'inverted values' rather than a selection of inverted regulatory norms. However, Nightingale's (1993) idea that hyper-identification combines with rejection, used by Hallsworth (2005), Hayward (2004), and Young (1999, 2007) in his interesting concept of social 'bulimia', is again for us too simplistic, because the courting of rejection seems to be the vital centrifugal aspect of the dynamic tension that capitalist culture has over its life-course developed into a very sophisticated energy-generating mechanism. One is encouraged from an early age to court the ubiquitous forces of rejection and alienate oneself from one's fellow human beings in 'society'; the trick is doing it in a legal and profitable way that allows one to eventually rejoin in a position of distinction.

We can see quite clearly that one of the fundamental problems in recent social theory is a rather hasty and totalising appraisal of what has changed and what has not in the transition from classical capitalism to advanced capitalism. In our formulation the actual movement has been considerably more complex and less clear-cut. In the period of classical productive capitalism the containment and harnessing of conflicting interests in a homogenising productive economy converted an already existing combination of thymotic social struggle and ethical social conflict to linear economic momentum, which, as it progressed historically through the Lacanian categories of the Imaginary, the Symbolic and the 'passion for the Real' in the twentieth century, carried with it the danger of transcendence beyond these banal yet vital generative conflicts and the unification of mutual interests as a political force (Badiou 2002). We have now reached an advanced stage in the process where an economy driven by consumer culture requires the artificial production, intensification and proliferation of the types of thymotic conflict that have always been known by capitalism's more alert agents (see Frank 1997) as those which can be readily sublimated and harnessed by the economy. In an economy that has transcended needs, and in a group of societies that were on the road to dampening down conflict in the post-war social democratic period, what were once readily available as non-transcended legacies from the past must now be artificially provoked into existence, customised and sustained. In other words, in order to replace the needs, conflicts and narcissistic desires capitalism was in the process of losing as vital economic drivers – specifically because of its own partial success at transcending them – consumer culture had to systematically construct, diffuse and ignite simulations of these needs, conflicts and narcissistic desires for the specific purpose of their conversion into economic energy; it had exhausted its natural fuel deposits and was thus forced to manufacture artificial ones. Thus what has changed is everything formal and nothing substantive.

Continuous and systematic attempts are now made as a matter of course to customise conflict for this purpose, and the anxious struggle for identity by means of social distinction in the swirling cross-currents of the permanently disrupted and postponed collective is the most suitable raw material. Thus Young's (1999, 2007) further claim that we face a greater range of life choices could also be countered by the suggestion that, at the deepest level, if we want to avoid humiliation and insignificance, we have no alternative than to seek a distinguished individual identity in the consumer market with a proliferating range of means of conforming to it, identifying with it and achieving marks of social distinction within it. The more the range of choices inspires our imagination the more pressure it places on the competitive core, the more the new super-ego imposes its guilt on those who might miss opportunities and the more the lifestyle industry expands. This, as we see in more detail in the following chapter, does not give the subject an identity, but traps it in an interminable process of compulsory identification (Lacan 2006; Žižek 2006a, 2007) in which it can never feel content. The alleged new world of 'greater difference' is thus more homogeneous, restrictive and compulsive than ever, and the 'differences' that he suggests should be accepted while kept at a distance are actually being forced to come closer together in a mêlée of over-proximity as they compete as suppliers of cultural tools for individuals who are absorbed in their quests for social distinction. Young's (1999, 2007) and Bauman's (2001b) conception of the mid stage of modernity as an inclusive, assimilative society misses the dynamic tension created by the accompanying centrifugal force generated by the constant threats of insecurity, poverty and insignificance, and it is thus too static; overall stability was an impression given by the relative stability of the economic dynamic, like a smooth-running nuclear reactor belying the turmoil occurring beneath its surface.

To recapitulate briefly, we must not forget that liberal-capitalism's 'cool individual' is scared stiff of both social inclusion in the 'herd' and the cultural and economic exclusion that denies him the ability to achieve a position of distinction in some sort of spectacularly eccentric orbit around it. Liberal-capitalist economic dynamism was created in the tension between the threats of social inclusion and culturo-economic excision – which, as well as being undesirable and therefore aversely provocative, were impossible and therefore unattainable as pure conditions of existence – and thus manifested as the competitive individualist desire to alienate the self in an effort to eventually escape inwards to the eye of calm in the centre of the storm by amassing wealth, achieving distinction and buying freedom. The basis of the dynamic movement is the interplay of enclosed centripetal and centrifugal forces. The upshot is that status and distinction became associated with escaping inclusion in the system's social obligations and mundane economic tasks, yet the escape could only be achieved by first deeply immersing the self in the economic system – thus providing it with a vital shot of energy – in order to secure the necessary means. The criminogenic effect of this set of highly effective functional values, norms and practices is obvious, and crime is often fantasised as a means of short-circuiting the whole process to the terminus of a premature retirement to an anti-social life of leisure decked out with the social symbols of status, distinction and booty. Our data shows clearly that so many of capitalism's subjects, no matter how lowly their positions and how numerous their failures, imagine themselves to be on that road.

However, despite these critiques and the reflexive reservations that permeate his own work, Young (2007: 6) has stuck to his guns; in more recent works he continues to argue that we live in the midst of a genuine cultural revolution in which negative consequences are outweighed by positive ones:

> [The] cultural revolution, of course, preceded the economic crisis, as indeed did the rise in the crime rate, which began in most advanced industrial countries before the early 1970s and then continued to rise, often at a greatly augmented rate, as the economic recession began to bite.

In the light of all we have said, we might ask, along with Frank (1997) and others: 'what cultural revolution?' We are unsure that what could easily be portrayed as a regression back to eighteenth-century romantic, pre-political individualism organised by the marketing industry and its abject creation the 'counterculture' can be described as either 'cultural' or 'revolutionary'. Apart from skinheads and other marginal proletarian groups, from the Teddy Boys in the 1950s to the New Romantics in the 1980s, these strikingly narcissistic fashions harked back to the faux-aristocratic leisure classes and urban dandies who appeared in various phases of classical industrial capitalism and its run-up. This bogus revolt, the *avant-garde* preparing the ground for a new phase of the spectacle on behalf of the marketing industry, might have preceded the economic crisis of the 1970s, but it certainly did not precede the marketing industry's knowledge – honed in the bitter aftermath of the Great Crash – that capitalism always existed in the shadow of an economic crisis waiting just around the corner. It was this fearful knowledge that spurred the agents of consumer culture to lobby with great success the West's culturo-legal apparatus with a plea to allow the individual out of the straitjacket of functional morality, shifting the dynamic interplay between repression and sublimation. In other words, the so-called 'cultural revolution' was itself a product of powerful entrepreneurial and political agents' knowledge of the capitalist market economy's inherent tendency to instability, crash and recession, and the 'cultural revolution' was organised alongside other complementary economic and macro-fiscal measures aimed at boosting demand and stabilising the globalising financial system (Harvey 2007). All this, of course, was also spurred on by the Cold War, the constant threat that the Soviet Union's command economy might continue to evolve and win a huge ideological battle if the Western capitalist economy once again crashed or failed to deliver individual prosperity and 'freedom', its main selling points. There were specific reasons, deeply embedded in econ- omic logic and ideological imperatives, why hedonism had to be encouraged as the types of politically harmless and economically functional freedom that could boost consumption. The cultural water- sheds were the mainstream promotion of overtly sexual popular music and art forms in the USA from 1955 and the release in Britain in 1961, after a court case, of the erotic novel Lady Chatterley's Lover as a cheap paperback available for mass consumption. From that point onwards the floodgates of hedonism as commercialised sensuality were open. Almost everyone wanted a piece of the action as a producer, a promoter or a consumer, and society did not become more 'exclusive' or 'plural', but ever more homogeneous and seductively inclusive in the senses of identity and desire, which created more competition and hostility in the socio-economic sense. Many lost in this competition, for sure, but, given the huge amount of money spent on education, housing, social security and other public services, and the daunting power of consumer culture to assimilate individuals into the Dream, we must challenge the claims that capitalism's losers were 'excluded' from society to positions where any more than a tiny politicised minority 'resisted' the game that most continued to want to play.

This is not to deny that life at the periphery is also uncomfortable. Now that intoxicating substances and extreme symbolic images are cheap and in plentiful supply the terror of insignificance can combine with the risk of *jouissance*, the painful realm beyond excess itself. Yet, seductive and terrifying dreams of these extremes still haunt the subject to combine with the terror of insignificance, prompting restless ambition in perpetual motion. Thus it is the capture of the agent's struggle against being swept up by either centrifugal or centripetal forces that creates energy, and although the inability to escape life on the precipice or survive life as a subject of *jouissance* can be an accidental by-product, it is neither the intention nor the functional prerequisite of consumer capitalism and its attendant welfare state; the system requires the energy of the subject's constant motion, and Foucault's (1984) 'micro-resistances' and Deleuze and Guattari's (1987) 'lines of flight' are always already harnessed as energy sources as they bring themselves into being. There is no 'outside', thus there can be no exclusion, and, with moral prohibitions relaxed, credit available to most and virtually unlimited consumption possible, the hedonistic excess of total inclusion becomes not the realm of *eros* but of the death-drive. The vast majority of consumer subjects are still mentally, emotionally and practically bound up in the circuits of the consumer-service economy no matter how near the imaginary precipice they might be. As temporally and morphologically distinct entities the 'inclusive society' of old and the 'exclusive society' of the present are both myths. What we are looking at is a permanently suspended and conditional form of inclusion that constantly implies and threatens exclusion at the slightest loss of performative value (see Lea 2002) but never really allows it to happen. The real exclusion that might revive the dangerous politics of true opposition can never come into being, and neither can the true inclusion that can exist only with the unconditional membership of a community rather than the conditional and fragile membership of a fantasised, individualised performance elite. Thus the system ensures that the assimilated agents of advanced capitalism are cyclists that dare not stop pedalling lest they wobble, stall and crash either inwards or outwards.

For these cyclists on their orbital pathways there is no loss of ontological security or a genuine sense of the 'chaos of reward' (Young 1999 2007), but an intensification and outward spread of the strangely predictable uncertainty of a culturo-economic system whose populations are learning rapidly to be ontologically secure about what to them is the platitude that the ontological insecurity and chaos caused by constant 'progressive change' constitute the natural order of things. Put simply, not knowing what's what, feeling the ground underneath one's feet constantly shift and sensing chaos in the air has become normality, cancelling out any political passion to establish or restore a stable, egalitarian social order; Klee's *Angelus Novus* has become entirely accustomed to life in the storm that blows him forward in time with his back turned to the future and his eyes permanently fixed on the wreckage mounting in the past and defining the reality of the present. Almost anything is better than being trapped in a static identity and sensing this wreckage building up and threatening to bury the self, so most individuals are more than willing to up their anchors and sacrifice themselves to the storm. The whole purpose of our chaotic, multi-paradoxical life is to generate immense energy as it compels the permanently deracinated subject to struggle constantly in search of a distinguished identity in the impossible imaginary community that dissolves itself as soon as one joins. The unstable competitiveness that has always existed at the core of capitalist culture, among its elites, has now been diffused right through the social body to the periphery. Consumer capitalism, it would seem, has performed the remarkable feat of splitting and tapping the psychodynamic atom.

Chapter 8

Consumerism, narcissism and the reorientation of the Western super-ego

Times, both real and intellectual, have changed markedly since the early 1970s. In the light of the nascent rethink of the relationships between the social dynamics of consumerism, the marketing industry and the individual, which we have discussed in previous chapters, the claim made by liberal-pluralists that older forms of critical theory were simply reductionist and wrong because they posited human engagement with consumer capitalism as determined, reactive and adaptive rather than free, transgressive and creative (Becker 1967; Taylor *et al.* 1973) – once regarded as a paradigm-shifting critique – now cuts very little ice. As we have seen, this is merely one pole of a false dichotomy, a dichotomy that can no longer be overcome by simply claiming, as Giddens (1984) does, that human agency is creative in a social structure that can be both restrictive and enabling. In many cases simply inverting received ideas is the mark of adolescent contrarian sophistry, but for us Giddens's formulation is so wrong-headed that it might well be permissible to claim that in the reality of advanced capitalism the relationship is almost the inverse; the scope of human agency is severely restricted in a fluid and competitive structure that is enabling only in a very narrow economistic sense. By the 1960s the consumer marketing industry had learnt how to harness in a very efficient manner the individual's readily given creative energy, which is generated in the quest to identify with the icon of 'cool', rugged individualism. As we have seen, the consumer economy is now energised by the tension between the centrifugal force of the individual quest for distinction from the reviled 'herd' and the centripetal force that prevents the escape from actually occurring for anything more than a brief, agonising moment of simulation; the individual generates energy by splitting itself as it oscillates between two points – community and individuality – that loom large in the imagination yet in reality deny each other's existence. This alternating current of centrifugal and centripetal forces is a product of consumer culture's ability to recycle utopian images of non-existent positions of freedom and social distinction to which the individual wants to escape as he reconstructs 'community' as a decomposing pile of failed attempts to achieve these incompatible and contradictory positions, from which he constantly feels the need to escape.

As we have tried to make clear, the individual subject of advanced capitalism is not, as Presdee (2000: 114) suggests, caught up in 'the tensions that emanate between regulation and rebellion', but the tension that is systemically generated between distinct yet complementary centripetal and centrifugal forms of bogus rebellion enclosed in an energy trap. Each time an individual attempts to conform to the command to rebel in the normative order, a shot of energy is contributed to the competitive individualism, fetishistic desire and economic growth that together constitute the underlying ethical and practical orders. The problem for the system's regulators is to keep these micro-revolts and the temporary forms of quasi-cultural diversity they create within the law, and sufficiently sanitised/simulated to the extent that the constant little cuts they continue to make in the Symbolic Order's 'rationalised' skeleton do not cause irreparable damage to society's increasingly flimsy fabric. Taboos, prohibitions and symbols of the sacred disappear every day, and the flimsier the fabric becomes the more the social management machine must implement techniques of micro-intervention to manage the ensuing 'risks', an expensive and bothersome task that state-averse and tax-averse neo-liberals would rather do without; far better to sucker the sub-intellectual residue of dying socialism into performing this unpopular task, further tarnishing its reputation. However, in a personal effort to minimise these risks and avoid the discomfort and insecurity that pervade the reality of life on the margins, the individual must take care to travel to the edge only in the imagination to obtain some mass manufactured souvenir of a brush with edginess, thus allowing her to harness the centrifugal force generated in a brief outward trajectory as a sort of slingshot, which, in turn, generates the centripetal force of 'rebellion inwards' towards a position of approved social distinction; in other words, the individual generates both poles of the alternating current required to drive forward the economic system. Failure to take care, to be carelessly too real about one's transgressions, can result in a real drop down into the real margins, where the same game is played in a far more robust manner.

Radical criminology's major ontological inversion of 'common sense' was to rename deviance as a proto-political leap for existential freedom while renaming conformity as collusion with the repressive 'system'. This, as we have argued, completely misrecognised the shape and underestimated the complexity of advanced capitalism's dynamic socio-economic relations. In today's social reality, exploitable forms of deviance have been fully unleashed from the elite social circles of yesteryear and diffused throughout the social body as the system's main drive, while conformity, in the sense of compliance to the collective decisions that real politics once had the potential to make in a more democratic manner, has become the system's mortal enemy. The inversion was made possible only by systematically underplaying the crucial distinction between regressive and progressive modes of conformity and deviance. Consumer culture and law now lie at awkward tangents to each other. In consumer culture, controlled deviance is now regarded as healthy and conformist, while conformity to collective decisions that threaten to place restrictions on self-gratification is seen as pathological and deviant, denounced as oppressive, totalitarian and so on. In law, as much controlled deviance and conformity as possible has been legalised, while most forms of uncontrolled deviance and conformity that are impossible to harness to the economy have been criminalised. Despite the constant revising of ethico-legal categories and the blurring of boundaries, the basic (mis)shape is holding firm, and in Habermasian terms the relation between system and life-world has never been more misaligned and perplexing for citizens and administrators alike. In both ethical and rational terms, social life in advanced capitalism has become a set of paradoxical categories and relations that as a whole make very little sense, and the relations between culture, law and criminality probably make the least sense of all. Postmodern pluralism was not a movement for progress, or even romantic regression, it was simply a chorus of sighs of resignation to life in a system whose internal paradoxes were making firm and durable interpretations and moral positions almost too difficult to contemplate, yet which precisely because of that chaotic situation were functioning better than ever in generating and harnessing economic energy on a gargantuan scale.

At the heart of this hopeless misrecognition and misalignment is the fact that Left and Right variants of liberalism are fighting a *ghost revolution* on behalf of the individual against the tyranny of a feudal elite that was vanquished a very long time ago. The battle continues to be fought, with foot-soldiers spurred on by the demonisation of anything that smacks of collective authority placing unnecessary restrictions – beyond those legitimised by a core of consensual morality stripped down to its bare bones (see Henry and Milovanovic 1995) – on the creative freedom of the individual, which is increasingly defined less as a right and an end in itself and more as an instrument that should be applied to the furtherance of the individual's economic and hedonistic aims;

rather than 'having' freedom *per se*, we have the freedom to do this, that and the other. Socratic negative freedom – where the individual is freed from the tyranny of desires and fetishes – is notable only by its virtual absence in popular culture. A huge current of psychosocial energy generated on the battlefield can be harnessed by a consumer economy that has honed to perfection the art of selling the individual the comforting signs that she has made it in her struggle to actually be an individual distinct from the fearfully repressive 'herd'. While this was once indeed a noble call for the exploited producing classes to battle against genuinely illegitimate oppressors and gain the self-respect and dignity of *amour-de-soi*, in today's western world of *amour-propre* it has become a toxic and destructive force programmed to seek and destroy all forms of collective authority. Thus, with a little ideological guidance from busy neo-liberal agents, it now targets the legitimate collective authority that was in the early stages of construction in the social democratic era (Reiner 2007; Barber 2007), casting the world of everyday people into a condition of chronic insecurity that constantly dampens enthusiasm for radical reform, radical subjectivity or genuine rebellion (Boltanski and Chiapello 2007). As life in the neo-liberal era becomes more unstable and insecure as legitimate authority's steadying hand becomes more tentative and weak, reactions and adaptations to this instability and insecurity become more desperate and extreme, pushing a mainstream culture highly energised by the paradoxical tension of conformity and controlled deviance towards uncontrolled deviance. This educes more unpopular, draconian measures from hamstrung governments unable to approach the culturo-economic roots of social tension and criminality (Reiner 2007), and the principle of collective governance collapses towards a critical point of illegitimacy. The enduring ghost revolution is successfully eroding our ability to govern ourselves and control our own destiny as citizens of a political body, and it is the single most influential cultural force operating on behalf of the current handover of power to the forces and institutions of the global market.

There is no real 'structuration' or 'symbolic interaction' to speak of here; in a culture where conformity to collective decisions made about issues outside the minimised core has become deviant, the majority of individual actors are only lightly involved in the 'uncool' political task of creating social meanings, rules and institutions – a task now monopolised by the mass-media and the para-political risk-management bureaucracy – but heavily involved in creating ephemeral lifestyles from which eventual escape is compulsory as they too become 'uncool'. What radical-liberal theorists did not understand in the early post-war era was that the marketing industry and its child the 'counterculture' were demolishing the social democratic system, a political entity that was already in the throes of demolishing the old conservative order, and much of the hegemonic edifice that had become 'common sense' within it, in the construction of a stable socio-economic platform on which a new cultural order with a heightened level of sociability might have brought itself into being. Žižek (2008), talking about the recent riots in the poorer French banlieues, is correct to depict the current socio-political condition of European social democracies as parlous, almost as capable as neo-liberalism is of creating the non-citizen of *homo sacer* (see Agamben 1998), but he fails to mention that these nations have now been severely compromised by the intrusion of neo-liberal political and economic practices. Whether or not social democracy has 'had its day' and the baton can be picked up by social movements or the radicalised 'new human' is too big a question to answer here, but it is certainly worth pondering Boltanski and Chiapello's (2007) important point that sustainable and enduring progressive socio-political change tends not to occur under conditions of chronic insecurity. However, there is no doubt that radical liberals did little to prevent the destruction of the fledgling social democratic order, with its proven ability to set up and maintain conditions of economic security for individuals, thus clearing the way for the emphatic return of classical liberal-capitalism in its new seductive form of consumerism serviced by neo-liberal politics. Fraternity, security and social justice were relegated to the position of possible bonuses entirely reliant on the unlikely emergence of Young's (1999, 2007) consensual meritocracy within the fluid and unstable market system, perhaps one of Žižek's (2000) 'impossible dreams' that distract the radical imagination while protecting the para-politicians from the stigma of constantly failing to have anything real to offer. Back came the game of economic dynamism energised by harnessed chaos, an explosion of activity as myriad individual actors tried to cash in their recirculated promissory notes of unlimited personal freedom, pleasure and prosperity and seek their positions of social distinction. Nothing is more accomplished than the veteran power of liberal-capitalism in the art of manipulating the conditions of our existence in order to generate and harness apposite forms of individual desire.

Although we can accept the current and very timely critique of the 'counterculture' that we discussed earlier (Frank 1997; Heath and Potter 2007), it provides little insight into the source of the primal desire for 'positional goods' that signify social distinction, the raw form of psychosocial energy that fuels the whole process by catapulting the individual back and forth across the gap between rebellion and conformity. That both positions are unattainable as static singularities brings into being the unified, paradoxical and therefore dynamic position of 'social distinction'. This absence leaves us with the suspicion that the authors, along with Weber and Durkheim, might assume it to be an aspect of

Plato's *thymos*, the supposedly natural human proclivity that stands in a tripartite relationship to reason and desire and drives the individual to seek recognition among peers by taking part in noteworthy activities. However, even if indeed we are all slaves to *thymos*, surely we must question the idea that its current narrow, consumerist form is a true legacy from the past and acknowledge that it seems to be generating its psycho-emotional energy and socio-economic dynamism in a context of values and functions very different from those that structured the ancient or classic modern worlds. Arriving at parties in expensive cars and eye-catching outfits might furnish individuals with moments of socially elevating distinction and admiration, but it is hardly of the same order as holding off the Persian army at Thermopylae or coming up with a cure for cancer, which is just our rhetorical way of suggesting that the social values which inform distinction have changed quite radically; some might say they are significantly less demanding in the sense of the efforts and sacrifices that must be made by the individual (see Lasch 1991). Today's money-culture seems to encourage the short-circuiting of effort and sacrifice, which puts the cart before the horse in a crucial way that allows the imagination to bypass the symbolic order, which begins to disintegrate through disuse.

What is the generative source of consumerism's intense but rather narrowed down and domesticated form of thymotic energy? Is it simply the same fear of insignificance and lust for immortality that seemed to drive our ancestors? To begin to answer this question we must look briefly at the major alterations that occurred in the transition from the world of the warrior/producer to that of the consumer (Bauman 2001a). Baudrillard (1993) was unerringly right when he insisted that needs rooted in biology, function and cultural tradition have been displaced, or 'layered over', by those which are a product of the identities that structure consumerism's sign-system. Miller's (1987) claim that material goods, whether or not they function, are sought and displayed by individual consumers as signifiers of sexual display, or 'fitness indicators', suggests that the aesthetic and socially distinguishing aspects of the goods are now primary, while their technical functions, along with the character and deeds of the individuals who display them, are secondary. The advertising industry is alert to this – in fact some would argue that it was instrumental in bringing about this state of affairs (Frank 1997) – and within its production of signs, the functional utility of the goods and the character and reputation of the owner often come a poor second to the aesthetic display of the goods themselves, the way one 'wears' them (Barber 2007). This has established a fairly solid monopoly on identity construction and erotic attraction (Stratton 2001). The display of power and the performance of 'great deeds' and practical functions were once the basis of recognition and status for the 'heavy-weight' inhabitants of the significantly earthier class-structured cultures of our past (Hall 2000), but now elite class power and communal service have both been displaced by the more sublimated and unstable form of performance in the marketplace, which has now become 'sexy' and firmly associated with the aesthetic and erotic dimensions of culture. The threats of performative failure and symbolic insignificance now override the traditional threats of loss of reputation, functional redundancy and poverty as capitalism's main 'motivations'. Thus consumerism erodes all anterior senses of identity, respect and motivation grounded in customs, social class, and the service of communal/practical needs, and the actor is forced under threat to become constantly active in the tasks of performing in the market and creating an identity in the ornamental culture's aesthetic competition. Few regret the passing of an often brutal old world – although the question of whether or not it has really 'passed' will be brought up in the final chapter – but is what we have today a significant improvement? It seems that the terror of insignificance, of remaining unrecognised by others, might now reign supreme as the most potent and extractable source of human energy, and, for the majority of today's worker/consumers who will never perform 'exceptional deeds', significance is determined primarily by the ability to obtain and display the right type of consumer goods.

The major problem with most constructivist explanations of the consumerist dynamic is that they are based on a conception of the desiring individual as a weightless and flexible cipher in a system of signs, and thus they lack an analysis of the unconscious roots of desire and the connection between the body, the unconscious and the social (see Williams 2001). In order to be fully absorbed into consumerism, Deleuze and Guattari (1994) recognised that individuals must become 'desiring machines', although this was a rhetorical device rather than a serious analytical description; machines can produce neither symbols nor desire. What they meant was that the system required individuals who are 'machine-like' in the sense of being consistently and predictably energetic in their desire for endlessly proliferating consumer goods and symbolism. However, as we shall see shortly, such predictability and specificity are not the products of the allegedly inexhaustible energy of creativity, polymorphous desire or love of novelty, but dependent upon the formation of the unconscious in a specific mode of identification with external objects and signs in early childhood, and – as suggested by many of those who from a number of perspectives now see the need for a revived critical approach to consumerism – the maintenance of that mode throughout the subsequent stages of the life-course (Žižek 2000, 2007; Virilio 2005; Barber 2007; see also Lasch 1991, for a classic account).

This specific mode of identification and desire, motivated by the terror of helplessness and insignificance that afflicts each prematurely born and maladapted human being in early childhood, is, of course, *infantile narcissism*, and it creates and sustains precisely the types of unconscious desires and drives that consumer culture and its para-political civic life require. Most cultures that preceded consumerism were equipped with functional Symbolic Orders replete with the moral prohibitions and reality-testing mechanisms that can engender a maturation process. As the individual enters such an order the unconscious can be brought under control, and consequently the incessant and insatiable demands of the infantile narcissist tend to be pushed into the background throughout the later stages of the life-course (Žižek 2000), to be displaced by passions for art, science, politics and love (Badiou 2002). The infantile narcissist does not die, and lapses must be tolerated, but its mode of desire is eventually outweighed and diminished by more important and mature concerns. Thus we must suspect that consumerism somehow interferes with the maturation process, preventing the individual's interest from being drawn towards objects and signs – especially those which are ethically, politically or scientifically charged and thus attractive only to the mature individual – that lie outside the consumer sphere. The subject of consumerism must not meet prohibitions and demands that make too many Lacanian 'cuts' in the childish imagination and its ongoing process of narcissistic identification, allowing critical reflection and engendering a desire to move beyond the infantile desire that consumerism finds so useful. Thus the Law of the Father, the tradition at the heart of the Symbolic Order, must be defeated and prevented from reviving itself for reasons in relation to which the political challenge to the conservative patriarchal order – radical liberalism's great enduring crusade – appears to be secondary. Unfortunately, this means that any movement that assisted in the destruction of the old order without constructing a replacement also assisted in opening the floodgates through which consumerism and its infantilising culture poured (Barber 2007). Once fully unleashed, as it was in the 1960s, consumer culture simply betrayed, brushed aside and demolished the weak forces of the liberal-left, whose rather apologetic appeals to social justice and meritocracy and half-hearted support for the democratic socialist political movement that was attempting to *properly* replace the old order could not compete with consumer culture's immensely seductive imagery and economic dynamism in the competitive public tender to be the ultimate provider of security, freedom and pleasure. Although often accompanied by prematurely optimistic caveats warning of organic resistance about to burst forth from consumerism's frothy inferno any minute now, acknowledgement of the sheer extent of consumerism's victory and an accompanying urge to revive a critical approach to its totalising mission are beginning to seep back slowly into criminological theory:

> This relationship between consumer goods and the construction of self in late modernity is of great importance. So encompassing is the ethos of consumerism within (late) capitalist society that, for many individuals, self-identity and self-realisation can now only be accomplished through material means – money (in the form of commodities) as 'self laundering'? Thus, identity, as Christopher Lasch (1991) brilliantly pointed out, takes on the form of a 'consumption-oriented narcissism'. Twenty years after Lasch's seminal monograph, the full force of his message is only now being felt. (Hayward and Yar 2006)

To unpack this further we need to inspect concepts such as infantile narcissism and the Symbolic Order in more depth and detail. However, before we do, it is worth saying that we should not become too maudlin when exploring gloomy and sinister-sounding phenomena such as narcissism and fetishism. The fashion industry's breathless attempts to produce something 'distinctive' for the narcissist's wardrobe, and the glitches that occur in individuals' efforts to stroke the ego born of *amour-propre*, obey the fetish's commands and preen the body and its immediate living space into a beacon of social distinction and erotic attraction that leaves everyone else standing, can often be very funny indeed. However, the vital economic functions these phenomena perform in the maintenance of commodity circulation and the postponement of crisis by overproduction, downturn in demand, disinvestment and mass unemployment – along with the social atomisation, cultural degeneration and relentless psychological drives they help to bring into being – must be taken very seriously.

Heidegger (1962) was right that capitalism is 'unbearably radical', and Western radicalism's sociocultural process is not a product of the post-war era but is in fact very old, dating back to the liberal-individualist revolt against feudal, religious and state authorities during the birth of the capitalist/modernist project. Before Protestant asceticism really took root as the rather dour cultural ordering system (Mellor and Shilling 1997; Barber 2007), the original form of liberal-capitalist individualism was the prototype counterculture, wrapped up in its essentially bourgeois origin as the swashbuckling aristophile's search for social distinction as a spectacularly 'free' individual in the process of gentrification (Hall 2000, 2007). The psychosocial drive behind this long individualist revolution was much more complex and socially embedded than the crude notion of *thymos*. In Hegelian terms it was the mimetic quest of the slave for the master's recognition and an identification with the master's power, but using the more detailed Lacanian formulation we might speculate that it was a product of the aspiring entrepreneur's envious identification with an *ego ideal* that was inspired by the aristocratic warrior's surfeit of free time, space and autonomy, a space in which the individual could perform acts and cultivate marks of distinction in all aspects of the social: economy, politics, culture, war, sport, sexual conquest, charity and so on, but nevertheless a space that was physically and symbolically carved out at the expense of others, in the true tradition of *amour-propre*. There were two main ways of achieving individual distinction in the gaps opening up in the Symbolic Order's social prohibitions: first, the gentry's direct method of using money to mimic the aristocrat's wealth, power and status; the simulated aristocrat; and secondly, the theatrically shabby Bohemian's indirect method of aligning with the unaltered essence of aristocracy as it faded away in a valiant quixotic fight against the crassness of the new order of money, markets and technocracy; the undead aristocrat. What occurred in the post-war era was the final phase of the democratisation and diffusion of a cleverly constructed combination of these two principal techniques of identification as a method of prolonging narcissism and boosting consumerism; not a 'conspiracy', of course, simply a logical reworking of extant and traditionally seductive categories of rebellious identification. Rather than a break with feudalism, as Foucault (1980, 1991) and others suggested, we are witnessing the democratised and commercialised continuation of a historical line of culture and subjectivity that stretches into the dim past of the West's imperial settlements (Hall 2000), Veblen's barbarian order (1994), which of course Freud saw internalised as the rather violently impulsive and aggressively self-preserving core of the psyche around which cultural history has layered a protective and fragile insulation (Elias 2000; Mestrovic 1993).

The concept of 'self-preservation' is, of course, crassly instinctualist and simplistic (Fromm 1973); there are many ways to preserve the self and many complex feelings about why the self might regard itself as worthy of preservation, or not, as the case may be. We need a more detailed exploration of what lies at the unconscious core of the being that consumer capitalism and preceding forms of socio-economic organisation have tapped with such potent and surprisingly predictable results. This has been the subject of a protracted investigation by philosophy and science. Far too much has been written to discuss fully here, but perhaps we can pick up the story with Hegel's conception of the 'night of the world', the pre-symbolic domain of partially formed phantasmagorical drives, as the most deep and radical self-experience, depicted by the paintings of Bosch, Munch and others. This pre-exists language, and it has been named in today's cutting-edge neuroscience as the *proto-self*, the original disturbed animal that reacts to and registers the sensory irruptions of the real external world as a set of partially formed interactive emotions, feelings and images arranged around the basic friendly/hostile, seductive/repulsive dichotomies, seeking to either merge with them or destroy them in an attempt to return the organism to a condition of homeostasis (see Damasio 2003). Consumerism, like most other charismatic ideological and religious forms, seeks to keep this proto-self as alive and active as possible throughout the life-course as a constant energy source for the narcissist who emerges in a relationship of exclusive primary identification with the seductive and responsive objects of reality, preventing the symbolic law and the maturing subject's developing rationality and emotionality from leaving it behind to wither and reduce in significance.

Hegel (1979) talked about the 'sublation' of natural needs by cultural conventions, disconnecting satisfaction from nature and turning it into a set of 'lethal passions' that exist beyond the natural circular connection between needs and satisfactions. However, for us it was Jacques Lacan's neo-Freudian explorations that advanced this premise and furnished the intellectual world with the analytical tools required to make some sense out of consumer culture's 'capture' of the individual. The basis of Lacan's schema is *prematuration*, the biological fact that compared to most other animals humans are born too early and therefore immediately develop unavoidable proto-feelings of helplessness and incompleteness, which offers an explanation of neuroscience's observations of the proto-self's tendency to react with fearful emotions to the irruption of external disturbances upon the senses. The world is not made for the infant; it can be an uncomfortable and frightening place over which the infant feels no sense of control. Lacan (2006) argued very persuasively that the human being's mimicry of the environment as 'disguise' is not simply for survival, and thus it cannot be fully explained by Darwinian evolutionary biology. Following Roger Caillois (1961), Lacan argued that the organism is somehow 'captured' by the environment, perhaps for aesthetic reasons, an urge to lose the proto-self's fear or satisfy its sense of wonder in the act of unification or simply to be associated with other organisms who do seem to succeed in exercising some sort of control, and with the objects that are in turn associated with these others. Competent others and their objects together offer a symbolic sense of completeness and control that the helpless infant craves, and this is perhaps the basis of the primary desire to seek signs of recognition from them and identify with them. In order to construct some sort of preliminary understanding of this 'capture', and to relate it to our explanation of the young individual's capture by consumer culture, along with its criminological implications, we need an understanding of the three basic Lacanian realms: the Real, the Imaginary and the Symbolic.

The Real, the irruption into the senses of reality, the external world of objects in which the child finds itself, is unattainable in any symbolic sense; it is indeterminate and resists language and comprehension, yet it intrudes forcefully in the subject's sensory world. It is impossible to imagine and impossible to integrate into the Symbolic Order, the set of customary signs and moral prohibitions that, by cutting gaps in the Real and the Imaginary and providing chances for reflection, guides us through reality's disturbing irruptions and helps us to make at least *some* sense out of them and what we imagine them to be. Yet, as the proto-self – the alarm-system of Freudian self-preservation – is disturbed by the proximity of something that is not understood (Damasio 2003; Žižek 2000), it immediately becomes charged with powerful emotions and feelings. The Real cannot be known in language or imagination, yet its presence is felt, which initially makes it a source of terror and insecurity as well as wonder. The Real forcefully solicits the attention of the neurological and emotional core of the psyche, which could explain why the virtual reality of the systematically ambiguous yet ultra-realistic 'thing-images' that populate today's communications, entertainments and marketing strategies (see Lash and Lury 2007) – especially in the new generation of graphically sophisticated computer games (see Kirkpatrick 2005) – and the hyper-reality of our simulated theme-park existence grab the attention with so much power. In essence, virtual reality is an enduring simulation of those first irruptions of the Real's materiality that grabbed our fearful and wondrous intuition during the first six months of our lives; the preserver of infantile emotions and processes of identification *par excellence*. The Real is the basis for and the opposition to the Symbolic and the Imaginary. It is not 'reality' itself, the contents of the external world that are at least partially knowable in the phenomenological sense by means of symbols and concepts, but the structural effect of the disruption of the phenomenal world by the irruptive proximity of abstract and unknowable 'thingness', and the first glimmer of intuitive pre-symbolic self-knowledge is the incomplete and helpless being's fear of its inability to understand and cope with the mysterious irruptions of the Real.

The Imaginary reigns in the first six months of life as the human infant seeks a sense of completeness by identifying with images outside of itself. The ego constitutes itself in an early, alienating identification with these external images. This 'split' ego struggles against its sense of incompleteness by constructing a false and very fragile sense of completeness in a narcissistic identification with an important 'other' who first responds to the ego's demands for recognition, usually the mother. From the very beginning, the human psyche is trapped in a delusional treadmill, oscillating between the alienating external image, in which it sees itself recognised and reflected as something other than its real self, and a sense of its fragmented internal body. The Imaginary is comprised of unarticulated fantasy images and idealisations that build the ego and can eventually be articulated; the articulation of some of the deeper, more hidden and troubling content is the basic aim of psychoanalysis. As soon as it is articulated, according to orthodox psychoanalysis, it destroys itself and can be absorbed into the Symbolic Order, but this, of course, assumes that some sort of Symbolic Order that creates sufficient distance between itself and the Imaginary is in operation in the sociocultural world, which is one reason why psychoanalysis has perhaps been less successful for individuals inside the clinical setting yet far more successful when its principles are used in macro-cultural practices such as art, politics or mass-marketing, orders of symbols that must engage in struggle with each other for the subject's imagination. The Imaginary, in that sense, is fragile and because it is a constant seed-bed for the Symbolic it must keep remaking itself to maintain its existence, which it does internally with memory but also in its frequent contact with the irruptions of the Real, which are the primary sources for the contents of memory. Again, we can see how consumer culture, posing as the Real with the irruptive effects of its imposing audio-visual culture, can colonise the ongoing Imaginary by supplying it with constant irruptions to cut through its borders; the more forceful, spectacular and mysterious the better. Topologically, in its relationship to the other two orders, and diachronically, in the sense of the stage of child development in which it appears, the Imaginary is the intermediary between the experience of the Real and the eventual entry into the Symbolic Order.

Entry into the Symbolic Order should follow if the mirror stage and the Oedipal complex are successfully negotiated (see Lacan 2006: 75–81; Evans 1996; Žižek 2006a). In the mirror stage, a sense of self more complex than the proto-self and the narcissistic ego begins to emerge in the developing ability to distinguish the self from others, which commences a lifelong quest to return to the stage of primary narcissism where this differentiation did not exist. There is always an urge to regress pulling against the subject as it matures and joins the social order, where the salutary understanding that it is not the only self in the world dawns upon it and the super-ego develops alongside the more reflective ego to regulate the individual's social conduct. This goal of returning to the primary narcissistic relation is impossible, but a simulation of the goal is possible in the formation of the *imago* or *ideal ego* (not to be confused with the *ego ideal*), the fantasised image of the self that becomes the imaginary essence of identity and allows the subject to reduce real and symbolic differences to the difference between imaginary identities. We might suspect that consumer culture, recirculating the subject endlessly in a simulated journey back to what promises to be a primary narcissistic relation, is geared to the maintenance of the *imago* as a primary yet flexible means of identification. This allows the self's split ego to continue to imagine its difference, and thus create its self-identity, against the imaginary differences of others, preventing complete entry into the Symbolic Order and drawing energy from the subject as it incessantly repeats its attempts to achieve its impossible goal; consumer culture is, in other words, a supplier of a procession of *imago* models that promise to recognise and reflect the self in a primary narcissistic relation, yet, ultimately, are unable to keep their promises.

Following on from this it should not be too difficult to understand how consumer culture takes advantage of the fact that the mirror stage, which initially occurs between six and eighteen months, is not a stage that the subject passes through and leaves behind. Because the child's motor control, symbolic competence and understanding are undeveloped and it thus feels helpless in its efforts to understand or do anything about its situation in the Real beyond surrendering to its own feelings and imaginings, the mirror stage is restricted to vision and imagination. The child projects its imaginary and rather fearful conception of itself outwards where it recognises itself, either in a real mirror or in the imitative actions of someone else (Evans 1996: 190), as recognition by the other, usually the mother, which means that the child's concept of itself in its developing ego is split between itself and its double, although it nevertheless recognises both at the same time. The child's own reflection therefore becomes another irruption of the Real that floods the intuitive imagination with fear and wonder, but the intuitive perception of wholeness as the duality of the split ego unifies in the reflection is a source of trauma as it contrasts starkly with the proto-self's perception of its own helplessness, yet is also a source of potential comfort as the possibility of the unified and competent self is perceived if the child can become its reflection. This has many implications, but for our purposes the main one is that the child from this very early stage will develop an affection for and a wish to model itself upon whatever 'imagined other' – which is now a reflection of the self on the surface of another human being who seems whole and competent – more effectively recognises it and reflects back wholeness to its imagination and embryonic ego. It is very difficult to overestimate the power of identification in the imaginary order and its reverberation across the remaining life-course as it exerts 'a captivating power over the subject, founded in the almost hypnotic effect of the specular image' (Evans 1996: 83). Also, because it is based on the interchangeability of self and other and the primary *méconnaissance* (misunderstanding) this creates during the construction of the 'I', the childhood fantasy of self is inherently alienating. The subject is caught up in a captivating form of identification that takes it from a forlorn and fearful sense of bodily fragmentation to the fantasy of a complete yet alienated self, and thus 'the mirror stage is a drama whose internal pressure pushes precipitously from insufficiency to anticipation ... which will mark with its rigid structure the subject's entire mental development' (Lacan 2006: 78).

What occurs in the mirror stage is beyond the mere wishful thinking of the fantasising infant. The identification with the *ego ideal*, which is the wish to become *like* an admired other driven by an ego and super-ego that have matured as they enter the Symbolic Order and grapple with its prohibitions and reflexive gaps, is mild and tractable compared to the earlier dramatic identification with the *ideal ego*, which convinces the subject that it actually *is* the specular other. Thus it is this earlier phase of self-identification – with its much greater captivating power, which is sustained throughout the life-course as the subject strives to achieve the impossible goal of returning to it – in which the marketing industry via consumer culture attempts to intervene and keep intervening with all the techniques available to it. Because the mirror stage is so captivating and it is never truly left behind, consumerism can, right up to early adulthood, compete with its procession of *imagos* against all the significant others who represent family, community, art, science, politics and all other actors and institutions of the Symbolic Order, including the radical alternative Symbolic Order that could grow in the existing one as the embryonic antithesis in the Hegelian dialectic. A growing body of social critics from the Left (see, for example, Barber 2007; Bauman 2001b, 2007) are now arguing that with each passing generation mature adulthood is being delayed until later in the life-course. According to Virilio (2005: 94), we now live in a nursery, surrounded by the virtualised toys and games of overgrown spoilt children, the icons of infantilised fetishists who have no skill in the art of reflexively deciphering the content of their imaginations or existing like responsible adults in the finite and fragile real world:

As early as the first half of the twentieth century, Witold Gombrowicz and a number of his contemporaries had noted that the mark of modernity was not growth or human progress, but rather the refusal to grow up. 'Immaturity and infantilism are the most effective categories for defining modern man,' Gombrowicz wrote. After the telescopic metamorphoses of Alice, we had reached the Peter Pan stage – the stage of the child stubbornly determined to escape his future. It seemed no longer possible to make the transition to adulthood, which was primordial in ancient societies, in a civilisation in which everyone carried on playing without any age limit ... anyone or any activity which did not have aspects of puerility would be dubbed 'elitist' and rejected as such.

To gain advantage in the competition with the Symbolic Order and its inbuilt maturation process, consumer culture must manipulate its objects and their associated iconography to a position in the line of vision where they, complete with their signifying and distinguishing objects, appear to be the most 'competent others', the most successful performers and therefore the most efficient and enthusiastic reflectors of wholeness to young people in crucial stages of their life-courses. In that case the most effective strategy is to gain control over the life-course stages themselves by using mass-media and other marketing techniques as providers of the most paradoxically fearful and wondrous, disturbing and seductive irruptions of the Real to create an Imaginary populated by suitably competent and responsive *imagos*, with which young people who are painfully aware of their continuing incompleteness can sustain the enduring promise of the recovery of narcissistic identification. However, since this recovery is impossible, the feeling of incompleteness is sustained in the constantly shifting contexts of consumer culture in preparation for capture by another *imago* that promises to perform the task, and so on *ad infinitum*. What we can see clearly here is a process of identification that allows the most potent and competent aspects of the contextual environment into which the infant experiences the early stages of its development to capture its emotional allegiance in a form that endures across the life-course. The structural essence of the series of images, as a pivot of successful performance, can therefore represent the central value that the agents of liberal-capitalism's Symbolic Order wish to promote: the master-signifier of the rugged, 'off-road' hyper-individualist competing in the market and eschewing all forms of collectivism and collectivist politics – the attractive, exciting but essentially apolitical and immature reluctant citizen known as the 'cool dude'.

Thus the consumer subject's fantasising ego, just to remain as what it thinks it is, becomes trapped in the illusion of difference as it is driven to gather more and more superficially different instances of the impossible, alienating *imago* as they are carefully circulated in front of it. This extends an intensified form of narcissism right across the subject's life-course in liberal-capitalist culture (Lasch 1991; Virilio 2005; Barber 2007). Homogeneity appears as difference and mundanity as enchantment, and each 'quilting point' of identification is initially felt to be a success that soon fades into disappointment, which drives the subject to seek yet another isomorphic resemblance. It is at this point that the narcissist also becomes a fetishist as it is driven in the unending quest for the objects that express 'different' aspects of what it thinks it should be. The twist here is, of course, that the principal icon in the capitalist collection, the collective *ego ideal*, is the 'cool', successful individualistic performer in the market, and the powerful current of mimetic admiration merges with the *ideal ego* as it is represented in our culture as the iconic representation of the fantasy of the complete person. Thus in this merger and takeover all traditional forms of *ego ideal* are overpowered. Parents and peers are forced to comply with it in the process of mutual misrecognition if the wish to be simultaneously the other in which the subject can recognise itself and the subject that can recognise itself in the other is to be fulfilled; in other words, if parents and peers seek relations of mutual respect with the young consumer subject they must imperson- ate the structural value at the centre of the system's preferred form of subjectivity. Children are empowered and parents risk disempower- ment, so everyone must act like a 'cool dude'. The subject's *ego ideal* thus becomes a continuation of the fantasising child's *ideal ego* and the critical break that could possibly occur, as the process of misrecognition is partially corrected in the Oedipal stage, is neutralised by the homogen- ising effect of the fact that the consumer capitalist Symbolic Order's core icon is a concatenation of stylised resemblances – and, latterly, an opportunity to create one's own from the memory of one's previous imaginings – of the fantasising child's original *ideal ego*. For the subject weaned on its images, consumer iconography is thus an endlessly expanding procession of isomorphic variations of the original fantasy of the complete self as it was created by the original recognition in and identification with the core icon as the quintessential representation of completeness. There is no 'true self' to find, but, if we are to understand the constitution of the subject, we must leave behind the myth that the subject's primary and durable form of identification is its entry into language and the Symbolic Order; Lacan did not mean that in a way unqualified by all that occurs *before* that stage.

Thus the Imaginary, with its narcissistic process of identification, is the primary site for the formation of the durable identity preferred by an enclosed system of fantasies such as manufactured consumer culture. In the absence of an imposing Symbolic Order that provides the critical language necessary to cut reflective gaps in the Imaginary, the narcissist can continue into adult life to confront a world of images and language that actually reinforce its phantasmagorical identity, rather than chal- lenging it with the demands of maturation. Lacan took Saussure's concept of the arbitrary relationship between the signifier and signified as the basis for his theory of the way that the social operates as an essentially symbolic form, a principle he borrowed from Mauss and Levi-Strauss. It is the signified, the mental image triggered by the signifier, which is influenced by both biographical experience and cultural hegemony. Barthes (1972) used this relation as the basis of his concept of the connotative order. What is important here is to recognise that in vital ways the intuitions and fantasies underneath the signified in the connotative order precede the reception of the signifier, which means that there are pre-existing emotional tendencies to interpret signs in specific ways, and, without the vital support of a healthy alternative Symbolic Order, the narcissistic subject's ability to resist in the realm of the signifier is not as well developed as orthodox reception theorists such as Stuart Hall (1988) suggest. The presence of such emotions and preferred fantasies – which by now we can call not just narcissistic but fetishistic in their search for objects that signify in ways that reflect aspects of the imaginary self – places the subject in a position of extreme interest but also hermeneutic restriction when interpreting signs that reflect the imaginary self, and extreme disinterest in signs that do not.

Consumer culture is underpinned by the triumph of the inherently unstable syntagmatic metonym (Jakobson 1956; Evans 1996) over the more stable paradigmatic metaphor. Jakobson's concept of the split between the paradigmatic order and the syntagmatic order was based on the recognition of two distinct types of aphasia that afflicted some people. The paradigmatic axis is based on metaphor, the fixing of meaning by substitution, while the syntagmatic axis is based on the order in which signifiers are combined. In the standard textbook interpretation (see Fiske 1989) the signifier, as a striking material representative of other signifiers that represent abstract concepts, often designated by the 'logic of the concrete', passes over from the denotative order to the connotative order where it invokes a mental image, suggested by the metaphor's vehicle, to the object in mind. The metaphor is the fundamental building block of the split ego in the Imaginary because it works by compression, substitution and resisting full symbolism. Where the paradigmatic order and the metaphor are based on the synchronic substitution of signifiers that carry a similar meaning, the syntagmatic order is based on the diachronic ordering of different metaphors that carry different meanings. As a horizontal movement or slippage (*glissement*) along the chain of signification, it perpetually defers meaning (one of the bases of Derrida's (1976, 1978) *differance*); unless it is a transparent cliché from near the beginning, the meaning is not clear until the chain comes to a halt, like the revelation in the final paragraph of a detective story. This is the order where complex meaning is created, but it is inherently unstable. Only at specific 'quilting points' where imaginary identification is allowed to cut through does the necessary illusion of a fixed meaning emerge as a temporary clarification (Žižek 2006a; Evans 1996) where the deep meaning of the metaphor can disrupt the integrity of the Symbolic Order.

Without these anchor points the whole signifying chain can dissolve into psychotic self-referentiality, where the metaphorical reference to the Real is lost. Desire could be seen as the wish of the subject, as it is drawn along the chain of signification and its deferred meanings, to reach anchor points and regain its metaphorical hold on the Imaginary's now legendary narcissistic identification with its reflection in the Real. In a stable social order of meaning, this means that the subject will always be drawn back to the initial recognition of the self by the mother and other significant primary carers, and, as a supportive point of recognition, identity and symbolic reflection, the subject's post-Oedipal entry into the Big Other, the set of social prohibitions, laws and customs that reproduce and are represented by the Symbolic Order. The unstoppable diachronic movement of the signifying chain prevents fixity of meaning between signifier and signified or sign and referent, and prevents the settlement of meaning between signifieds in the chain itself. It is a temporal movement that must give the subject the seductive impression that meaning, and thus the meaning of the self and its place in the world, might be waiting at some point in the future. This, of course, energises desire. Unless the Symbolic Order can prohibit the flow by inserting positive quilting points, the subject remains caught up in it. It is not necessarily a linear flow, an impression that our common understanding of modernity and our life-courses as constant progress might give us, and it can move in either direction, endlessly returning to the infantile binary primal symbolisation between the presence and absence of the first objects that the self recognises as recognising itself, to the extent that each shift in signification can be a repetition of it. However, because each signified presence in the binary scheme marks an absence that haunts it, desire is always combined with the alienation that shadows it in the subject's relationship with all other objects that it encounters.

Signifiers seek affirmation by a signified, which, in the case of the human subject that has already begun its process of subjectivisation with intuitive reactions to the original disturbance of the proto-self, the innate sense of lack and incompleteness and the split ego's narcissistic identification with the *imago*, already exists in a proto-hermeneutic form; that is, a form already in a state of emotional prefabrication with tendencies to select specific signifiers out of their paradigmatic and syntagmatic struggle with each other for distinction and apply to them specific interpretations. The total arbitrariness of the relationship of 'slipping signifiers' to each other, the basis of post-structuralism, cannot exist in a world of subjects in pre-existing emotional states; that arbitrariness will always be tempered and shaped by already existing hermeneutic tendencies. The real twist here is that the pre-symbolic emotional condition of the proto-subject, if it can be prolonged in such a way that it does not drift too far in the background, fuels the dominant bourgeois-individualist culture. The narcissistic desire for the significant other – as well as the desire to be the significant other's object of desire and to desire and be the desire of the objects that the significant other desires – is harnessed *via* the intrusion of the Master Signifier of the 'cool individual' to fuel a quest for recognition by acquiring the signifiers of distinction in a rebellious posture that is actually a fake that masks absolute conformity to the tamed and harnessed rebellion that is capitalism's economic driver and the real grounded and socially structured identity of the Master Signifier itself. We are left with a process of prefabricated arbitration as consecutive generations of subjects are trapped by the fetishistic desire to continually seek distinctive signifiers to 'feed their habit'. Thus a stable socio-political Symbolic Order is impossible as it is kept in permanent kaleidoscopic flux by the fundamental desire shared by the bulk of its subjects as they seek the signifiers of fake distinction. The narcissist-fetishist's sheer disinterest in symbols and discourses that say nothing about his imaginary split self is thus capable of collapsing a whole traditional Symbolic Order and its potential of dialectical change into a liberating political movement because it fails to say anything complimentary or comforting about his new cool image. Hegel's third-stage *negation of the negation* commences just before the vital second stage negation gets off the ground; goodbye and good riddance to everything that fails to reflect my imaginary 'I'.

Despite this capture of the narcissistic ego by its sources of reflection and recognition in the environment, and the durability of the wish to sustain the attractive option of primary narcissistic identification, in a healthy culture with a rich and mature Symbolic Order all is not lost. The Symbolic is the site of language, the sludge of slipping signifiers that refer to each other and to the signified in the connotative order's receptacle. At the end of the mirror stage, although the primary fantasy does not disappear, accession to the Symbolic Order should at least provide the individual with the linguistic and conceptual means of reflecting critically on the fantasy itself, its source, its functions, its politics and its consequences for the self's autobiographical future. During the entry into the Symbolic Order at the end of the dominance of the mirror phase and at the beginning of the Oedipal phase, the child, who has become accustomed to the pleasure of primary narcissistic identification with his mother's body and her recognition of his identity and physical needs, must accept that the father's rights to the mother's body take precedence. This is the first experience of the deep prohibition of primary desire, much more profound than the minor behavioural prohibitions that the parents and significant others have already introduced. This is not the prohibition of affective bodily contact but the withdrawal of what the child imagines to be exclusive rights to pleasure and identification through pleasure and the traumatic realisation that the primary object also recognises and gives pleasure to others. This paternal intervention, expressed verbally, is the first indication that the Law is constituted by prohibitions and taboos that disallow narcissistic identification as the primary sense of being, but in doing so it opens up the reflective, symbolic gap in the narcissistic connection between the Imaginary and the Real. In simple terms, this is a command to 'put away those childish things', to start growing up and engaging with symbolism that allows reflection of the self as a social being; to grow up and consider others. It demands entry into the structure of laws and language that constitute the Symbolic Order as a social code. Better the infant enters a conservative Symbolic Order – with the hope that he or she might one day turn its linguistic-conceptual tools back on it in a dialectical challenge – than none at all. The alternative is the narcissist's joyride driven by the fetishistic command to circle permanently around objects associated with others who seem to offer vague recognition of the self and represent a concrete form of competence in the immediate environment.

Put simply, this should be the first stage of maturation, of growing up. Engagement with the world should transcend the sensory irruptions of the Real and the narcissistic fantasies of the Imaginary to reach a position where the subject can mobilise phenomenological concepts to represent reality in increasingly sophisticated ways as part of a truth project (see Badiou 2002). Maruna (2001) noticed that whereas persistent offenders were fatalistic, deterministic, backward-looking and needed the 'lucky strike' or 'big score' to stop offending, desisters tended to adopt an evangelical posture regarding the subject's ability to reject a fake former self and rediscover the 'real self' in an act of redemption. The desisters had found solace in a personalised Symbolic Order and a renewed autobiographical self-narrated path, marked by newly discovered prohibitions, towards a new purpose. This echoes the need for alternative objects, truth-projects and visions that can inspire emotional commitment. Critical conceptualisation of what exists is the wellspring of the Hegelian dialectic, and nurturing this ability should always be the main task of education in schools, families and communities. However, if consumer culture's iconography – introduced to the subject as the structural significant others' primary symbolic objects of desire – remains in place as the unconditional and flexible reflector of the primary narcissistic fantasy, the work of the mother and other significant others who attempt to introduce the child into the Symbolic Order at the end of the mirror stage can be undone, which threatens the reproduction of the orthodox Symbolic Order and its radical potential. This destruction is backed by liberal postmodernism, whose agents accentuate the relativistic and mythological aspects of mental and cultural life, working towards the evaporation of the very idea of a Symbolic Order, with all its political truth projects, orthodox or radical.

The failure to enter the Symbolic Order means that the subject never really learns what is impossible, and only by doing this can the individual become a true subject rather than a narcissistic ego-self prone to immersion in proliferating fantasies. What the Symbolic Order designates as impossible must be tested in reality, as Freud said, but at least the true subject has a rough guide. This is what Žižek (2000, 2007) is referring to when he notes that the politicians' constant offer to perform what is impossible under the current politico-economic circumstances is the basis of the continuation of liberal-postmodernist para-politics because it prevents the emergence of the prohibitions with which a dialectical shift in the political order could be mobilised, thus creating a cynical population, prone to ritual, that stops caring anyway (see also Sloterdijk 1988). The constant breaking of promises is a winning strategy. However, more importantly for us, the subject's failure to enter the Symbolic Order and communal-political life as a citizen (see Barber 2007) ends up in a life dominated by the desires of the primary narcissistic fantasy, its carefully manufactured resemblances and its fetishistic drive to obtain the objects that reflect, affirm and comfort the alienated 'imaginary I'.

The child's provocations constitute a demand to set a limit, a product of the underlying desire to be recognised by the agent of a Symbolic Order. The limit does not repress but liberates the subject; it is the possibility of unlimited desire represented by close proximity to the endless appearance, irruption and disappearance of circulating objects that terrifies and suffocates the subject:

> [F]ar from frustrating us simply because it sets no limits, *the absence of explicit limitation confronts us with the limit as such, the inherent obstacle to satisfaction*; the true function of the explicit limitation is thus to sustain the illusion that, through transgressing it, we can attain the limitless. (Žižek 2006b: 296, original italics)

The Kantian project was about self-governance, to replace the external Master after passing through the Symbolic Order to absorb its prohibitive techniques; the mature human being is a self-limiting individual capable of achieving satisfaction when the limit is reached and she is no longer in need of a Master. However, no transgression of the narcissistic identity is possible without preliminary prohibitions that break up the happy couple of the ego and its primary *imago*, and not only does the Symbolic Order sever the relationship but it creates desire in the absence of what it has destroyed. The child has no *choice* but to grow up at the same time as it develops the absence-constituted *desire* to grow up, as the narcissistic rug is pulled from under its feet. The symbolic father's intervention creates a rivalry that, if sensitively handled, creates the possibility for a reflexive, critical relationship with cultural customs and commands. If intervention is firm and accompanied by the rapid assimilation of linguistic skills that eventually move the child's powers of understanding from the concrete to the abstract (Piaget 1966), the child cannot recoil from the intervention and return to the cloying comfort of the narcissistic relation, it must go forward into a Symbolic Order that has offended against it and must be accepted or resisted with a gradually maturing means of symbolic dissent. The Symbolic Order, which originates in the social tradition and is thus inherently and unavoidably inter-subjective, insists on communication, opening channels between its members. This propels the slightly wounded but rapidly more self-assured and sociable child towards the political, and hopefully towards the dialectic as he or she wishes to 'kill' the Big Other that the father represents yet simultaneously becomes immersed in its techniques of meaning; this risks the reproduction of the tradition, but it also creates the possibility of informed, collective and potent opposition.

Entry into the Symbolic Order thus opens an initially painful gap in the primary narcissistic relation, in which the subject must accept the impossibility of returning to its condition of closure and the comforts of the mother's body, the constant reflection of the self in the *imago* and the associated feelings of pleasure and relief. It is here that consumer culture offers its initial compensation, the maintenance of an *imago* in its reflective objects, which also represents the structural Master Signifier and can stay with the subject for the rest of the ride. Thus the transition from the Imaginary to the Symbolic, from the period of the mysterious and alienated external self to the period of the mystery solved and the alienation cured by the attachment of words and meanings, is now largely arranged by consumer capitalism's marketing apparatus, operating *in loco parentis*. Not only does this prolong the reign of the narcissistic ego, it also recruits the developing super-ego, transforming the source of guilt from the failure to engage creatively with the Symbolic Order's prohibitions to the failure to sustain the desire for narcissistic identification with the imaginary Ideal and its Master Signifier of the cool, hedonistic individual, along with its associated symbolic objects:

> The disintegration of paternal authority has two facets. On the one hand, symbolic prohibitive norms are replaced by imaginary ideals ... on the other, the lack of symbolic prohibition is supplemented by the re-emergence of ferocious superego figures. So we have a subject who is extremely narcissistic – who perceives everything as a potential threat to his precarious imaginary balance ... 'post-modern' subjectivity thus involves a kind of direct 'superegoization' of the imaginary Ideal caused by a lack of proper symbolic Prohibition. (Žižek 2000: 368)

The Real remains mysterious and external, as the source of *jouissance*, that which exists outside of symbolisation and meaning, yet which keeps returning to stimulate unbearable excitations in our unconscious drives, promising satisfaction yet never delivering it, and making many excursions into the painful reality just beyond its Real. The mass-media's icons represent the mystery of the Real and its outlying reality. They seem to be living real lives and achieving real satisfaction by performing as successful competitors in the market and owning and displaying consumer culture's symbolic objects, yet the subject of consumerism constantly fails to emulate them in achieving that satisfaction, coming back obsessively time and time again. The symbols that can shed some light on reality, and reveal so many of its mysteries as spectral impostors, have been foreclosed, and the subject is lost in its repetitive fantasies. There is no resistance, because the seductive and dangerous force of *jouissance* combines pain and discontent with a sense that it is in the subject's own best interests to live its whole life suffering the repetitive pangs of desire. All the traditions that minimised *jouissance* as a primary drive have been abolished. Lacan's schema cannot be reduced to language, as it often is; the relationship of language to *jouissance*, the form in which the Real enters the psyche, is still the primary research problem.

Conflicts between the id's pleasure principle and the super-ego's prohibitions can usually be maintained by the secret codes that forge the relationship in the unconscious, supported by the ego's consequentialist reality principle. However, at the extremes of consumerism's sociocultural order the subject is driven beyond the pleasure principle – which, because too much pleasure is painful, is not unlimited – by the reoriented super-ego's injunction to take enjoyment beyond its limits, to gorge the self with pleasure; put very simply, the super-ego that once made us feel guilty about doing excessive and risqué things now makes us feel guilty about *not* doing them. With the super-ego now reoriented from the repression of desire to the repression of that which represses desire, the subject, as Wouters (2002) recognised, now relies more on the ego's awareness of consequences as 'risks' to control its actions. Unless the ego is very strongly developed in the socialisation process and the subject is truly in awe of society's formal prohibitions, the subject can often lose the battle with the super-ego that has displaced and reworked the standard libidinal desires of the id with its own morally charged drives, and which now seeks to repress the prohibitive aspects of the Symbolic Order, to repress the repressive mechanism, collapsing the Lacanian 'gap' and sustaining the subject as an anxious narcissist-fetishist. Žižek (2000: 367) suggests:

As we become dedicated to pleasure we become subjects of permanent anxiety, haunted by our potential failure to achieve the ultimate experience, and thus the . . . direct injunction 'Enjoy!' is a much more effective way to hinder the subject's access to enjoyment than the explicit Prohibition which sustains the space for its transgression.

The net loss of pleasure is now caused not by repression but by the painful experience of *jouissance* as the subject is propelled towards its realm, and in a cultural process of *desublimation* the traditional sublimation of libidinal energy becomes less important as unrestricted gratification becomes more routine in the commercial market. The end result is the fetishist whose painful experience is negated and whose aim is fulfilled by endlessly circulating through desire, pleasure and *jouissance*, circling the quasi-objects of desire that are formed by the moral injunction of the commodity. The symbolic gap is closed, and the subject becomes a lover of consumer culture's hyper-reality, the realm where the Imaginary and the Real have achieved closure, negating the Symbolic and replacing the sublimated Eros, the glue of friendship (fraternity) that holds society together, with the fetishist's unending lonely pilgrimage. Others simply become obstacles if they get in the way or temporary companions if they share the same tastes and methods of circulation.

Braithwaite's (1989) theory of crime reduction relies on the self-regulating conscience and its ability to be shamed. But now the super-ego is very different, no longer the exclusive creation of violence repressed and directed back into the subject, but a new hybridised mechanism wherein desire compelled by the 'new conscience' to seek its object is deflected back inside by its painful experiences in the realm of *jouissance*, where it merges with violence, both symbolic and, in some circumstances, real (see Žižek 2008) as it is propelled back outside as 'aggressive desire'. Put simply, the 'new conscience' has merged with the aggressive instinct that it has traditionally repressed. The conscience is overdeveloped, to be sure, not in the classic Adornian mode of the authoritarian personality, but in the new consumerist mode as a sling to propel aggressive desire back into hyper-reality as soon as inevitable disappointment causes it to recoil back inwards. This is, of course, the extreme, the pure consumerist ideal-type, but there is no doubt that where engagement with the market economy is at its most direct and enthusiasm for consumerism is at its most fervent, this new psycho-economic process is showing signs of displacing standard psychodynamic and psychosocial processes. The libertine quest to disrupt the principle of the Symbolic Order to eliminate traditional forms of prohibition, repression and guilt is not destroying society, as reactionary conservatives feared, but dissolving society for the purpose of merging it, with all its symbolism and desire, with the consumer economy.

Chapter 9

Conclusion: consumerism, crime and the pseudo-pacification process

As the data has clearly demonstrated, the lives of our interviewees were firmly framed by advanced capitalism's culture of ornamental consumerism, a shifting hierarchy of fantasised identities disembedded from practical reality and politics and only tenuously connected to traditional ethics (see Bauman 1995, 2001b). Even those who didn't display the energetic, 'go-getting' acquisitive ethos of the committed street criminal continued to conjure dreams of big-time criminality as an abbreviated means of obtaining symbols of social distinction, which were of vital importance to the individual in his field of social struggle. None of our respondents perceived themselves to be occupying a position of 'social exclusion', but constantly expressed a desire and a resolute determination to obtain symbols that reflected their fantasised identities back to themselves, and which represented their identities to others as individuals distinguished from the shameful 'losers', 'mugs' and 'muppets' who littered their living spaces. Their social identities and dreams were animated by the ambitions and symbols of *amour-propre*. Their central concerns reflected the attention-seeking narcissism deliberately cultivated by the post-war marketing industry. They dreamt of a pile of money just ahead, from a windfall, a big deal, a crime or a highly remunerative job that would miraculously come their way. They dreamt of moving up the mainstream ladder with extreme rapidity, surprising everyone around them, winners and losers alike, and shoving their success in everyone's face with a sudden and extreme bout of conspicuous consumption. The sole shame was in being seen to lose in the game and the sole merit was in being seen to win, and this was the only game in town. So complete has been the destruction of traditional culture, collective identity and politics in our interviewees' corners of the world that they were quite simply unable to identify with the urban poor of which they had been lifetime members, a position in which most of them were likely to remain for the foreseeable future. If our portrayal appears to be one-dimensional, which would be the predictable critique, all we can say is that, compared to consumer culture and a few vestigial aspects of local traditions, the influence of alternative sociocultural institutions – regional traditions, community, education, religion, politics and so on – on our interviewees' world-views was, to say the least, minimal.

Of course, 'social exclusion' has a phenomenological existence in the structural metaphors of sociologists and social administrators, and it's even possible to argue – depending on one's philosophical persuasion (see Hollis 1994) – that it has an objective existence in social reality. However, in the absence of a popular perception among the excluded themselves it is politically inactive, an extinct volcano, a useful illustration of why radical philosophy has shifted over the past fifteen years or so to the question of radical subjectivity and how it can be inspired to bring itself into being in the 'absent centre of political ontology' (see Žižek 2000). Like hydrogen, radical subjectivity has no natural existence on earth, and for over two hundred years radical political thought has been hampered by the assumption that it has; just like hydrogen must be manufactured, radical subjectivity must be inspired.

Nor could we detect any perception or understanding that an unfair socio-economic system might be the root of their problems, or that others like them were once part of a subjugated class, which has a long cultural history and until relatively recently had been in the process of politically constituting and asserting itself, even if the eventual purpose of this activity was its own partial dissolution as humanity attempted to elevate itself to an ethically higher plane of existence (see Badiou 2002). When we assessed the sum total of our data we were forced to conclude that 'social justice' has joined 'social exclusion' as little more than a memento of a previously active socio-political force. This was a life motivated by the individual's perception of a constant struggle with hostile others in a dog-eat-dog world, a 'war of all against all' in a Hobbesian state of nature. This situation is, of course, highly criminogenic, not in the sense of direct mechanistic causality but in the sense that if all else fails there is very little in the way of normative restriction on criminality as a particular means to a general end.

Extreme derogation of 'Aldi-bashers' and 'skip-rats' contrasted sharply with extreme veneration of the ability of sharp criminal businessmen to display symbols of status beyond plutocracy as the new aristocrats creating a brutal order in the midst of the market's 'creative destruction', especially those involved in the drug-trade. Echoing times past, the slaves seemed to be turning on themselves rather than the master and the master's system (Ames 2007), which the majority under decades of mass-mediated cultural hegemony have come to admire deeply and regard as natural and ethical; if the Old Left didn't know that the ontological centre of political subjectivity is hollow the New Right certainly did. Given the force of neo-liberal ideology over the past thirty years of its restoration, it is perhaps unsurprising that selections of flexible maxims and norms which predate the social democratic era are returning as the principal strategic means of dealing with dominant liberal-capitalist values and systemic imperatives. Our respondents showed a lack of trust in others, presuming them to be 'all out for themselves', and regarded life as an unforgiving business in which 'number one' must look after himself, a patchwork of temporary contracts that carry no guarantees and an ethical tradition that is at best makeshift and flexible. The constant endeavour to cultivate an aura and reputation of violence, or at least abrasive 'no-nonsense' toughness, was motivated by this mistrust and fear. Despite all the risks of hostility, violence and punishment that accompany crime, and a landscape littered with humiliated others who failed to make the grade, most of our respondents refused to doubt that one day very soon they would take their place among the tiny few who have 'made it'. Even those whose constant failure engendered a degree of fatalism just carried on doing it anyway, just in case their luck might change; in the absence of the ability to plan (Bauman 2001b) or even foresee a course of events, they had little choice but to keep on feeling lucky about the imminence of some vague upturn in their lives.

For our interviewees, the traditional social, political and ethical dimensions of life have virtually evaporated, and the personal trajectory appears in front of the narcissistic individual as the whole way and purpose of life, a narrow economised tunnel stretched into a complete cultural vista. The concept of relative deprivation, although perhaps quite adequate as a description of an objective socio-economic relation, is inadequate as a subjective motivation or 'cause of crime' because the linguistic, psychosocial and ethical contexts required for it to exist as a viable perceptual category among those who inhabit the objective position of relative deprivation itself are either impoverished or entirely absent. Our interviewees did not sense themselves to be the 'deprived victims' of social injustice, simply because there are no victims, there is no social, and there is no justice. Instead we are faced with the cold recognition that these supposed 'deprived victims' have in fact been drawn into a systemic struggle of the narcissists, with its simple Luhmannesqe (see Luhmann 1986) binary categories of luck and bad luck, cunning and stupidity, losers and winners. All that is left is a sense of distance from 'the bottom', which must be increased at all costs. 'The bottom' was understood in relation to a fantasy of life at the top, but those who populated the upper echelons were not yardsticks and certainly not the source of ethically driven discontent; they were 'arseholes' too, just like everyone else. It was the position of social distinction and the symbols and images it provided that were admired, rather than the actual individuals who occupied the position. This enabled our respondents to admire the symbolic constitution of the position and the strategies used to achieve it while resenting the actual individuals who occupied it. Our respondents were their own judges, and the judges of all others, and their narcissism allowed them to recognise only those others who reflected their images in ways they found satisfactory. To be judged harshly was thus a form of misrecognition on the part of the judge, not the product of a social hierarchy; the judge was a fool for misrecognising the self as a loser or a member of a 'lower class'. The sense of authority required for judgement is generated by the narcissistic belief that as one is reflected perfectly in one's *ideal ego* one already is a member of the upper echelons (or, with a bit of luck, very soon will be). Rather than simply admiring the elite in the way of the mature *ego ideal* and harnessing admiration as a spur for one's efforts, the *ideal ego* provokes the subject to exert far more pressure on itself for instant success and recognition in the order of signs. The far more potent fear of falling from an imaginary position has largely displaced the traditional fear that one will be unable to rise from the reality of a lowly position, thus sustaining the most perverse, misleading and politically destructive fantasy of them all; despite existing at the bottom of the pile, the subject sees itself one lucky break away from the top and thus unable to forge any political allegiance with the 'mugs' who, compared to oneself, really *are* at the bottom. This, we suggest, is a product of the false ideology of liberal 'rights' and 'equal opportunities' coupled with the narcissistic fantasies of consumer culture, because, of course, there are now allegedly no real systemic reasons why one should not reach the top, a sentiment regurgitated *ad nauseam* by mass-mediated popular culture. The advantage with which this situation furnishes the consumer economy is that everyday consumer products and their settings are now loaded with the vital symbolic meaning that can sustain the individual's relationship with the *imago*, for which individuals are willing to struggle and pay. The accompanying advantages for neo-liberalism are that collective identity and politics have crumbled into dust, and whatever once was social is now atomised, fantasised and politically neutralised. The disadvantage for us all is that in biographical, geographical and cultural situations where normative restrictions are weak and risks are worth taking, crime is possibly the most efficient way of obtaining the symbols required for the narcissist's dream of social distinction.

This paradoxical mix of fatalism and optimism expressed by many of our interviewees resulted in a cynical, nihilistic, occasionally dystopian and fatalistic yet highly enthusiastic world-view, but this bundle of conflicting sentiments tended to be oddly split: not simply between the social and the individual, but between ethics and hedonism. On the one hand, pessimistic fatalism was reserved for the chances of the individual or the social life-world getting anywhere at all in the furtherance of some sort of ethico-political project, while on the other, optimism was reserved for the opportunities for hedonistic excess and social distinction that might present themselves on the road to nowhere. The expectation of self-interest on behalf of others was so pervasive and naturalised that to pass it off as a 'technique of neutralisation' (Sykes and Matza 1957) – in other words an excuse, made after the event, for the individual's criminal act – or simply an overdramatised conception of the life-world and its inhabitants, is wholly inadequate. It was natural, accepted and therefore unimportant, as was getting constantly caught and prosecuted, which, of course, diminishes the individual's reputation as a criminal and a 'smart' individual. None of this really mattered; paramount was the money that can be earned from the stolen items and then converted into the appropriate consumer object bought from the appropriate place. Simply being able to buy the object in the right place, and being able to conspicuously display the object to let it be known as widely as possible that this prestigious 'magic moment' of consumption had actually occurred, was the primary goal, the real mark of distinction, the fetish that overrode all other considerations. As we explained, this 'goal' was not really a goal at all but the *aim* of the fetishist, which is to circulate endlessly around the 'goals' represented by consumerism's system of ever-changing objects of desire. In this way, the act of consumption/display was never over and done with, never complete, because the consumer fetishist must also let it be widely known that he or she will always be capable of performing this act of stylish purchase as many times as the incessantly turning wheel of the fashion industry dictates. The availability of relatively cheap consumer items and the ability to adopt and rework mainstream styles were not aids to liberation but to the multiplication of fetishistic moments of consumption.

To most of our interviewees, respect as a competent or feared criminal was not the primary objective but merely an agreeable addendum, a bonus that rendered the main prize all the more alluring. If the constant attempt to satisfy the consumer fetish was best served by shoplifting, then shoplifting it was; prestigious forms of crime were preferred but not essential. The individual could always imagine that the item had been bought in a prestigious shop and imagine that others will believe that too. The adventure, excitement and potential violence that could be experienced when committing more prestigious crimes was also preferred, and it added to the repute and mystique of the individual, but again this existed in a *secondary layer* of desire that our respondents had few regrets about bypassing if it required a major detour on the road to the fantasised destination. Desired objects could be either stolen or paid for with the proceeds of theft, but the latter was seen as a 'progression' and seemed to be preferred so that the real 'magic moment' of consumption in a prestigious shop could be added as a narcissistic bonus to conspicuous display, thus deepening the temporary gratification before it inevitably wore off. Every object could be traded or converted into cash because it was not the object that was desired but rather the image of being able to consume and display anything that was in vogue. This achievement signified a position of social distinction in a system where some sector of consumerism's artificial social environment had in the Lacanian sense 'captured' the individual in a narcissistic relation that disguises this capture as what in Western culture is now regarded as an irresistibly attractive combination of freedom, competence, success and distinction: a true 'rugged individual', the new libertarian aristocrat of the marketplace, unbound from the collective, its symbolic order and its 'nanny state'.

For most of our interviewees, police intrusion into their day-to-day activities was seen simply as an inconvenience. It was not seen in a context of social justice, of some battle between the inalienably free individual and the authoritarian state. As we suggested earlier, the notion that criminality is a set of misguided acts driven by some underlying emancipatory urge seems wide of the mark, and indeed some previous studies may be correct in claiming that some criminals possess even more punitive attitudes than the state and its agents; it is after all only others who commit real crimes, and all others, to the narcissist, simply get in the way of the self and deserve to be punished. Neither did attitudes towards other individuals who share the same geographical space and sociocultural group seem communal, charitable or imbued with empathy, solidarity and a sense of social justice and common fate. Poorer consumers able to buy only small amounts of drugs, and who lacked the means to acquire prestigious goods, were regarded as losers and insignificant irritants whose personal failings were the cause of their own downfall, rather than fellow human beings in social and financial distress who hailed from the same historical class. The locales in which our respondents lived were usually considered 'shit', not because of the absence of community and social justice, not because of their long-standing economic difficulties or indeed their lack of political agency and representation, but because they failed to live up to the dream of a world that drips with easy opportunities, and responds immediately and without question to the individual's desires. The only real source of complaint lay in the huge gap between actually acquiring the symbolism necessary to achieve a position of distinction in the locale's specific culture – usually a minor variant of the mainstream – and the means that low-level criminality can provide in order to perform this task as quickly and easily as possible.

Reaping the rewards and claiming the status that came with more profitable and professional forms of crime did not seem to diminish narcissistic desire. For most, the money vanished as quickly as it arrived, leaving them clinging on desperately to their hard-won positions as 'top criminals' and searching the horizon for new opportunities. Dreams of reaching the next step on the ladder still lingered, and the desire to reach yet further imaginary heights of conspicuous consumption, hedonism and social distinction would accompany them for some time to come. Like some pre-classical Greek myth, beyond the mortals were the Titans, but beyond the Titans were the Gods of Mount Olympus itself; ambition was never satisfied, even though a fatalistic attitude towards failure was also prevalent. Each activity was merely an instrument; there were no alternative Ideals, no higher purposes, and for some, even emotional commitments to other human beings were signs of weakness or at the very least a 'nuisance' that often impeded the fulfilment of personal wishes. In these locales the whole tradition of working-class values appeared to be dead, abandoned in favour of the most pure form of utilitarian individualism, and shorn of even the minimal social conscience demanded by Smith, Mill and other classical liberal philosophers. All social and political dreams seem to have regressed to a basic concatenation of exploitative rights, defensive security and distinction from the social herd, which characterised the cultural values and personal desires of the feudal barbarian, and which somehow have been revived in the context provided by advanced capitalism and its thoroughly depoliticised liberal-democratic system.

Previous attempts to explain this consumer-driven criminality have, on the whole, been less than successful. The incumbent tradition of critical criminology, heavily influenced by radical liberal-pluralist metaphysics and political philosophy (see Taylor *et al.* 1973; Scraton 1987; Arrigo 2001), was unprepared for the profundity of consumerism's influence on post-productivist society and culture. Eschewing the traditional social democracy that had evolved as the principal political regulator of market capitalism, a powerful riptide of American libertarian culture flooded into leftist discourse in the 1960s to produce a new and highly individualised transatlantic hybrid. The upcoming generations' ensuing rejection of collective political traditions as the means of dissent synchronised quite remarkably with a major shift in popular culture, orchestrated by the marketing industry, towards 'cool individualism'. Consumer desire, depoliticised rebellion and the craving of the socially disembedded 'cool individual' for social distinction as a paradoxical means of escape and social incorporation were assembled as a package by the combined efforts of the marketing industry and libertarian politics in the era of the 'counterculture'; by cultivating popular fascination with its basic principles and attractions, the way was being cleared for the return of classical liberalism as 'neo-liberalism'. Just as the 'new criminology' was positing crime as an unfairly labelled act of proto-rebellion driven by a latent and frustrated sense of social justice accompanied by needs for individual freedom and cultural diversity – in other words, a fundamentally noble reaction against the oppressive bourgeois state and cultural hegemony – individuals were being assimilated into this libertarian/consumer culture and encouraged to adopt an increasingly narcissistic bearing in an attempt to emulate and reproduce the classical bourgeois posture and its faux-aristocratic roots. In the reality underneath the new criminology's romanticism the whole aetiology of crime was shifting from the social and material needs and sense of injustice that drove Hobsbawm's concept of traditional 'social crime' to the newly reconstituted and amplified desires for consumption, narcissistic identification and social distinction that drive today's 'asocial crime'.

By the very nature of its hybrid liberal-pluralist and social structural ontology – which both in their own ways emphasised diversity and conflict – the 'new criminology' could do nothing but deny the inexorable absorption of huge numbers of individuals into consumer culture and the subsequent homogenisation of primary values and dissolution of cultural and class differences, a corrosive process that left behind only vestigial parodies of formerly substantive dissimilarities. History's most powerful culturo-economic force has with consummate ease succeeded in cultivating, modifying and harnessing the social 'conflict' and anthropological 'differences' that Gray (2007) posits as timeless, natural and fundamental to social relations. The liberal-pluralists misunderstood the dissimilarity and dynamic tension between norms and values in a capitalist era in which norms had broken away from anthropological values to become functional practices, not only to enact economised core values but also to keep them in check. Normative strategies were used to both conceal and practise the brutal core values with which all cultural groups, no matter how 'plural' and essentially 'different' they thought themselves to be, were forced to comply. The analytical focus was conveniently wrenched away from the value order to the normative order – where superficially 'plural', 'conflictual' and 'deviant' forms could be pointed out – and retained in a position as far as possible from the relentless, grinding force generated by free-market capitalism's underlying utilitarian values and economic imperatives. Core values based on competitive individualism and the individual's quest for social distinction had become *doxic*; customary and taken for granted as the primary culturo-economic context for the logic of practice (see Bourdieu 1990). Despite social democracy's modest success and the possibility of building upon it – a possibility that existed even in post-Soviet Russia (Cohen 2001) – we were constantly and sternly warned by neo-liberal ideologues that any attempt to alter or regulate these core values and practices would lead inevitably to a decline in economic growth, individual liberty and quality of life, and if not to brutal totalitarianism then to something far too close to it; liberal-pluralists responded with extremely faint protests or often none at all, and sometimes with a chorus of agreement. One of the resulting criminological trends from the late 1960s onwards was to constantly under-predict rising crime in Britain and the USA, largely ignore social democratic Canada's and Europe's success in keeping crime and imprisonment rates relatively low, play down rises in local crime rates, and concentrate on waging the liberal war against the 'totalitarian' state, even though Britain and the USA had never seen anything like a genuine totalitarian state. Ironically, it was only after two decades of collusion in neo-liberalism that the states in both Britain and the USA veered towards totalitarianism, caused not by the domestic crime problem but by the cultural and geopolitical tension and terrorism fomented by their own cultural exceptionalism, geopolitical aggression, inept foreign policies and hunger for oil; driven, of course, by the consumerism and the imperative of constant economic growth that had ceased to be real problems in the mind of the liberal-left. Radical liberal-pluralist crimi-nology was entirely unprepared, ontologically and theoretically, for the world that was emerging in this stage of advanced capitalism.

The liberal-conservative slugging match was a battle between the two iconic images of dread behind two potential moral panics (see Badiou 2002) – the pathologically authoritarian state and the pathologically unruly individual – and neither side was focused on the real underlying problem of pathogenic core values and practices, which meanwhile had mutated into a condition that was increasingly difficult to manage with traditional ethics and politics. The sheer force of neo-liberalism's abrupt revival and the imposition of these values and practices led to the exhaustion of political energies, the adoption of the pragmatic 'risk' doctrine and the vague hope that some 'third way' might evolve (see Žižek 2007). The political victim was the partially effective regulatory politics of social democracy that for a short time had penetrated and restrained the underlying culturo-economic causes of crime. There was to be no revolution, we were told (Lea and Young 1993), but what was really being consigned to the dustbin was the social democratic regulatory model, to make way for the neo-liberal state and its intrusive strategies of surveillance and risk management. Unlike social democracy, which in its latter stages had begun to develop a positive yet modest, patient and culturally sensitive notion of progress, for liberal-pluralism and its de-subjectified and de-centred postmodernist variants all political macro-conceptions of 'good' were negative; in other words 'good' was anything that could not be associated with the 'Big Evil' of modernity's failed Utopian projects (see Badiou 2002; Gray 2007), while all cultural micro-conceptions of 'good' were positive: anything that enhanced the individual's productive freedom *to* desire rather than freedom *from* desire. The result was theoretical and political inertia, except for the continuation of the long-running critique of the state and the 'disciplinary society', and a systematic eschewal and running down of the critical discourses that might have been mobilised to explain the emergence of the belligerent impotence and cynicism that manifested itself among the newly unrepresented population in a number of regressive forms, including predatory crime. The real destroyer of social democracy was, of course, not its own internal failings but economic competition from industries abroad, which furnished resurgent classical liberals with the 'rational' economic excuse to roll back state welfare, downsize industry and reintroduce broad social inequality and flexible labour to 'incentivise' the relatively poor, creating geographical areas of long-term recession, many of which never recovered. After a few faint protests, liberal-pluralists accepted these events with a shrug of the shoulders as a *fait accompli*, and began to alter the shape of their own meta-discourse, which in some quarters metamorphosed into a rather backsliding critique of working-class traditions and a celebration of the personal opportunities available in neo-liberalism's not-so-brave, not-so-new world.

In the period where social democracy was rejected by the population we saw constant eruptions of an atomised form of regressive barbarism as myriad instances of micro-fascism, the 'cruel innocence' that constantly seeps out of the system (see Badiou 2002). This revealed itself often in liberal discourse to be a conscious and resolute preference – hidden under the faintest and most painfully cautious praise for social democratic regulation (see Cohen 1985) – to even the outside chance of the return of the 'Big Evil', the authoritarian state, even though post-war Western European social democracies had never approached this condition. Liberalism seems to prefer to manage the constant stream of 'little evils' that seep out all over the place rather than grasp the chance to intervene democratically in the Big Evil of consumer capitalism's deep culturo-economic homogenising processes, and in doing so it fails to understand that the sum total of the risk strategies necessary to micro-manage and suppress myriad 'little evils' is in all probability considerably more oppressive and potentially 'totalitarian' than social democratic regulation of core economic and cultural practices and stabilisation of the 'business cycle' ever was, or is ever likely to be. It seems clear to us that liberal-pluralism has impoverished criminological theory and diverted it from its aetiological and political tasks.

At the same time, liberal-pluralist discourses were neglecting and underestimating the gravity of the twentieth century's most important cultural current. The release of the psychosocial forces of narcissism and the craving for social distinction generated the impetus consumer capitalism required, risking alienation and pathology in a social body that had in the social democratic period embarked on the first stages of a historical trajectory towards the sort of ethico-political solidarity, social stability and integration that could cope with ethnic and cultural diversity. However, social democracy was simply not sufficiently thorough, resolute or scrupulous to survive under pressure. The structural economic problems it encountered in a globalising world and the gradual corruption of the post-war political class combined in an internally corrosive process. The mass-manufactured symbols of counterfeit gentrification radically shifted the struggle from the structural axes of race, gender and class, which intersected the relations of production and political power, to culture and the individual means of personal freedom and social distinction, disintegrating collective politics at the same time as boosting desire and demand in the market. More and more individuals were enrolled into consumer culture, becoming ever more active in its reproduction and less interested in the politics of social democracy. Children are now remorselessly targeted in unethical marketing practices in an attempt to enrol them at the earliest possible age, before their own identities and their first political thoughts can form in their minds (see Barber 2007). The core consumerist strategy, gathering strength to burst up from underground and shatter the whole social ground on which we stand, was the rapid takeover of the processes of identity construction from political collectives, traditional proximal/significant others and local, grounded sociocultural groups; in George Ritzer's (2004) terms, from the 'something' of a real existence to the 'nothing' of 'grobalised' consumer capitalism. In the absence of any significant opposition – and seemingly with the blessings of many of the less insightful liberal theorists – the marketing industry got very busy indeed, focusing its formidable resources on the cultivation and prolongation of the infantile-narcissistic identification process that precedes entry into the Symbolic Order and the early stages of maturation. Our data revealed that for so many who are deeply absorbed in consumer culture, adulthood is now a continuation of narcissistic aspects of the infantile world, and as this simulated faux-adulthood is imposed on the child from an early age, we are seeing the end of both traditional childhood and adulthood: distinct life-course stages that are now melding into a single undifferentiated consumerist form.

The iconography of this ageless world is based on a sign-object system culturally constituted and reproduced by individuals who have learnt how to acquire and display consumer symbolism for the purpose of distinguishing themselves from the 'herd', despite not having done anything really distinguished. This signifies neither resistance nor co-option; individuals and street cultures are always already, from the very beginning of their identification processes, incorporated into the principle and practice of constructing images that ensnare them. What ends up being constructed on the 'street' in adolescence is based – like Tarantino's movies – on previous engagement with the consumer culture that has been internalised by individuals at an early age. The icon that represents neo-liberalism's core structural value of the 'cool', rugged individual thus gathers strength across the whole life-course in most locales, where it is adapted to local conditions and reinforced further as it generates market demand for yet more isomorphic images that represent this core value in novel and seductive ways. By the 1960s the principles of restraint and abstention were marginalised and reduced to a bare minimum in cultural life, in keeping with the logical demands of the advanced capitalist economy, and the rugged individual – now shorn of most of the disinterest, restraint and discerning tastes that character-ised the cool identity in its early stages – has more hedonistic options open to it than ever before. To many libertines this means quite simply that consumer capitalism has delivered its promises of real individual freedom, fun and prosperity, but this hasty assumption tends to distract attention from the far less euphoric fact that the marketing industry now controls culture, constructing dissent and resistance and limiting them to consumer capitalism's preferred, functional and para-political forms. A politically significant majority have been persuaded to trade the one important human freedom – the chance to change the sociocultural coordinates of existence and control our own collective destiny – for a proliferation of opportunities to indulge in hedonistic delights and distinguish themselves from the socio-political collective in a way that buries them deeper in the consumerist collective, in whose existence neither they nor liberal-pluralist intellectuals believe. The price of this pseudo-freedom is high; the emotional proclivity targeted by the marketing industry in order to spur the individual's constant efforts to leap from the collective identity of the past into the unstable, competitive individualist identity of the present is humiliation, the fear of being a loser, of having little significance, a social position that has now been moved from its traditional location at the bottom of the social order to a precarious imaginary existence circulating between the core and the margins. This has nothing to do with fun, creativity and freedom, which, when the dynamic mechanism is examined, appear not as consumer capitalism's rewards but as fleeting, superficial compensations for a life spent energetically absorbing pressure and avoiding humiliation.

The counterculture and the marketing industry simultaneously culti-vated the ethos of conspicuous disobedience as the mark of rebellion, inappropriately conflating the two terms. There was no conspiracy between two distinct groups here, because the counterculture itself was a product of the marketing industry, and it satisfied the demands of the hedonistic majority as well as absorbing the earnest minority who genuinely thought there was a revolution around the corner. Liberal-pluralist theory failed to see that the condition of ethico-political disorder and proliferating polymorphous desires is the most fertile soil in which consumer capitalism can best cultivate and reproduce itself. By casting such suspicion on collective politics, 1960s liberal-pluralism helped to keep the whole culture in tune with the underlying requirement of constant economic growth; the counterculture was reliant on that which it made so much noise about wishing to destroy. The consumer system stimulates specific desires in order to repress, sublimate and commercial-ise them, and the basis of these desires is the anxiety felt about lack of recognition and distinction as an individual. What looks like rebellion is an anxiety-fuelled urge to conform to the double bind foist upon subjects by consumer capitalism's rebellion/conformity hybrid, the imperative to stand out and fit in at the same time (Miles *et al.* 1998; Winlow and Hall 2008, forthcoming). Old mechanisms of recognition and distinction had to be dismantled and rebuilt in a deliberately unstable form, and thus consumption is not about freedom, it is a defence against humiliation and a response to this confusing double bind. This is what we could see throughout our interviews: the wish to avoid the humiliation heaped on those who fail to use symbols provided by consumer culture to distinguish themselves from the 'herd', the reviled, undifferentiated collective. Localised 'sub-cultures' were simply variants of this desire, some of whose members break the law if other means are not readily to hand and if socialisation into core values is strong but socialisation into socially and legally acceptable normative strategies weak.

Labouring under the delusion that it was heralding a revolutionary juncture on the road to the 'natural' condition of human freedom and diversity, liberal-pluralism cast doubt upon social intervention and helped to discredit and dissolve the traditional working-class identity and value system in preparation for its absorption into consumerism and neo-liberalism. The traditional working class was roundly condemned as racist, sexist and homophobic in ways that were intrinsic to its being, rather than in ways that could be left behind in its partial dissolution while leaving the better aspects of its cultural tradition intact to carry forward into the future (see Collins 2005). Neo-liberalism's tactic was to eliminate the sole source of militant non-utilitarian values and politics in the Western world; the cultural genocide of its sole dangerous foe. The export of Britain's manufacturing base in the 1980s destroyed the practical point of existence for large numbers of working-class people, the source of what little political strength and solidarity existed in advanced capitalism (Winlow and Hall 2006). Previously proud estates degenerated into sink estates in areas where economic development proved difficult, natural political leaders moved out and criminal markets flourished. Most individuals began to assess themselves as 'cool' individualist performers in the marketplace and the aetiological nature of crime changed quite radically. As crime rose with affluence and individualism it could no longer be posited as a reaction to injustice or a symbolic product of identification with a label, as it might well have been in earlier periods of the twentieth century. Most criminal acts were the products of avoiding humiliation in a dissolving, atomising culture where traditional or alternative means of dignified livelihood and identity were disappearing and consumerism had penetrated and colonised the hollowed-out culture with alarming ease. The result was a hostile and desperately competitive form of identification, which was also more likely than it had been throughout the twentieth century to manifest itself in acts of crime and violence if the well-researched biographical conditions conducive to criminality were prevalent. Crime was no longer an imaginary solution to a real problem, nor even a real solution to an imaginary problem, but an instrumental means of acquiring the symbolism required to construct an imaginary solution to an imaginary problem.

The deep values of the cult of barbarism – acquisitive individualism, narcissism and social distinction – have been revived, cultivated and fully democratised as primary fuel for growth in the post-productivist, post-social consumer capitalist economy. In the heat of this homogenising competition, differentiated identities are now constructed not in the realm of diverse values and politics but in proliferating normative strategies, and what were once deep cultural values and essential elements of sociability have now been relegated to the functional role of controlling capitalism's toxic competitive meta-culture as it is driven along generation after generation by the highly effective force of hybridised rebellion/conformity. Narcissistic subjects are the atomised energy sources for this force, trapped in a constant slingshot orbit around the poles of rebellion and conformity, oscillating between them and creating what is the social equivalent of an alternating current. Liberal cultural studies and radical criminology have for decades mistaken the belligerent impotence displayed by groups of losers in the struggle for distinction in the highly competitive and ethically homogenising culture of consumer capitalism as positive signs of subversion, resistance, transgression and proto-politics. It is in most cases simply the strategy of the disadvantaged narcissist. However, liberal-pluralism measures its evaluations of all crime and its means of reduction against their potential contributions to the return of the Absolute Evil, the totalitarian or fascist state that was the product of a conjuncture of political and cultural forces at a specific point in the twentieth century. It has also accepted the global market as the basis of the only feasible economic system. Thus, in this climate of political abdication, the serious interventionist measures that are needed to address the underlying ethico-cultural and socio-economic conditions that generate crime, from the boardrooms to the sink estates, can never be taken. Liberalism prefers to keep on trying to manage with a soft touch the fall-out that seeps from the toxic core of the wealth-generator on which it is entirely dependent.

While poring over available theoretical work over the years in order to explore our data it became obvious to us that structural, integrationist and 'radical' liberal-pluralist criminological positions have not been able to cope with the complex paradoxes and contradictions of consumer capitalism, the phenomena that indicate various aspects of the dynamic tensions that consumer capitalism has cultivated and harnessed in order to drive itself forward. Old social conflicts, individual struggles for freedom and existential struggles for authenticity and identity have all been assimilated, modified and burnt as fuel by the economic engine of liberal capitalism. The key source of motive energy was to be found in the merger of rebellion and conformity to create a dynamic hybrid form in the era of post-war consumerism. These ancient struggles were transformed from ends to means, wrenched out of the realm of cultural values to act as sublimated quasi-values that informed and motivated evolving and proliferating normative strategies, which now act in the dual role of motivation and insulation for the potentially toxic operation of liberal-capitalism's competitive values, social practices and functional economic drivers. It looks as though means have been energised by deracinated quasi-values to generate a dynamic force to motivate the primary end, which is, of course, successful participation in economic competition with a view to winning and driving forward the economic system as a whole. If the economic competition that generates growth needs these complex normative strategies – which are themselves energised by social and psychological forms of anxiety and competitive identity-seeking – to motivate what many see as a 'natural' human proclivity for competitiveness, it puts this 'naturalness' into question. It also highlights the fragility of normative strategies; because on balance they are being constituted and used more as motivation than insulation, it is far more likely that the motivating force will leak past its insulating boundaries and fuel criminal activity. The paradoxical form of conformity as controlled deviance is producing more uncontrolled deviance as the informal normative strategies that are expected to provide the control begin to fail in cultural locales where their maintenance and reproduction have become difficult.

We can see with some clarity that ancient forms of highly tractable and dynamic psychosocial forces have been retained across historical epochs (see Hall 2000, 2007), and because of the longevity of their cultivation they appear to us as natural, immutable human drives beyond mere proclivities. This suggests that we have not really made a clear-cut break from 'stable' modernity to 'unstable' postmodernity; rather, we have moved from an era in which social instability was confined to the top echelons, where it had been throughout the ancient and feudal worlds an inevitable product of the struggle for social distinction among the elite, to a reconfigured continuation of that era where this same struggle has been unleashed, democratised and diffused throughout the social body to be harnessed by the consumer economy. There never was real resistance to the power and status of old feudal elite in the liberal-bourgeois epoch or an endeavour to leave it behind, only an attempt to imitate and manipulate it from a standpoint of deep admiration. Now that there is no inconvenient, self-aware producer/warrior mass occupying with its distinct cultural and political presence the bulky bottom end of a social pyramid, everyone must struggle in the way that exclusive elites once struggled, to achieve a dynamic balance between centripetal and centrifugal forces, to remain in orbit in the gravitational field in the inherently paradoxical position of 'social distinction'; establishing the self as a highly valued part of the social by distinguishing the self as something *other* and *more* than a part of the social. Post-needs consumer capitalism, having exhausted its psychosocial fuel in the satisfaction of basic needs, must now manufacture it by organising a simulation of this traditional thymotic struggle in a way that is easily domesticated and commercialised. Genuine political resistance has been largely dissolved, and now the new neo-liberal elite are cultivating a permanently atomised, competitive and hostile milieu in their own image, an 'open competition' with big prizes, few winners and many losers, democratising and diffusing throughout the population the psychosocial forces that fuel the search for social distinction as self-aggrandisement. If the politically significant bulk of the population is tied to this hamster's wheel, we must question the received wisdom that advanced capitalism has allowed space for the transformation of subjectivity and more active citizenship, or that it alerts people to inequality and foments protest. Complaint is so often based on *amour-propre* and the inability to achieve distinction; our interviewees represent what we suspect is becoming a pervasive and normalised wish to have the chance to make others feel relatively deprived rather than equalise the structure of inequality in which relative deprivation, in a different ethico-political climate, could be perceived. So many believe in the palpably unreal fantasy that they are in the race to do precisely this, and that they are merely one lucky break away from success. It looks as though liberalism's ideology of formal equality, opportunity and classlessness has been swallowed whole.

In the effort to remain up and running, the true subject of consumer capitalism has become trapped in an endless process of identification, and it can neither settle on a single anthropological identity nor commit to truly radical subjective change that would launch the self in a completely different direction. Nor can it accept too many ethical prohibitions that might stand in the way of the acquisition of the symbols required to keep taking part in the identification process. If these symbols can be acquired legally, fair enough, but increasing numbers appear to be gravitating towards illegal methods; for our interviewees this has become a routine first resort in a normative strategy that has evolved in locales of permanent recession. This process generates the constant uncertainty and anxiety that feeds the consumer market's lifestyle industry and liberalism's para-political system of citizenship; subjective change becomes compulsory and always done in haste and fear, like dressing up for a short-notice invitation to a party. The subject must be constantly busy in the art of making sure that it is recognised, and thus it is trapped in an interminable struggle for identification in a social distorting mirror, whose shape, refractions and reflections constantly change, yet whose structural position remains the same. As our data suggested, in the awkward position of being ensnared in the paradox of a dynamic orthodoxy, the true consumer subject is equally terrified of the prospect of either too much inclusion or too much exclusion. Crime can allow the fearful subject to short-circuit the whole complex process of identification and compulsory contribution to the surplus labour and value that the system seeks to extract from its consumers as they work in order to consume; the new narcissistic aristocrats of the boardrooms (Henwood 2005; Mokhiber and Weissman 1999; Bailey 1991) and those of the sink estates (Hall and Winlow 2004) revel in their ability to simply take what they need in the way of symbolic objects that can establish their distinguished identities without the ignominy of having to labour like those in the 'bovine herd' they imagine to exist below them.

Individuals are becoming increasingly accustomed to the chore of constructing ephemeral, reflexive identities in a condition of social chaos and ontological insecurity that now constitutes normality; consumer capitalism has split and tapped modernity's unstable psychodynamic atom, feeding on its released energy. In this unstable normality, consumer culture's values and laws now lie at awkward tangents to each other, confused about deviance and conformity, where law is forced into a mode of living with socially destructive values and practices and being restricted to the task of monitoring the normative strategies that constitute the insulation. The result is a society hopelessly confused and misled about the roots of criminality, the real source of the 'fear of crime', which is much more than a crude authoritarian conspiracy to erode individual rights and freedoms and harass and label the 'other' (indeed for the most part there are no 'others' because domesticated 'otherness' is now 'cool' and functionally normal while oppositional 'otherness' has been largely crushed). The broader cultural current humming away underneath this confusion, generating psychosocial power and constantly misleading liberalism's metaphysical and political discourses, is the *ghost revolution*, the perpetual struggle against totalitarian forms of authority that were transcended long ago and the ideological association of the shibboleth of 'democracy and freedom' with the paradoxical assimilating dynamic relation between extreme individualism and social conformity. The ghost revolution continues to disparage all forms of collectivism, no matter how democratic they might be, and it has operated in tune with the logic of the competitive global market to destroy the post-war fledgling social democracies, more so in the USA and Britain, where the crime and imprisonment rates are far higher compared to Western Europe, which is still hanging on grimly to its various forms of social democratic governance under intense pressure from neo-liberal ideology and global economic competition (Reiner 2007; Harvey 2007; Sassoon 1997). Traditional post-war social democracy is possibly on its last legs, and already, as recent riots in Britain and Western Europe have indicated, it now seems incapable of providing the basis for the security, identity and significance it once promised (see Žižek 2008).

Our data have suggested that, in the midst of this dissolution of the real social and its politics, the majority of formal citizens are no longer actively involved in creating social meaning and institutions, only ephemeral lifestyles in a process of narcissistic identification. In the later chapters of this book we have tried to explain why so many willingly play this game, and what might be the source of the desire that generates this energy to fuel the specific identification practices that are so useful to consumerism. For us the most fruitful psychosocial theories are those proposed by Lacan and Žižek, based on the core phenomenon of infantile narcissism and its retention throughout the life-course, aided by the super-ego injunction to enjoy. The current assault on the principle of the symbolic order and its prohibitions is preventing individual maturation, because these prohibitions, rather than simply 'repressing' the subject, allow it the space it needs for reflexive appraisal. As the individual becomes more obsessed with seeking his own reflection in external objects he is permanently distracted from matters of intellectualism, citizenship, ethics and politics. The subject is trapped in the realm of the Imaginary, which is constantly stimulated by the irruptions of the 'thingish' virtualised reality (Lash and Lury 2007) that now prevails in consumerism's technologically sophisticated mass-mediated culture.

This entrapment of the subject in the Imaginary realm and its process of narcissistic identification allows consumer culture to inculcate and reproduce with consummate ease liberal-capitalism's most potent psychosocial dynamic force: the historical continuation of the gentry's mimicry of the aristocracy as the paragon of free, powerful and distinguished individuality. The primary urge of the premature and helpless infant to preserve its physical integrity and narcissistic relationship to the other has been prolonged throughout the life-course and harnessed to the consumer economy by constantly feeding the subject with stylised variations of the iconic image of the 'cool', rugged, transcendent individual who is best disposed to survival, success and distinction in liberal-capitalism's competitive culture. The tactic seems to be to diffuse this iconic image as a Master Signifier across all the intersecting structural orders of the social as the sole source of symbolic articulation and identification; no matter where one comes from in the sociocultural order, one can imagine oneself to be this individual. Consumer culture controls this process from early childhood by arranging the original irruptive stimulations that, by the time adolescence dawns, have locked the subject in a condition of permanent identification with this iconic, structural form of individuality as it struggles with dangerous and disturbing external stimuli. The emphasis on hedonism as the principal reward for work and the achievement of a socially distinct identity has over the past fifty years or so created a new form of super-ego, radically different from the one that prevailed in the traditional Symbolic Order, a super-ego that heaps guilt on the subject's failure to enjoy rather than her failure to abstain. This is the psychic source of the hedonistic drive, constantly reinforced by mass-mediated and peer-group culture, with which normative strategies must now cope. Its constant presence places huge pressure on parents as they attempt to socialise young children into normative strategies that must now guide desire and action in impossibly complex positive and negative relations to consumer culture's rebellion/conformity drive. In the face of this additional pressure we must not be too surprised that there can be a high failure rate among families that exist in a variety of difficult circumstances.

Our data lend support to the idea that we have entered an era in which many young people who regularly commit acquisitive asocial crimes – sometimes accompanied by intimidation and violence – have become in the Lacanian sense 'captured' as subjects by the consumer environment. What liberal-pluralists posit as different inter-subjectively created subcultural identities are very often shifting isomorphic images of the same structural-ethical principle of 'cool', rugged individualism, around which young people congregate and which has become fetishised and associated with the symbolism carried by consumer capitalism's products. Language and politics make very little impression as tools of critical reflection because the prelinguistic identification process is prolonged throughout the life-course, preventing full entry into the symbolic order that is the source of all critically reflective language. After all the sterling work done by the labour movement and the social democratic education system, intellectual reflection oriented to social and political affairs is in danger of once again becoming an elite activity as a high proportion of the consuming masses become distracted and disinterested; this disinterest is not merely a product of cynical spin-sodden para-politics but also a cause. Creativity in the reception of signs in the connotative order is stymied as the subject is constantly absorbed in the continuation of the bogus rebellion, in which the super-ego injunction to enjoy – to take pleasure beyond its limits into the painful realm of *jouissance* – combines with the marketing industry's strategy of expanding ways of seeking pleasure to fill the world with fetishes, along with all the petty misdemeanours and infractions that invariably accompany attempts to satisfy them. As hedonism, bogus rebellion, ritual cynicism, solipsism and narcissism become increasingly established as common aspects of normative strategies, which overwhelm the traditional insulating and restraining aspects of the norms that were to constitute the Smithian 'moral framework' and act as the main motivators and guides of competitive individualism, the general culture becomes latently criminogenic. Crime is manifested throughout the social order from cabinet meetings, boardrooms and offices to sink estates, differing in form and intensity according to opportunities and the extent that the insulating normative strategies are internalised by individuals in the socialisation process. The upshot is that the socialisation process receives a markedly lower level of support from the broader culture and community – and, of course, none whatsoever from underlying economic relations – which in many ways can now act against it with more pressure than we have ever seen, even in the chaotic urbanisation process of early nineteenth-century Western Europe. As the outside world becomes more brutally competitive the family-centred socialisation process becomes a fragile, privatised affair forced to bear the whole weight of responsibility itself with some support from ailing state agencies; thus the possibility of it breaking down in the variety of difficult circumstances that it has always faced – especially in unstable, economically impoverished locales – becomes increasingly likely.

Karl Polanyi, aware of the fundamental difference between toxic core values and insulating norms, was one among many who recognised that if free-market economies are not embedded with social norms that promote the common good then 'acquisitiveness and competition . . . achieve overwhelming dominance as cultural forces rendering life under capitalism as a Hobbesian "war of all against all"' (quoted in Pollin 2005: 16; see also Boltanski and Chiapello 2007). Young (1999, 2007) argues that the traditional social democratic method of placing capitalist markets under the authority of stabilising, redistributing governments is now 'contentious', mainly because of the resentment of egalitarianism felt by the civil service and the population at large. However, the para-political strategies – meritocracy, citizenship, equal opportunities, responsibilitisation and so on – that we now see emerging tend to be based on the assumption of a pre-existent radical subjectivity. This also assumes an intrinsic sense of social justice in the subject, rather than a crude sense of personal injustice fostered during the early stages of narcissistic identification. This fundamentalist liberal discourse neglects the crucial fact that the politico-cultural conversion of this negative, solipsistic sense of personal injustice to a sense of social justice is one of the crucial aspects of growing up as an individual in a sociocultural collective and its Symbolic Order; far better, we think, to take a more penetrating look at the real underlying reasons why the bulk of the Western population allow their resentment of egalitarianism to over-whelm their alternative proclivity for the higher sentiment of social solidarity.

Kant saw Enlightenment as humanity's growth out of immaturity, but he did not see that alongside that was a powerful counter-current of infantile narcissism, fostered and diffused by liberal-capitalist culture as an economic driver. This narcissistic historical current has its roots further back in European history, and is an aspect of a broader and more fundamental current we have named the 'pseudo-pacification process'. The finer details of this process have been outlined elsewhere (Hall 2000, 2007), but, to summarise briefly, the theory emerged from an attempt to explore the politico-economic dimension of Norbert Elias's 'civilizing process', which from this perspective appears not as a process driven by some suppositious blind, teleological civilising tendency but a pacifica-tion project cultivated by the nascent European bourgeoisie to help the system of market-capitalism to establish and diffuse itself in the midst of a culture whose tendency to arbitrary violence was inhibiting important factors essential to its growth. Most important among these factors were the establishment and protection of property rights, the safe and reliable distribution of money and commodities along the arterial trade routes that were proliferating in geographical space, and the cultivation among the lower classes of the personal ambition to achieve social distinction by pacified means; namely participation in the generation and acquisi-tion of wealth and the conspicuous consumption of its symbols.

The fundamental practical aim of the pseudo-pacification process was the evacuation from public life of as much arbitrary interpersonal intimidation and violence as possible. The ethos of peace for its own sake might have existed as an Ideal deep within the Christian code, but pacification was not diffused and applied as such. A modernist cultural code evolved wherein physical violence and overt displays of hostility were repressed and sublimated for two principal reasons: the protection of property and the conversion of the petty hostility and violence that characterised the social landscape of feudalism into aggressive social and economic competition. The fundamental value of aggressive competition that pervaded feudal Europe and most other forms of expansionary agricultural settlement was left undisturbed, but the normative strategies that guided the value's practices were inverted in the cultural hierarchy as the violence of the former warrior aristocracy was replaced by the pacified politeness of the rising bourgeoisie. However, because the underlying aggressive-competitive value system was undisturbed, this 'politeness' hid a kernel of tough aggression that reproduced itself in a sublimated form. This reduced everyday violence in the public sphere, yet it hid a lot of violence in the private sphere and it often erupted in spectacular forms of organised violence during the era of nation-building. As Europe emerged from feudalism – a notably brutal and spectacularly over-symbolised period in its history – there was no movement towards civilisation strictly for its own sake, only to the functional norms of pacification required to lubricate the move to the market; therefore there was no movement even towards pacification for its own sake, hence the term pseudo-pacification. All classes, whose historical entitlements to the use of violence had been highly differenti-ated, were to be brought under this purging principle.

However, violence is dimorphic (Hall 2000) in the sense that it operates in both the physical and symbolic dimensions (see also Bourdieu 1986; Žižek 2008), and the pressure brought to bear on physical violence in order to eliminate it from public life energised the sublima-tion process (see Fromm 1973) that converts the urge to physical violence into its symbolic form. Put very simply for the sake of brevity, the symbolic form of violence is the disparagement of the symbolic aspects of the other's being, and the objective of this sublimated 'violence' is subjugation or destruction by humiliation; the vigorously reactive struggle that this threat stimulates in the individual is the wellspring of the energy that can be harnessed by consumer capitalism if the atomised individual can be enrolled once his collective identity has been erased. The upshot is that throughout the capitalist project, from its mercantilist beginnings to its current stage, the entitlement to symbolic violence – once jealously guarded along with the complementary entitlement to physical violence by alliances of royal elites and priesthoods across the history of expansionary agricultural settlements – was democratised at the same time as the entitlement to physical violence was severely restricted in civil society and largely monopolised by the state. Demo-cratisation began with the gentrification process and the gradual outward spread of conspicuous consumption as a mark of social distinction, which became associated with wealth accumulation and flamboyant individualism rather than public service and civic virtue. Capitalism is an immensely powerful machine for expanding wealth, but its concomitant claim to be the great expander of freedom is questionable. What it seemed to do was diffuse the right of the individual who had achieved a position of freedom by performing in the market to pour scorn on the less successful who lacked the symbolism required to represent success and defend their identities; thus freedom's symbolism became wrapped up with an ugly form of personalised supremacist gloating. Acting as a restraint on this socially corrosive tendency, Protestant asceticism contained within its cultural code the moral command not to display the symbolism of personal economic success in bouts of spectacular consumption, and not to humiliate less successful others and massage one's narcissistic ego in public. However, too many broke this rule, unable to resist opportunities to savour their success in the market and lord it as consumerist *Übermenschen* over the losers. Although the personal struggle to achieve the means of symbolic violence was establishing itself as a powerful economic driver throughout capitalism's mercantilist beginnings by creating demand in the marketplace, capitalist economic growth throughout its classical-industrialist period was driven chiefly by the innovation and manufacture of products designed to meet basic needs, and asceticism functioned reasonably well as a fragile stabilising mechanism to at least restrain and reduce the interpersonal social hostility that symbolic violence can so easily provoke.

The emergence of the pseudo-pacification process predates Foucault's state-administered 'bio-power' and is perhaps more fundamental to the capture of the body and its passions. Despite asceticism's reasonably successful attempt to dampen the alienating, antagonistic and divisive effects of systematised symbolic violence, the symbolic practice of spectacular gentrification continued to infect the culture of Europe as everyone and anyone came to believe that they could achieve a position of magnificent social distinction by means of money and the display of purchased possessions, first in the form of land and buildings and eventually consumer goods as smaller luxury items became more common. By the eighteenth century consumerism was spreading outwards quite rapidly, and here we see the birth of fake revolts into style, commercialised simulations of what was once an important cultural aspect of the resistance to Puritanism in the English Civil War, which helped to deter the English from violent revolution after the successful constitutional bourgeois revolution of 1688. Symbolic violence was harnessed as the most potent economic driver on the demand side of the equation, and it also operated quite effectively on the productive side as a growing number of people became willing to sacrifice surplus labour to acquire more consumer goods and their social symbolism. As what

American business commentators like to call rather euphemistically 'motivation', this began to displace the traditional threats of absolute poverty and arbitrary violence, and in essence it was the continuation of aristocracy by other means, namely the democratisation and diffusion of its symbolic violence and its practices of encultured narcissistic identification. As physical violence was further reduced in civil society in the late eighteenth century, it cleared the way for the gradual and comparatively safe accelerated diffusion throughout an atomising society of the symbolic violence and narcissistic identification processes that prevailed in elite culture. Powerful emotions of admiration, desire, competition and envy were being fostered as dangerous but extremely useful by-products of the repression of collective sentiments. Interpersonal hostility had, of course, existed to a notable degree in the often argumentative and violent peasant cultures of the feudal era (Gurr 1981), but the point is that the pseudo-pacification process was not an attempt to eliminate this petty squabbling by constructing a maturational Symbolic Order, but rather to capture and systematise it as a cultural driver for the economy; thus the pseudo-pacification process gave petty squabbling and all the feelings of envy and insecurity that underpin it shape, meaning and authorisation. It became necessary to prolong the life of the infantile-narcissist alongside the subject of the prohibitive Symbolic Order, and the dynamic schizoid modernist subject was born. As basic needs were fulfilled and luxury products became essential to commodity circulation and profitability, the creature of childish desires grew in the shadow of the serious worker, socio-political citizen and public servant. The warrant of the infantile narcissist grew in an underlying current, a shadow *Zeitgeist* that was to burst upon us as the dominant culture from the 1960s. The more ambitious Randian subjects of liberal-capitalism imagined themselves as little aristocrats lording it over their inferiors, a characteristic we can now see pervading the hierarchal criminal culture from Conrad Black and Nicholas von Hoogstraten right down to the more successful minor criminals who lord it over the unsuccessful 'mugs' and 'Aldi-bashers' on sink estates.

Even in Nazism and Stalinism we saw the elevated lower middle classes' abject mimicry of the aristocracy that modernity had allegedly deposed; as Brecht once remarked of early Nazi supporters, 'bankrupt shopkeepers dreaming of Siegfried' (Jacoby 1999). This terrifying institutionalised variant of narcissism, allied to other pathogenic forms such as racism, nationalism and so on, is not what liberal-capitalism's agents intended, but it remains a constant risk when whole cultural groups are subjected to humiliating losses of status and subjugation (see Žižek 2007; Fletcher 1997; Bourdieu 1986). However, it is not this but the *atomised* variation of narcissism that liberal-capitalism prefers, which functions more efficiently in its economy and which has been culturally rather than politically institutionalised in its practices of glorifying the successful self. The tragedy of liberal-capitalism is that the more the opportunity for narcissistic identification is prolonged throughout the life-course and diffused throughout the social body to drive economic growth, the more the social and cultural dimensions of life are poisoned. Asceticism had discharged its duties with reasonable success, and in the mid nineteenth century in Britain the proletarianised working classes, with a combination of Methodism and tough labour politics, had constructed a non-utilitarian, collectivist symbolic order that was proving ominously successful as a cultural socialising agent and a political motivator (see Sassoon 1997). However, by the 1920s the culture of narcissism was quite systematically revived by an embryonic marketing industry taking advantage of further technological innovations in production and communications. Capitalism entered a new and more efficient phase in its democratisation of narcissism and its assimilation of everyday individuals into conspicuous consumption and the competitive individualist ethos. The visual culture of mass media, focusing from the beginning on the glamorous lives of the rich and famous, began to spread the virus, and the successful entrepreneur and ostentatious displayer of symbols of social distinction was released fully from all the shackles of cultural restraint, ethical doubt and caution that had characterised capitalism's earlier ascetic periods; the lid on Pandora's box was flung fully open. Crime rates rose slowly but ominously in Britain and the USA from the early 1920s, accelerating in the 1960s and exploding in the 1980s (Reiner 2007).

As the twentieth century progressed, the state-managed relative stability of the social democratic era in Britain and the USA helped to slow the growth of crime and violence quite considerably as its institutions acted as a brake on social atomisation, not by reviving the principles of asceticism but by expanding the opportunities to indulge in consumption while retaining a semblance of collective political identity and solidarity among the working class and cultivating a heightened sense of common fate across the class, race and gender orders. However, this fragile stability, already weakened by burgeoning consumerism in the 1960s and by global economic forces in the 1970s, was lost in the 1980s when, after bouts of working-class militancy, the bourgeois Restoration arrived in both nations with a bang (Badiou 2002; Lea 2002; Harvey 2007). The economies were ruthlessly rationalised and working-class cultural traditions and political solidarity began to disintegrate just as the culture of narcissistic identification and conspicuous consumption was reaching its heights of intensity. Class solidarity was sufficiently eroded for traditional political opposition to be brushed aside and consigned to the fringe with relative ease. There was an explosion of media and marketing across the globe, and alongside this appeared the

215

further advance of infantile narcissism and the erosion of the traditional 'politics of commitment' and the principle of public service. Consumption became the major site of personal identification, and the infantile narcissist's proliferating desires and ambitions began to overpower the prohibitions of the Symbolic Order, which had already been weakened in the 1960s as a functional requirement for the purpose of increasing market demand, reducing it to a skeleton. In a rapidly depoliticising environment where protest was being displaced by resignation and admiration, a quite remarkable amount of wealth and power was transferred to the top strata of society, allowing the elite to relight their beacon of conspicuous consumption and let it burn at its maximum candlepower before the masses for the first time since the 1920s. Simultaneously, however, the proliferation of cheap imported luxury goods and the expansion of opportunities for budding entrepreneurs allowed consumer culture to assume the most democratised form that had yet been seen. On both sides of the Atlantic, many young working-class people abandoned politics, class loyalties and egalitarian ethics to embrace opportunities to emulate the new self-made superstars of Thatcherism and Reaganism. Chaotic, impoverished spaces of long-term recession were thrown up by this process in the 1980s and crime joined entrepreneurialism and higher education as a means of pulling oneself off the bottom, where the terror of permanent social insignificance and mounting consumer debt – echoes of urban life in the late eighteenth century – had replaced absolute poverty as the main motivating factors. Rather than a primary cause of 'crime as misguided rebellion' based on a sense of social justice and a clear perception of relative positions in a structure of social relations, 'relative deprivation' was a sociological category that emerged as a superficial explanation of the deep culturo-economic and psychosocial processes that were increasing both consumption and crime during this period. When the Right complain about the 'politics of envy', they are complaining about what they consider to be an unwelcome collectivised manifestation of their own principle strategy of social atomisation, cultural assimilation and economic dynamism; the driving force at the heart of their way of life: envy is fine as long as it is not politically organised. Even when it is, of course, it does not create anything truly different or radical at the core of our way of life.

In the Anglo-American world since the 1960s the stock market and the service and entertainment industries have become the loci of personal wealth accumulation, and there has also been a vast expansion in gambling alongside significant rises in crime and violence. This signifies the emphatic return of the short-cut mentality that preceded the Victorian insistence on the ethos of productive work and savings as the link to reward. One unintentional and rather ugly consequence of consumer capitalism's need to stoke up a dynamic culturo-economic force in a post-needs economy was that the burgeoning super-ego injunction to enjoy became entangled with the democratisation of the entitlement to symbolic violence to create a corrosive psychosocial force that encouraged individuals to enjoy the act of using conspicuous consumption to indulge in simulated acts of subjugating and humiliating others. We emphasise the term 'simulated' because we must not forget that none of this is real and all it takes to oppose and demolish it is to stop believing in it; consumer culture is at root a belief system founded on the belief that one can perform the impossible task of actually *becoming* the *imago* with which one has narcissistically identified, and if one appears not to be this *imago* then this temporary situation must be false and it needs to be rectified as efficiently as possible with the means at one's disposal. It was the expression of this psychosocial force that we could see most clearly as a consistent and pervasive phenomenon in our data, and the corollary is that, for those whose entry into a reflective Symbolic Order has been at best partial, the act of acquiring consumer symbolism in an effort to avoid humiliation and insignificance becomes a pressing necessity; so pressing that it unconsciously provokes the short-cut mentality and increases the likelihood of crime or other means of cheating the system. What is seen as rational and conscious by utilitarian rational choice theorists is at its root actually irrational and unconsciously motivated. If frustrated, the consumer narcissist who is determined to save face by deploying what has now become the customary method of symbolically upstaging those around him – we must not forget that in advanced capitalist culture equality and humility have little value – can be a notably unpleasant individual. A dwindling band of individuals – fewer than ever since the hundred years between the mid nineteenth and mid twentieth centuries, we might speculate – are now socialised into a reflective Symbolic Order that directly prohibits and cuts reflective gaps in capitalism's acquisitive, competitive and narcissistic core values, giving the subject space to forge an alternative perspective, ethos and identity. The consumer narcissist thus becomes both the product and agent of an intrinsically criminogenic culture, still largely latent but increasingly active. Decent behaviour towards others has become largely dependent not on common culture but on state deterrents supported by privatised methods of socialisation into a fragile and confusing normative code that acts as a bulwark against the robust practice of core values, which are based at the deepest level on sublimated violence and the narcissistic struggle for social distinction. It is not that the Anglo-American West's civilising process is failing; it is simply that as an end in itself it was never really begun. Perhaps this is a little task we might consider putting on the 'to do' list in the near future. Some would take the opportunity to quote Gandhi at this point of closure, but we will resist and leave it there.

Glossary of terms

Aldi-bashers a reference to the discount food store. People who use this store are derided as 'Aldi-bashers', usually a reference to the dispossessed urban poor; those with little overt concern for the status associated with specific shops and labels on goods.

bairn child

bamp tramp

banged-up imprisoned

bint woman, female

bird woman, female

bizzy police officer

blagging stealing

blow up to lose one's temper

boffing as in 'boffing petrol', meaning inhaling the fumes from petrol

bother usually meaning 'trouble'

bottle bravery, nerve

box 'the box', meaning television

brown in this context, often a reference to heroin

canny nice, pleasant

carve-up in this context, usually a reference to stabbing or cutting someone

charlie cocaine

chippy in this context, a fish and chip shop

chucky credit, debt

clock keep an eye on, watch

coke in this context, cocaine

coz because

cush good, nice

dafties persons of low standing, unintelligent

Dam the 'Dam', an abbreviated reference to the city of Amsterdam

dipping often used to refer to shoplifting or theft, e.g. 'we used to go out dipping' means 'we used to go out stealing/shoplifting'

dirty brown stuff heroin

divvies persons of low standing and intelligence

dog's lives a reference to the dispossessed urban poor; those with little overt concern with consumer signification

dole a reference to various forms of welfare payment; also used to refer to the Job Centre, where welfare claims are assessed

draw in this context, often a reference to weed, cannabis

ez derived from 'us', but in most cases meaning 'me'

fatha father

factory 'the factory', a reference to prison

fizzie a 'Honda fizzie', a reference to a small-engined Honda motorbike

fucked over ripped off, cheated

gear clothes or just general 'stuff', but occasionally a reference to drugs

gelt gold

graft/grafter means work/worker; often used to refer to illegal forms of work

grand/s often used to refer to one thousand pounds, or units thereof

granda grandfather

Henry 'a Henry', meaning an eighth of an ounce of cocaine, 3 and a half grams

knot often used to refer to a wedge of cash

lush meaning top quality, nice, impressive

manky meaning of poor quality

minging meaning smelly; often used as a reference to scruffiness, dirty

minted rich

nana grandmother

naughty in this context, usually an ironic reference to seriousness; for example, a 'naughty lad' might be a reference to someone who is either particularly skilled at violence or someone involved in very serious crimes.

nash to go quickly, flee

nine bar a common unit of sale for Cannabis resin.

nipped arrested

no-mark in this context, a reference to the dispossessed urban poor; an insignificant 'other' with little self-respect or concern for consumer signification

nowt nothing

nutter implies someone with some kind of mental dysfunction, but in this context usually a metaphorical reference someone who is expressively and unpredictably violent, who uses violent for no apparent reason

old doll/old lady mother

old man father

on bail on credit

ower yon over there

owt anything

quid/s one pound, or units thereof

'perfect nick' meaning 'perfect condition'

pills in this context, usually a reference to ecstasy tablets

pisshead a drunk or an alcoholic

rammy sexy, attractive

rock crack cocaine

sat nav a satellite navigation system

sarnies sandwiches

screw in this context, a reference to burglary e.g. screwing houses

scoping out looking at; often means 'to criminally appraise'

skip rats in this context, a reference to the dispossessed urban poor; those with little self-respect or concern for consumer signification

skunk skunk cannabis, weed as opposed to resin

smoke 'a smoke', often used to refer to an amount of cannabis e.g. 'get a smoke in' means 'get in some cannabis to smoke'

snide fake, counterfeit

swag traditionally meaning 'stolen goods', but often used to refer to 'stuff' generally e.g. 'all the best swag' means 'all the best stuff'

tabs cigarettes

tom jewelry

topping 'to top', meaning 'to kill'

top notch high quality

touch often used as a noun, 'a touch', meaning a criminal score

turn-over to rob violently or to assault violently

waster inactive dispossessed urban poor; those with little self-respect

web money

wedge a considerable amount of money

why aye emphatic yes

window-lickers a disparaging metaphorical reference to the mentally handicapped; also used to refer to the dispossessed urban poor, those with little self-respect or overt concern for consumer signification

wor our

References

Agamben, G. (1998) *Homo Sacer: Sovereign Power and Bare Life.* Stanford: Stanford University Press.

Aichhorn, A. ([1925]1935) *Wayward Youth.* New York: The Viking Press.

Ames (2007) *Going Postal: Rage, Murder and Rebellion in America.* London: Snowbooks.

Angell, I. (2001) *The New Barbarian Manifesto.* London: Kogan Page.

Arrigo, B. (2001) 'Critical Criminology, Existential Humanism, and Social Justice: Exploring the Contours of Conceptual Integration', *Critical Criminology*, 10(2): 83–95.

Badiou, A. (2002) *Ethics: An Essay on the Understanding of Evil.* London: Verso.

Badiou, A. (2007) *The Century.* London: Polity.

Bailey, F. (1991) *The Junk Bond Revolution: Michael Milken, Wall Street and the Roaring Eighties.* London: Fourth Estate.

Bagguley, P. and Mann, K. (1992) 'Idle Thieving Bastards? Scholarly Representations of the Underclass', *Work, Employment and Society*, 6(1): 113–126.

Bakan, J. (2005) *The Corporation: The Pathological Pursuit of Profit and Power.* London: Constable and Robinson.

Barber, B. (2007) *Consumed: How Markets Corrupt Children, Infantilize Adults and Swallow Citizens Whole.* London: Norton.

Barthes, R. (1972) *Mythologies.* New York: Hill and Wang.

Bataille, G. (1992) *Accursed Share.* London: Zone Books.

Baudrillard, J. (2005) *The System of Objects.* London: Verso.

Bauldrillard, J. (1994) *Simulacra and Simulation.* Michigan: University of Michigan Press.

Baudrillard, J. (1993) *The Transparency of Evil.* London: Verso.

Baudrillard, J. (2001) (ed. by M. Poster) *Jean Baudrillard: Selected Writings.* London: Polity.

Bauman, Z. (1995) *Life in Fragments.* Oxford: Blackwell.

Bauman, Z. (2001) *Work, Consumerism and the New Poor*. Buckingham: Open University Press.

Bauman, Z. (2001) *The Individualized Society*. Cambridge: Polity.

Bauman, Z. (2004) *Wasted Lives: Modernity and its Outcasts*. Cambridge: Polity.

Bauman, Z. (2006) *Liquid Fear*. London: Polity.

Bauman, Z. (2007) *Consuming Life*. Cambridge: Polity.

Beck, U. (1992) *Risk Society: Towards a new Modernity*. London: Sage.

Beck, U. and Beck-Gernsheim, E. (2001) *Individualization: Institutionalized Individualism and its Social and Political Consequences*. London: Sage.

Becker, H. (1967) *Outsiders: Studies in the Sociology of Deviance*. London: Free Press.

Boltanski, L. and Chiapello, E. (2007) *The New Spirit of Capitalism*. London: Verso.

Bonger, W. (1916) *Crime and Economic Conditions*. London: Little Brown.

Bourdieu, P. (1986) *Distinction: A Social Critique of the Judgement of Taste*. London: Routledge.

Bourdieu, P. (1990) *The Logic of Practice*. Stanford: Stanford University Press.

Bourgois, P. (1996) *In Search of Respect: Selling Crack in El Barrio*. Cambridge: Cambridge University Press.

Box, S. (1987) *Recession, Crime and Punishment*. Oxford: Palgrave Macmillan.

Braithwaite, J. (1989) *Crime, Shame and Reintegration*. Cambridge: Cambridge University Press.

Brandson. R. (2006) *Screw it, Let's Do it*. London: Virgin Books.

Brown, P. and Hesketh, A. (2004) *The Mismanagement of Talent: Employability and Jobs in the Knowledge Economy*. Oxford: Oxford University Press.

Byrne, D. (1989) *Beyond the Inner City*. London: Open University Press.

Callois, R. (1961) *Man and the Sacred*. London: Free Press.

Carter, M. and Jephcott, A. (1954) *The Social Background of Delinquency*. Nottingham: University of Nottingham Press.

Cashmore, E. (2002) *Beckham*. London: Polity.

Castells, M. (1997) *The Power of Identity, Vol. 2: The Information Age: Economy, Society and Culture*. Oxford: Blackwell.

Chaplin, L. and John, D. (2005) 'The Development of Self-Brand Connections in Children and Adolescents', *Journal of Consumer Research*, 32: 119–129.

Clayre, A. (1977) *Nature and Industrialization: An Anthology*. Oxford: Oxford University Press.

Cloward, R. and Ohlin, L. (1960) *Delinquency and Opportunity: A Theory of Delinquent Gangs*. Glencoe, IL: Free Press.

Cohen, A. (1955) *Delinquent Boys: The Culture of the Gang*. Glencoe, IL: Free Press.

Cohen, S. (1985) *Visions of Social Control: Crime, Punishment and Classification*. London: Polity.

Cohen, S. (1986) 'Community Control: To demystify or to reaffirm?', in H. Bianchi and van R. Swaaningen (eds) *Abolitionism: Towards a non-repressive approach to crime*. Amsterdam: Free University Press.

Cohen, S. (2002) *Folk Devils and Moral Panics*. London: Routledge.

Cohen, S. F. (2001) *Failed Crusade: America and the tragedy of post-communist Russia*. London: Norton.

Collins, M. (2005) *The Like's of Us: A Biography of the White Working Class*. London: Granta.

Cross, G. (2000) *An All-Consuming Century: Why Commercialism Won in Modern America*. New York: Columbia University Press.

Currie, E. (2005) *Road to Whatever: Middle-Class Culture and the Crisis of Adolescence*. London: Metropolitan Books.

Damasio, A. (2003) *Looking for Spinoza: Joy, Sorrow, and the Feeling Brain*. Orlando, FL.: Harcourt.

Debord, G. (1984) *Society of the Spectacle*. London: Black and Red.

De Certeau, M. (1984) *The Practice of Everyday Life*. Berkeley: University of California Press.

Deleuze, G. and Guattari, F. (1994) *What is Philosophy?* New York: Columbia University Press.

Deleuze, G. and Guatarri, F. (1987) *A Thousand Plateaus: Capitalism and Schizophrenia*. Minneapolis: University of Minnesota Press.

Dennis, F. (2006) *How to Get Rich*. London: Ebury Press.

Dorling, D. (2004) 'Prime Suspect: Murder in Britain', in P. Hillyard *et al. Beyond Criminology: Taking Harm Seriously*. London: Pluto.

Downes, D. (1966) *The Delinquent Solution: A Study in Subcultural Theory*. London: Routledge & Kegan Paul.

Downes, D. and Rock, P. (2003) *Understanding Deviance*. Oxford University Press.

Durkheim, E. (1992) *Professional Ethics and Civic Morals*. London: Routledge.

Durkheim, E. (1984) *The Division of Labour in Society*. London: Palgrave Macmillan.

Eagleton, T. (1994) *Ideology*. London: Longman.

Eagleton, T. (2000) *The Idea of Culture*. Oxford: Blackwell.

Ehrenreich, B. (2002) *Nikel and Dimed: Undercover in Low-wage America*. London: Granta.

Ehrenreich, B. (2006) *Bait and Switch: The Futile Pursuit of the Corporate Dream*. London: Granta.

Ehrlich, I. (1973) 'Participation in illegal activities; a theoretical and empirical investigation', *Journal of Political Economy*, 81: 521–63.

Eisner, M. (2001) 'Modernization, Self-control and Lethal Violence: The Long-term Dynamics of European Homicide Rates in Theoretical Perspective', *The British Journal of Criminology*, 41: 618–638.

Elias, N. (2000) *The Civilizing Process.* Oxford: Blackwell.

Engdahl, O. (2008) 'The Role of Money in Economic Crime', *British Journal of Criminology*, 48(2): 154–70.

Engels, F. (1987) *The Condition of the Working Class in England.* London: Penguin.

Engels, F. ([1844]1958) *Condition of the Working Classes in England.* Oxford: Basil Blackwell.

Evans, D. (1996) *An Introductory Dictionary of Lacanian Psychoanalysis.* London: Routledge.

Featherstone, M. (1995) *Undoing Culture.* London: Sage.

Ferrell, J. (2002) *Tearing Down the Streets: Adventures in Urban Anarchy.* London: Palgrave Macmillan.

Ferrell, J. (2006) *Empire of Scrounge: Inside the Urban Underground of Dumpster Diving, Trash Picking, and Street Scavenging.* New York: New York University Press.

Fiske, J. (1989) *Understanding Popular Culture.* London: Unwin Hyman.

Fletcher, J. (1997) *Violence and Civilization.* Cambridge: Polity.

Foucault, M. (1991) *Discipline and Punish.* London: Penguin.

Foucault, M. (1980) *Power/Knowledge: Selected Interviews and Other Writings, 1972–1977.* New York: Pantheon Books.

Foucault, M. (ed. by P. Rabinow) (1984) *The Foucault Reader.* London: Harvester Wheatsheaf.

Frank, T. (1997) *The Conquest of Cool: Business Culture, Counterculture and the Rise of Hip Consumerism.* Chicago: University of Chicago Press.

Fraser, N. (1994) 'After the Family Wage: Gender Inequality and the Welfare State', *Political Theory*, 22(4): 591–618.

Friedman, T. (2000) *The Lexus and the Olive Tree.* London: HarperCollins.

Fromm, E. (1973) *The Anatomy of Human Destructiveness.* New York: Holt, Rinehart and Winston.

Fukuyama, F. (1993) *The End of History and the Last Man.* London: Penguin.

Gadd, D. and Jefferson. T. (2007) *Psychosocial Criminology.* London: Sage.

Galbraith, J. K. (1991) *A History of Economics: The Past as the Present.* London: Penguin.

Galbraith, J. K. (1999) *The Affluent Society.* London: Penguin.

Garland, D. (2001a) *The Culture of Control: Crime and Social Order in Contemporary Society.* Chicago: University of Chicago Press.

Garland, D. (ed.) (2001b) *Mass Imprisonment: Social Causes and Consequences.* London: Sage.

Geertz, C. (1973) *The Interpretation of Cultures: Selected Essays*. New York: Basic books.

Gerbner, G. and Gross, L. (1976a) 'Living with television: The violence profile', *Journal of Communication*, 26: 172–199.

Gerbner, G. and Gross, L. (1976b) 'The scary world of TV's heavy viewer', *Psychology Today*, 10(4): 41–89.

Giddens, A. (1984) *The Constitution of Society*. Berkeley: University of California Press.

Giddens, A. (1998) *The Third Way: The Renewal of Social Democracy*. London: Polity Press.

Giddens, A. (2007) *Over to you, Mr. Brown: How Labour can Win Again*. London: Polity.

Gilbert, E. (1957) *Advertising and Marketing to Young People*. Pleasantville, NY: Printer's Ink Books.

Girard, R. (2005) *Violence and the Sacred*. London: Continuum.

Goldthorpe, J., Lockwood, D., Beckhofer, F. and Platt, J. (1968) *The Affluent Worker*, Vols 1–3. Cambridge: Cambridge University Press.

Gouldner, A. (1971) *The Coming Crisis of Western Sociology*. London: Heinemann.

Gray, J. (2007) *Black Mass: Apocalyptic Religion and the Death of Utopia*. London: Allen Lane.

Grayling, A.C. (2007) *Truth, Meaning and Realism: Essays in the philosophy of thought*. London: Continuum.

de Grazia, V. (2005) *Irresistible Empire: America's Advance Through Twentieth-Century Europe*. Cambridge, MA: Harvard University Press.

Gurr, T. (1981) 'Historical Trends in Violent Crime: A Critical Review of the Evidence', *Crime and Justice*, 3: 295–353.

De Haan, W. and Loader, I. (2002) 'On the Emotions of Crime, Punishment and Social Control', *Theoretical Criminology*, 6(3): 243–254.

Hall, S. (1997) 'Visceral Cultures and Criminal Practices', *Theoretical Criminology*, 1(4): 453–478.

Hall, S. (2000) 'Paths to Anelpis: Dimorphic violence and the pseudo-pacification process', *Parallax*, 6(2): 36–53.

Hall, S. (2007) 'The Emergence and Breakdown of the Pseudo-Pacification Process', in K. Watson (ed.) *Assaulting the Past*. Cambridge: Cambridge Scholars Press.

Hall, S. and McLean, C. (forthcoming 2008) 'A Tale of Two Capitalisms: A preliminary comparison of murder rates in Western European and Anglo-American market societies', *Theoretical Criminology*.

Hall, S. and Winlow, S. (2003) 'Rehabilitating Leviathan: Reflections on the State, Economic Regulation and Violence Reduction', *Theoretical Criminology*, 7(2), 139–162.

Hall, S. and Winlow, S. (2004) 'Barbarians at the Gate: Crime and Violence in the Breakdown of the Pseudo-Pacification Process' in J. Ferrell, K. Hayward, W. Morrison and M. Presdee. *Cultural Criminology Unleashed*. London: Glasshouse Press.

Hall, S. and Winlow, S. (2005) 'Anti-nirvana: Crime, Culture and Instrumentalism in the Age of Insecurity', *Crime, Media, Culture*, 1(1): 31–48.

Hall, S. and Winlow, S. (2007) 'Cultural Criminology and Primitive Accumulation: A formal introduction for two strangers who should really become more intimate', *Crime, Media, Culture*, 3(1): 82–90.

Hall, S., Winlow, S. and Ancrum, C. (2005) 'Radgies, Gangstas and Mugs: imaginary criminal identities in the twilight of the pseudo-pacification process', *Social Justice*, 32(1).

Hall, S. (1988) *The Hard Road to Renewal: Thatcherism and the crisis of the left*. London: Verso.

Hall, S. (1980) *Popular Democratic versus Authoritarian Populism*. London: Lawrence and Wishart.

Hall, S. (1985) 'Authoritarian Populism: A reply to Jessop *et al.*', *New Left Review*, I/151 (May/June).

Hall, S. and Jefferson, T. (eds) (2006) *Resistance Through Rituals*. London: Routledge.

Hallsworth, S. (2005) *Street Crime*. Cullompton: Willan.

Harvey, D. (2007) *A Brief History of Neoliberalism*. Oxford: Oxford University Press.

Hayward, K. and Yar, M. (2006) 'The 'Chav' Phenomenon: Consumption, Media and the Construction of a New Underclass', *Crime, Media, Culture*, 2(1): 9–28.

Hayward, K. (2004) *City Limits: Crime, Consumer Culture and the Urban Experience*. London: Glasshouse.

Hayward, K. and Young, J. (2004) 'Cultural Criminology: Some Notes on the Script', *Theoretical Criminology*, 8(3): 259–274.

Heath, J. and Potter, A. (2007) *The Rebel Sell: How the Counter Culture Became Consumer Culture*. London: Capstone.

Hebdige, D. (1979) *Subculture: The Meaning of Style*. London: Routledge.

Heidegger, M. (1962) *Being and Time*. New York: HarperCollins.

Hegel, G. W. F. (2005a) *Philosophy of Right*. London: Dover Publications.

Hegel, G. W. F. (2005b) *Philosophy of History*. London: Dover Publications.

Hegel, G. W. F. (1979) *Phenomenology of the Spirit*. Oxford: Oxford University Press.

Henry, S. and Milovanovic, D. (1995) *Constitutive Criminology: Beyond Postmodernism*. London: Sage.

Henwood, D. (2005) *Wall Street*. London: Verso.

Hirsch, F. (1976) *Social Limits to Growth*. Cambridge, MA: Harvard University Press.

Hobbs, D. (1989) *Doing the Business: Entrepreneurship, the Working Class and Detectives in the East End of London*. Oxford: Oxford Paperbacks.

Hobbs, D. (1995) *Bad Business*. Oxford: Oxford University Press.

Hobbes, T. (2005) *Of Man*. London: Penguin.

Hobbes, T. (2007) *Leviathan*. London: Longman.

Hobsbawm, E. (1989) *The Age of Empire, 1875–1914*. London: Abacus.

Hobsbawm, E. (1995) *Age of Extremes: The Short Twentieth Century 1914–1991*. London: Abacus.

Hochschild, A. (1983) *The Managed Heart: The Commericalization of Human Feeling*. Berkeley: University of California Press.

Hodgkinson, T. (2008) 'With friends like these . . .', *The Guardian*, 14 January.

Hoffman, A. (2000) *The Autobiography of Abbie Hoffman*. London: Four Walls Eight Windows.

Hoffman, J. and Simon, D. (1996) *Run Run Run: The Lives of Abbie Hoffman*. London: Putnam.

Hoggart, R. (1957) *The Uses of Literacy: Aspects of Working-Class Life, With Special Reference to Publications and Entertainments*. London: Chatto and Windus.

Hollis, M. (1994) *The Philosophy of the Social Sciences*. Cambridge: Cambridge University Press.

Holt, D. (2002) 'Why Do Brands Cause Trouble? A Dialectical Theory of Consumer Culture and Branding', *Journal of Consumer Research*, 29: 70–90.

Horne, R. and Hall, S. (1995) 'Anelpis: A Preliminary Expedition into a World without Hope or Potential', *Parallax*, 1: 81–92.

Hubert, H. and Mauss, M. (1981) *Sacrifice: Its Nature and Function*. Chicago: Chicago University Press.

Hughes, G. (1998) *Understanding Crime Prevention: Social Control, Risk and Late Modernity*. Buckingham: Open University Press.

Hutton, W. (1996) *The State We're in: Why Britain Is in Crisis and How to Overcome It*. London: Vintage.

Hutton, W. (2003) *The World We're In*. London: Abacus.

Hughes, G. (1998) *Understanding Crime Prevention: Social Control, Risk and Late Modernity*. Buckingham: Open University Press.

Jacoby, R. (1999) *The End of Utopia: Politics and Culture in an Age of Apathy*. London: Basic Books.

Jakobson, R. (1956) 'Two Aspects of Language and Two Types of Linguistic Disturbances', in R. Jakobson and M. Halle, *Fundamentals of Language*. The Hague: Mouton.

James, O. (2007) *Affluenza*. London: Vermilion.

Jameson, F. (1992) *Postmodernism, or The Cultural Logic of Late Capitalism*. Durham, NC: Duke University Press.

Karstedt, S. and Farrall, S. (2006) 'The Moral Economy of Everyday Crime: Markets, Consumers and Citizens', *The British Journal of Criminology*, 46(6): 1011–1036.

Katz, J. (1988) *The Seductions of Crime*. New York: Basic Books.

Kirkpatrick, G. (2005) *Critical Technology: A Social Theory of Personal, Computing*. Aldershot: Ashgate.

Kivetz, R. and Simonson, I. (2002) 'Self-Control for the Righteous: Toward a Theory of Precommitment to Indulgence', *Journal of Consumer Research*, 29(2): 199–217.

Lacan, J. (2006) *Ecrits*. London: Norton.

Landesco, J. (1979) *Organized Crime in Chicago*. Chicago: University of Chicago Press.

Lane, R. E. (2001) *The Decline of Happiness in Market Democracies*. Yale: Yale University Press.

Lasch, C. (1991) *The Culture of Narcissism: American Life in an Age of Diminishing Expectations*. London: Norton.

Lasch, C. (1996) *The Revolt of the Elites and the Betrayal of Democracy*. London: Norton.

Lash, S. (1994) 'The Making of an Underclass: Neoliberalism versus Corporatism', P. Brown and R. Crompton, *Economic Restructuring and Social Exclusion: A New Europe?* London: Routledge.

Lash, S. and Lury, C. (2007) *Global Culture Industry: The Mediation of Things*. London: Polity.

Lasn, K. (2001) *Culture Jam: How to Reverse America's Suicidal Consumer Binge – and Why We Must*. London: HarperCollins.

Lea, J. (2002) *Crime and Modernity*. London: Sage.

Lea, J. and Young, J. (1993) *What Is To Be Done About Law and Order?* London: Pluto Press.

Lemert, E. (1967) *Human Deviance, Social Problems and Social Control*. Englewood Cliffs, NJ: Prentice-Hall.

Lewis, D. and Brigder, D. (2005) 'Market Researchers make Increasing use of Brain Imaging', *Advances in Clinical Neuroscience and Rehabilitation*, 5(3): 35–44.

Luhmann, N. (1986) 'The Autopoiesis of Social Systems', in F. Geyer and J. van der Zouwen (eds) *Sociocybernetic Paradoxes*. London: Sage, pp. 172–192.

Lyng, S. (2006) *Edgework*. London: Routledge.

McGuigan, J. (2006) 'The Politics of Cultural Studies and Cool Capitalism', *Cultural Politics*, 2(2): 137–158.

McKendrick, N., Brewer, J., and Plumb, J.H. (1983) *The Birth of Consumer Society: The commercialisation of eighteenth-century England*. London: Hutchinson.

Mailer, N. (1968) *The Idol and the Octopus: Political Writings on the Kennedy and Johnson Administrations*. New York: Dell.

Matthews, R. (2002) *Armed Robbery*. Cullompton: Willan.

Maruna, S. (2001) *Making Good: How Ex-Convicts Reform and Rebuild their Lives*. Washington, DC: American Psychological Association.

Marx, K. (1999) *Capital: An Abridged Edition*. Oxford: Oxford University Press.

Mayhew, H. (1985) *London Labour and the London Poor*. London: Penguin.

Mays, J. B. (1954) *Growing Up in the City*. Liverpool: Liverpool University Press.

Mellor, P. and Shilling, C. (1997) *Re-forming the Body: Religion, Community and Modernity*. London: Sage.

Merton, R. K. (1938) 'Social Structure and Anomie', *American Sociological Review*, 3(5): 672–682.

Messner, S. and Rosenfeld, R. (1997) *Crime and the American Dream*. Belmont, CA: Wadsworth.

Mestrovic, S. (1993) *The Barbarian Temperament: Toward a Postmodern Critical Theory*. London: Routledge.

Miles, S., Cliff, D. and Burr, V. (1998) 'Fitting In and Sticking Out': Consumption, Consumer Meanings and the Construction of Young people's Identities, *Journal of Youth Studies*, 1(1): 81–96.

Miller, D. (1987) *Material Culture and Mass Consumption*. Oxford: Basil Blackwell.

Miller, W. (1962) *Lower Class Culture as a Generating Milieu of Gang Delinquency*. Indianapolis: Bobbs-Merrill.

Mills, C. W. (1959) *The Power Elite*. Oxford: Oxford University Press.

Mokhiber, R. and Weissman, R. (1999) *Corporate Predators: The Hunt for Mega-Profits and the Attack on Democracy*. London: Common Courage Press.

Montanari, I. (2000) 'From family wage to marriage subsidy and child benefits: controversy and consensus in the development of family support', *Journal of European Social Policy*, 10(4): 307–333.

Morris, T. (1957) *The Criminal Area: A Study in Social Ecology*. London: Routledge.

Mouzelis, N. (1995) *Sociological Theory: What Went Wrong?* London: Routledge.

Murray, C. (1988) *In Pursuit: Of Happiness and Good Government*. London: Simon & Schuster.

Murray, C. (1990) *The Emerging British Underclass*. London: IEA.

Murray, C. (1994) *Underclass: The Crisis Deepens*. London: IEA.

Murray, C. (1997) *What it Means to Be a Libertarian*. New York: Broadway Books.

Murray, J. (2002) 'The Politics of Consumption: A Re-Inquiry on Thompson and Haytko's (1997) "Speaking of Fashion"', *Journal of Consumer Research*, 29(3): 427–440.

National Consumer Council (undated) 'Shopping Generation', available at:. http://www.ncc.org.uk/nccpdf/poldocs/NCC088_shopping_generation.pdf.

Newman, K. (1999) *No Shame in My Game: The Working Poor in the Inner City*. New York: Alfred A. Knopf.

Nightingale, C. (1993) *On the Edge: A History of Poor Black Kids and Their American Dreams*. New York: Basic Books.

O'Brien, M. (2005) 'What is Cultural About Cultural Criminology?', *The British Journal of Criminology*, 45(5): 599–612.

O'Brien, M. (2007) 'The Deviance of the Zookeepers', paper delivered to the British Society of Criminology Conference, 18–20 September. London School of Economics.

Ofcom (2007) http://www.ofcom.org.uk/media/news/2007/12/nr_20071219.

Palmer, S. (2006) *Toxic Childhood: How the Modern World is Damaging Our Children and What We Can Do About It*. London: Orion.

Philo, M. and Miller, D. (2001) *Market Killing: What the Free Market Does and What Social Scientists Can Do About It*. Harlow: Longman.

Piaget, J. (1966) *The Growth of Logical Thinking*. London: Routledge and Kegan Paul.

Polanyi, K. (2002) *The Great Transformation*. London: Beacon Press.

Pollin, R. (2005) *Contours of Dissent: US Economic Fractures and the Landscape of Global Austerity*. London: Verso.

Presdee, M. (2000) *Cultural Criminology and the Carnival of Crime*. London: Routledge.

Punch, M. (1996) *Dirty Business: Exploring Corporate Misconduct*. London: Sage.

Raban, J. (1975) *Soft City*. London: Fontna.

Rainwater, L. (2005) *Poor Kids in a Rich Country*. London: Russell Sage Foundation Publications.

Reiner, R. (2007) *Law and Order: An honest citizen's guide to crime and control*. Cambridge: Polity.

Reisman, D. (1953) *The Lonely Crowd*. London: Doubeday.

Ridderstrale, J. and Nordstrom, K. (2002) *Funky Business: Talent Makes Capital Dance*. London: Financial Times/Prentice Hall.

Ritzer, G. (2004) *The Globalization of Nothing*. London: Sage.

Rojek, C. (2001) *Celebrity*. London: Reaktion Books.

Rorty, R. (1989) *Contingency, Irony and Solidarity*. Cambridge: Cambridge University Press.

Rose, J. (2002) *The Intellectual Life of the British Working Classes*. London: Yale Nota Bene.

Rose, N. (1996) *Inventing our Selves: Psychology, Power, and Personhood.* Cambridge: Cambridge University Press.

Roszak, T. (1969) *The Making of a Counter Culture: Reflections on the Technocratic Society and its Youthful Opposition.* Garden City: Doubleday.

Rousseau, J.-J. (1990) *Rousseau, Judge of Jean-Jacques.* Hanover, NH: Dartmouth College Press.

Runciman, W. G. (1966) *Relative Deprivation and Social Justice: A Study of Attitudes to Social Inequality in Twentieth-Century England.* Berkeley: University of California Press.

Sassoon, D. (1997) *One Hundred Years of Socialism: The West European Left in the twentieth century.* London: Fontana.

Sassoon, D. (2005) 'From Buddenbrooks to Babbitt', in *New Left Review*, 36, Nov–Dec.

Schor, J. (1998) *The Overspent American: Upscaling, Downshifting, and the New Consumer.* New York: Basic Books.

Schor, J. (2000) 'The new politics of consumption', in J. Cohen and J. Rogers (eds) *Do Americans Shop Too Much?* London: Beacon Press.

Schur, E. (1973) *Radical Non-Intervention: Re-thinking the delinquency problem.* Eaglewood Cliffs, NJ: Prentice-Hall.

Schumpeter, J. (1994) *Capitalism, Socialism and Democracy.* London: Routledge.

Scraton, P. (1987) *Law, Order and the Authoritarian State: Readings in Critical Criminology.* Milton Keynes: Open University Press.

Scull, A. (1984) *Decarceration: Community treatment and the deviant.* Cambridge: Polity Press.

Sennett, R. (1998) *The Corrosion of Character.* London: Norton.

Sennett, R. (2006) *The Culture of the New Capitalism.* London: Yale University Press.

Shulman, B. (2003) *The Betrayal of Work: How Low Wage Jobs fail 35 million Americans.* London: The New Press.

Sloterdijk, P. (1988) *Critique of Cynical Reason.* London: Verso.

Slotkin, R. (1998) *Gunfighter Nation: The myth of frontier in twentieth-century America.* Norman: University of Oklahoma press.

Smith, A. ([1759]1984) *The Theory of the Moral Sentiments.* Indianapolis: Liberty Fund.

Stedman-Jones, G. (1976) *Outcast London: A Study in the Relationship between Classes in Victorian Society.* London: Penguin.

Stratton, J. (2001) *The Desirable Body: Cultural fetishism and the erotics of consumption.* Chicago: University of Illinois Press.

Sumner, C. (1994) *The Sociology of Deviance: An Obituary.* Milton Keynes: Open University Press.

Sutherland, E. (1985) *White-Collar Crime: The Uncut Version.* London: Yale University Press.

Sykes, G. and Matza, D. (1957) 'Techniques of Neutralization: A Theory of Delinquency', *American Sociological Review*, 22(6): 664–670.

Taylor, I. (1999) *Crime in Context: A Critical Criminology of Market Societies*. London: Polity Press.

Taylor, P. and Bain, P. (1999) 'An Assembly Line in the Head: Work and Employee Relations in a Call Centre', *Industrial Relations Journal*, 30(2): 101–117.

Taylor, I., Walton, P. and Young, J. (1973) *The New Criminology*. London: Routledge.

Thompson, E. P. (1991) *The Making of the English Working Class*. London: Penguin.

Thrasher, F. (1963) *The Gang*. Chicago: University of Chicago Press.

Tombs, S. and Slapper, G. (1999) *Corporate Crime*. London: Longman.

Toynbee, P. (2003) *Hard Work: Life in Low-pay Britain*. London: Bloomsbury.

Toynbee, P. and Walker, D. (2005) *Better or Worse? Has Labour Delivered?* London: Bloomsbury.

Veblen, T. (1994) *The Theory of The Leisure Class*. London: Dover Publications.

Virilio, P. (2005) *The Information Bomb*. London: Verso.

Wacquant, L. (2002) 'Scrutinizing the Street: Poverty, Morality, and the Pitfalls of Urban Ethnography', *American Journal of Sociology*, 107: 1468–1532.

Warburton, N. (2006) *Philosophy: The Classics*. London: Routledge.

Weber, M. (1991) *From Max Weber: Essays in Sociology*. London: Routledge.

Welshman, J. (2006) *Underclass: A History of the Excluded*. London: Hambledon/Continuum.

Williams, R. (1971) *Culture and Society, 1780–1950*. London: Penguin.

Williams, R. (2005) *Culture and Materialism*. London: Verso.

Williams, S. J. (2001) *Emotion and Social Theory: Corporeal reflections on the (Ir)rational*. London: Sage.

Williamson, J. (1988) *Consuming Passions: The Dynamics of Popular Culture*. London: Marion Boyars Publishers.

Willis, P. (1977) *Learning to Labour*. Farnsborough: Saxon House.

Willis, P. (1990) *Common Culture*. Milton Keynes: Open University Press.

Wilson, J. Q. (1975) *Thinking About Crime*. New York: Basic Books.

Wilson, W. J. (1987) *Truly Disadvantaged: Inner City, the Underclass and Public Policy*. Chicago: Chicago University Press.

Wilson, W. J. (1997) *When Work Disappears*. New York: Alfred A Knopf.

Winlow, S. (2001) *Badfellas: Crime, Tradition and New Masculinities*. Oxford: Berg.

Winlow, S. and Hall, S. (2006) *Violent Night: Urban Leisure and Contemporary Culture*. Oxford: Berg.

Winlow, S. and Hall, S. (2008, forthcoming) 'Living for the Weekend: Instrumentalism, consumption and "individualism" in youth identities in North East England', *Ethnography*.

Woodiwiss, M. (2005) *Gangster Capitalism: The United States and the Global Rise of Organised Crime*. London: Constable.

Wooten, D. (2006) 'From Labeling Possessions to Possessing Labels: Ridicule and Socialization among Adolescents', *Journal of Consumer Research*, 33: 188–198.

Wouters, C. (2002) 'Changing patterns of social controls and self-controls: On the rise of crime since the 1950s and the sociogenesis of a "third nature"', *The British Journal of Criminology*, 39: 416–432.

Yar, M. and Penna, S. (2004) 'Between Positivism and Post-modernity? Critical Reflections on Jock Young's The Exclusive Society', *The British Journal of Criminology*, 44: 533–549.

Young, J. (1987) 'The Tasks Facing a Realist Criminology', *Crime, Law and Social Change*, 11(4): 337–356.

Young, J. (1999) *The Exclusive Society*. London: Sage.

Young, J. (2002) 'Radical Criminology in Britain: The Emergence of a Competing Paradigm', *The British Journal of Criminology*, 28(2): 159–183.

Young, J. (2004) 'Crime and the Dialectics of Inclusion/Exclusion: Some Comments on Yar and Penna', *The British Journal of Criminology*, 44(4): 550–561.

Young, J. (2007) *The Vertigo of Late Modernity*. London: Sage.

Young, M. and Willmott, P. (1962) *Family and Kinship in East London*. Baltimore: Penguin Books.

Zimring, F. and Hawkins, G. (1995) *Incapacitation: Penal Confinement and the Restraint of Crime*. New York: Plenum Press.

Žižek, S. (2000) *The Ticklish Subject: The Absent Centre of Political Ontology*. London: Verso.

Žižek, S. (2002) *Welcome to the Desert of the Real*. London: Verso.

Žižek, S. (2006a) *How to Read Lacan*. London: Granta.

Žižek, S. (2006b) *The Parallax View*. Boston: MIT Press.

Žižek, S. (2006c) *On Belief*. London: Routledge.

Žižek, S. (2007) *The Universal Exception*. London: Continuum.

Žižek, S. (2008) *Violence*. London: Profile Books.

Name index

Subject index